Choosing
Correctional
Options
That Work

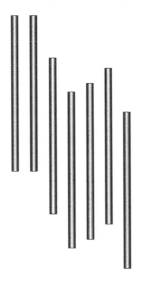

Alan T. Harland
editor

Choosing Correctional Options That Work

Defining the
Demand and
Evaluating
the Supply

Foreword by
Francis X. Hartmann

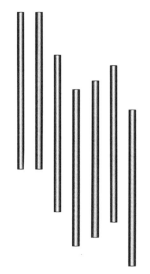

SAGE Publications
International Educational and Professional Publisher
Thousand Oaks   London   New Delhi

For information address:

SAGE Publications, Inc.
2455 Teller Road
Thousand Oaks, California 91320
E-mail: order@sagepub.com

SAGE Publications Ltd.
6 Bonhill Street
London EC2A 4PU
United Kingdom

SAGE Publications India Pvt. Ltd.
M-32 Market
Greater Kailash I
New Delhi 110 048 India

Printed in the United States of America

Library of Congress Cataloging-in-Publication Data

Main entry under title:

Choosing correctional options that work: Defining the demand and
    evaluating the supply/edited by Alan T. Harland.
        p.   cm.
    Includes bibliographical references and index.
    ISBN 0-8039-5930-3 (cloth: alk. paper). — ISBN 0-8039-5931-1
(pbk.: alk. paper)
        1. Corrections—United States.   I. Harland, Alan T.
HV9471.C474   1996
365'.973—dc20   95-35751

This book is printed on acid-free paper.

95   96   97   98   99   10   9   8   7   6   5   4   3   2   1

Production Editor: Gillian Dickens   Typesetter: Christina Hill

Contents

Foreword

The publication of the papers collected as chapters in this book is a further step in a process that deserves to be roundly celebrated. The process is one in which the International Association of Residential and Community Alternatives (IARCA), representing a broad range of private sector and governmental community corrections practitioners, put hard questions to researchers about the work of community corrections. In November 1993, the practitioners and the researchers met in a working conference at which early drafts of some of the chapters in this volume were presented. To facilitate and broaden the conversation about the research, a consensus panel of criminal justice practitioners—including judges, a prosecutor, a former legislator, a government official, a member of a group representing the community, and the head of the Vera Institute of Justice[1]—was formed and asked to address the researchers' findings. The consensus panel was to press the researchers: Exactly what is the researcher saying? What are the implications of the research for correctional policy? What programmatic decisions might be based on the research? On what findings might criminal justice decision makers most confidently depend? The objective was to produce, by way of the three-way conversation among researchers, community corrections practitioners, and other criminal justice decision makers, the beginning of agreement about the principles on which community corrections operates. I had the privilege of chairing the consensus panel.

The panel developed a statement that focused on the important lessons from the researchers to the field and from criminal justice decision makers to the field and to the researchers. We first addressed the context in which community corrections operates:

> The social contract of the society is changing; its grip on many members of society has loosened. The instruments of criminal justice are insufficient to right this situation. Criminal justice can support the social contract; it cannot create it where it does not exist or where it is tenuous. Community corrections did not create this situation, and its practitioners and proponents cannot feel fully responsible for restoring balance to the society. The corrections system cannot be the primary instrument for achieving social justice. Prevention will always be more powerful than any after-the-fact strategy.

Given that context and caveat, what can and should community corrections do? Before all else, for community corrections to be useful and effective, proponents must develop and articulate a vision of just what it is, what it is about, and in what terms and ways they propose the field to be effective. This vision must include a clear definition of goals—what is to be accomplished. As the consensus panel stated,

> Your vision must attend to what you *are* rather than what you are not. Your place in corrections is often stated negatively as something short of prison or as an alternative to or reaction against incarceration. There is so much more to the value of delivering correctional services in a community than a reaction against prisons, and you must articulate that value that you bring to the society.

For example, community corrections offers the objective and genuine hope of *restoring* people to their community. Institutional corrections merely *returns* people to the community. Other measures that address broader goals, more important than recidivism, must be developed. Changing the criteria by which community corrections is held accountable, to measures that are consistent with the goals and capacity of the field, and that are understood and valued by the public, is critical.

In these chapters, the researchers state that treatment has been demonstrated to be a necessary part of the process of helping offenders learn how to be citizens. Corrections efforts that work only to punish or incapacitate are unlikely to meet any of the broader utilitarian goals emphasized in this book. The knowledge that treatment is vital to success is basic to the articulated vision of community corrections and, at the same time, distinguishes community corrections from the majority of institutional approaches that are primarily defined by bricks and mortar. The research community can and must help practitioners to identify the elements of successful efforts.

Research can also tell those in the field how to use efficiently the capacities that the field now has. Another message that the panel extracted from the research is that community corrections resources are better utilized with higher-risk offenders than those now targeted by many programs. Community capacity is insufficiently used if used primarily with very low risk offenders. One of the goals for the field must be to target scarce resources on higher-risk offenders and away from those who are of negligible risk to the community. Researchers must also further the working conversation about the benefits of community corrections in comparison with the costs.

There must be a theoretical basis for the work of community corrections and for the vision of what it can be. At the same time, if programs are to be implemented successfully, the ideas that inform them must fit the environment within which the programs operate. Community corrections programs are likely to be most effective when they are interactive—that is, if they regularly adapt to the changing situation and circumstances of all concerned: clients, the community, and relevant agencies. One of the valuable contributions of researchers is as colleagues with practitioners in the conversation about the relationship between the theory and practice of corrections strategies. This is an arena in which theory and practice must engage each other if good practice is to thrive, particularly in an era in which the first and easiest response is to use prisons.

Articulating and communicating the vision of community corrections is not only for the benefit of those professionals active in the field but for its many stakeholders—citizens who care about their community, legislators who are thoughtful about the response to crime, members of organizations who are willing to support sensible policy and programs. Without them, those invested in the field are isolated and weakened. There must be regular communication with the public in general and with decision makers, including legislators, judges, prosecutors, community members, budget analysts, and the media. There is a great need for sharing what is done in the field and done well. Without this ongoing engagement and education, community corrections cannot have the impact that is possible.

By way of example, several years ago I was in Georgia speaking with corrections professionals responsible for the significant changes in correctional policy that Georgia had been able to accomplish. I asked several of them how much time they spent in the community talking about their work. The answer, on average, was that about 30% of their working time was devoted to

speaking and listening to community groups—churches, fraternal associations, any organization willing to give them a platform. They talked about the
work of corrections, what they were trying to accomplish, and why. And at
the same time, they listened to the citizens. The inestimable gain was that they
learned what was possible, and they brought about the change they wanted
with the support of the public. They bought immense credibility and protected
their work against the unpredictable solitary event or scandal that drives so
many systems.

Some forces—family, labor market, schools, and communities, to name a
few—will always be more powerful than probation or parole officers or
community corrections programs. Research must tell us how to reorganize
and reorient crime control and criminal justice strategies to take better
advantage of those strong forces in our society that affect the lives and choices
of individuals. We need the researchers to generate hypotheses about human
behavior and about the institutional forces that we can bring to bear on that
behavior. We need the researchers to challenge the practical experience of our
efforts to further extract lessons learned. They must help practitioners live the
examined life. It is crucial that they play interactive roles with the people
whose work they examine.

The initial conversation between IARCA members and the researchers
whose work is included in this book was a feeling of the way into uncharted
territory. The word that first comes to my mind about this beginning conversation is *courage.* I see courage in the community of practice in asking
outsiders to take a hard look at them and what they are about. I see courage
in the researchers in writing not just for colleagues but for those whose
professional work is at stake and, in so doing, putting themselves in an arena
in which their research will be subject to considerably different types of
challenge and criticism.

As the consensus panel of criminal justice decision makers stated, "We
begin by applauding this exciting and wholly appropriate conversation. In it,
researchers are actively engaged with criminal justice system decision makers
and with community corrections practitioners." This is admirable and praiseworthy work, and it was my privilege to be part of it.

Francis X. Hartmann
Executive Director and Senior Research Fellow
Program in Criminal Justice Policy and Management
John F. Kennedy School of Government
Harvard University

Note

1. A consensus statement regarding correctional research and policy is not analogous to that produced by a medical consensus panel. In the latter, the group votes for a particular finding—for example, whether a given dosage of aspirin is the appropriate treatment for a particular illness. The work of this panel reflects the current conversation among researchers, practitioners, and other decision makers in the criminal justice system about the work, direction, and capacity of community corrections and its place within the criminal justice process and the community. Members of the panel were the Honorable Legrome Davis, supervising judge, Criminal Division, Philadelphia Court of Common Pleas; Madame Andree Ruffo, family court judge, Quebec, Canada; Andrew L. Sonner, state's attorney, Montgomery County, Rockville, Maryland; Ms. Patricia McGovern, former state senator, Massachusetts, Goulston and Storrs, Boston, Massachusetts; Arden Thurber, director general, Case Management and Community Corrections, Correctional Service of Canada; Ms. Lee Soto-Thomas, director, Aboriginal Justice Consulate, Native Council of Canada; Michael Smith, president, Vera Institute of Justice, New York City.

Introduction

Alan T. Harland

This book is intended to respond to one of the most persistently voiced but consistently unmet needs in the entire field of criminal justice—the fervently expressed but often ill-defined demand by criminal justice professionals, policymakers, and the general public for correctional options that work. As the subtitle suggests, the book addresses the issue on two separate but related levels:

- First, the aim is to make more sense of the demand itself, via greater conceptual and operational specification of its two central components—examining a variety of possible meanings within the term *correctional options* and defining more precisely some of the unarticulated effectiveness, efficiency, and fairness concerns that are inherent in the search for "what works."
- Second, the book is intended to respond more directly and immediately to the demand in three specific areas, providing critical reviews of relevant theory and empirical evidence to ask what works in terms of selected diagnostic and assessment techniques, intervention and sanctioning options, and program implementation approaches.

By simultaneously clarifying the meaning of the *demand* for options that work and establishing a baseline of information derived from a critical review of past attempts to *supply* these demands, our overarching aim is to improve the odds that key decision makers will, in fact, be more likely to choose correctional options that work in the future.

The need to make this choice arises in a variety of contexts. At one level, it is part of the case management decision making of individual judges, probation officers, and other practitioners. Increasingly, however, it surfaces also in the work of legislative or other policy development groups. These include broadly charged state or local criminal justice coordinating or planning commissions and, in a slightly narrower context, task forces concerned with jail or prison overcrowding and looking for alternatives to incarceration. Usually, the need is felt in the routine and crisis-driven planning activities of administrators within a particular correctional or related agency in the criminal justice system.

By clarifying the range of correctional options and the goals and information needed to make sensible judgments about whether they work, our aim is to enhance the process of making choices in each of the foregoing settings. This involves improving the level and quality of dialogue and collaboration between the key players on the corrections field and providing administrators, policymakers, and practitioners with better insights, information, and tools for communicating their ideas and interests to the researchers, evaluators, planners, and program design personnel charged with developing the methodologies for implementing, monitoring, and evaluating the options identified. It is a major theme of the book that greater collaboration between these respective groups is an essential forerunner to more successful development of correctional and other criminal justice options in the future. Thus the lessons and messages it contains are offered for all of the following consumers:

- Administrators in the fields of probation, parole, community corrections, and institutional corrections, all of whom are under constant pressure to develop new and better options for dealing with the offenders and victims under their jurisdiction

- Legislators and other policy-making authorities, such as the many intermediate sanctions policy teams that have sprung up all over the country as a result of initiatives by the National Institute of Corrections, the State Justice Institute, and more recently, the Bureau of Justice Assistance. Similar groups include the criminal justice coordinating commissions that function as standing planning bodies at many state and county levels, as well as ad hoc task forces, commissions, and special masters seeking alternatives to reduce overcrowding in state and county correctional facilities.

- The leaders and membership of organizations such as the American Probation and Parole Association (APPA) and the International Association of Residential and

Community Alternatives (IARCA), whose U.S. and Canadian sponsors supported the early development of many of the chapters in this book

- Sentencing and supervision practitioners who are involved in the day-to-day decision-making task of identifying and selecting appropriate options for handling criminal caseloads, including judges, prosecutors, defenders, pre-sentence investigators, and the growing body of independent sentencing advocates who influence sentencing decisions via case-specific plans that attempt to match offender needs and risks to available sanctioning options

- Researchers, evaluators, and program planners engaged in the design, monitoring, and evaluation of correctional options

- Students in criminal justice, psychology, sociology, and social administration, in courses on sentencing, corrections, justice policy, planned change, and statistics and research methods, who will be the future leaders in all of the preceding spheres

Overview of Contents

The eight chapters that follow stir the "what" and "works" ingredients of the what works recipe in a number of directions. In the opening chapter, I have attempted a conceptual elaboration of the extensive range of possible lines of inquiry that are subsumed under the deceptively simple sounding title of the book—*Choosing Correctional Options That Work.* Through seeing the task framed in ways that go beyond its treatment in this volume, by the establishment of a more expansive context from the outset, the reader may appreciate the exact scope and limitations of the remaining chapters of the book and the implications for further inquiry that they suggest.

In Chapters 2 and 3, for example, Jim Bonta and Peter Jones bring their scholarship and extensive applied experience to the question of risk and need assessment and to the development and use of statistical risk prediction techniques. The limitations of available tools are documented in these two chapters, and a comprehensive review of diagnostic approaches would extend to include a wide variety of additional, more narrowly focused options, such as specialized assessment instruments and clinical techniques for particularly difficult subpopulations such as sex offenders and substance abusers. The lucid and thorough analysis of the more general topic by Bonta and Jones, however, clearly shows the relevance of better *targeting* in program planning, stressed by Frank Hartmann in the Foreword, and the issues of *differential treatment* and *matching* (of offenders, interventions, and providers) that deservedly constitute such an important theme of the later chapters, particularly those by Paul Gendreau and Ted Palmer.

For a field that by almost anyone's definition is so centrally involved in the management of risk and in responding to criminogenic needs of offenders, the continuing neglect or inadequate appreciation of the importance of this area in so many correctional agencies is little short of astounding. The role and responsibility of administrators that Peter Jones has identified as being critical to the development and proper use of statistical risk assessment tools is an excellent example of the need for the type of researcher-practitioner collaboration raised throughout the book and advocated so firmly and explicitly by Joan Petersilia in her closing chapter.

After this examination of what is known about the prediction of risk, discussion turns in Chapter 4 to a review of a variety of approaches, largely associated with U.S. corrections, to managing that risk via surveillance, punishment, and control in community settings. Chapter 4, "Control in the Community," by Frank Cullen and his colleagues, offers a thorough and critical assessment of research findings on such options as electronic monitoring, home confinement, boot camps, and intensive supervision probation programs. Although less dismissive of these approaches than Paul Gendreau is in the next chapter, Cullen et al. emphasize the pervasiveness and apparent importance of treatment components operating behind the facade of punitiveness and control that undoubtedly accounts for much of their political and popular support. They also highlight the fact that many of these seemingly singular options are really large black boxes whose programmatic contents are often so similar to each other as to make the overall programs virtually indistinguishable in all but the name or label attached to the lid. Under such circumstances, it becomes almost meaningless to ask whether one works better than another or whether "they" work at all, because they (e.g., electronic monitoring programs) mean many different things depending on what specific components happen to be dominant in the particular site examined.

Taking the lid off the black box of correctional interventions, as a prerequisite to finding out whether they work, is a central theme also of the next two authors, Paul Gendreau and Ted Palmer. In Chapters 5 and 6, these two leading authorities examine the extensive body of information that is accumulating as a result of meta-analyses and reviews of the correctional treatment research literature. Although covering some of the same ground, the two chapters offer important contrasts in terms of both style and result. Gendreau's presentation, in Chapter 5, is couched in terms of general principles, blending his interpretation of the published research results with more clinically based—and with respect to the types of programs reviewed by Cullen et al., perhaps ideologically tinted—judgments of what does and does not appear to reduce recidivism. In Chapter 6, Ted Palmer delivers the kind of meticulous and scrupulously balanced assessment of the published research that readers of his responses to Martinson and his other classic earlier works have come to expect. Importantly, however, Palmer goes well beyond an update of extant knowledge on the topic of what works and offers detailed and challenging prescriptions for the research and practitioner communities to follow if significant inroads are to made in filling gaps in that information base in the years to come.

In Chapter 7, Philip Harris and Stephen Smith tackle the question of what works in corrections from a very different but absolutely vital perspective. Applying a planned-change perspective that has its foundation perhaps as much in lessons from the *Harvard Business Review* as in the criminal justice literature, these two authors examine the correlates and principles of successful *implementation* of correctional programs. After so many lamentable failures to capitalize on seemingly promising intervention strategies in criminal justice over the years, it is common to hear that many of them were "never really given a chance" to work. Negative evaluations under such circumstances can be attributable to the failures of program implementation rather than to deficiencies in program theory or design. Even the most rigorous evaluation agenda will be futile, if it is wasted on interventions that are incompletely or inappropriately implemented to begin with. Harris and Smith illustrate the kind of knowledge and insight that practitioners need to bring to the question of what it takes to innovate successfully.

In the closing chapter of the book, the theme of joint practitioner-researcher commitment and action as an important factor in solving the what works equation, is forcefully taken up by Joan Petersilia, one of the most prolific exponents in the United States of such collaboration as a vehicle for improving correctional knowledge and practice. As Frank Hartmann notes in the Foreword, the interaction of individuals from the realms of correctional research and administration that occurred in the commissioning, presentation, and discussion of early drafts of the chapters that form the nucleus of this book is a step in this process that deserves to be celebrated. Let us hope that the baseline of information and the challenges to improve on it that the authors in this volume have set down will encourage systematic extension of the process and a corresponding increase in our understanding and supply of correctional options that work.

Correctional Options That Work

Structuring the Inquiry

Alan T. Harland

Against an unrelenting backdrop of crowded institutions and probation and parole caseloads, criminal justice officials are under considerable external and internal pressure to develop and use a greater range of correctional options, especially community-based alternatives. Although this is a vital first step toward the rational assessment and allocation of correctional resources, it should be axiomatic that it is not enough and indeed, that it may ultimately be counterproductive for jurisdictions simply to generate an ever-expanding array of pretrial, sentencing, and revocation options. Without clear guidance to structure discretion as to how and for whom the variety of options might best be applied, such expansion may make the decision maker's task even more difficult and confusing, opening greater chance for idiosyncratic and otherwise inappropriate results. Increasing the range of choices expands the prospect of improving correctional practices, but it also makes the task of deciding on the "right" selection an even more complex and challenging proposition than in the past.

Expansion of options without clear definition and a corresponding set of principles and standards to guide in their selection, application, and evaluation raises the prospect of faddish adoption and unstructured discretionary use—

AUTHOR'S NOTE: Portions of this chapter are reproduced from Harland (1993). Defining a continuum of sanctions: Some research and policy implications. *Perspectives, 17*(2), 6-15. Reprinted with permission from the American Probation and Parole Association.

and abuse. This, in turn, escalates the risk of applying them to inappropriate target populations and the corollary dangers of trivializing them, weakening their treatment and public safety impact and introducing other threats to their integrity and credibility, such as net widening, cost overruns, breaches of desert principles, inequity, undue disparity, and so on. The latter dangers are more acutely of concern as the types of community-based sanctions being introduced become more and more onerous as implementers strive to approximate the punitiveness and control associated with the terms of incarceration with which these alternatives are designed to compete (Petersilia, 1990b).

A central theme in expanding the range of correctional options, especially in the area of intermediate sanctions, is the persistent but poorly defined demand for "correctional options that work" (Byrne & Pattavina, 1992). Whether such calls are raised by the general public, the media, politicians, victims groups, or corrections and other criminal justice professionals, attempts to identify options that work or to develop new ones are likely to proceed more systematically and expeditiously if the different elements of the demand are clearly defined. Corrections practitioners are engaged in a broad range of case-specific activities, from bail and presentence investigations to diagnostic services and sentence recommendations and supervision, surveillance, enforcement, and service delivery and brokerage for both pretrial and convicted populations. In addition, they are involved in the related tasks of developing, implementing, administering, and monitoring the increasing array of correctional programs within which the preceding activities are conducted and managed. The scope of correctional agency work is being expanded further to address the reparative and other needs of victims of crime as well as the more traditional and still dominant focus on offenders (see, e.g., the 1994 special issue of *Perspectives,* the quarterly publication of the American Probation and Parole Association, devoted extensively to victim services within community corrections).

Within each of the foregoing spheres of activity, considerable room for variation obviously exists in the nature and scope of different "options," as well as the meaning attached to notions of how well or poorly each "works." A dominant theme of most public, political, and practitioner demands for options that work, for example, is undoubtedly the basic utilitarian interest in reducing crime. This translates into a plea for greater public safety via improvements in any and all of the foregoing aspects of the correctional enterprise that might contribute in some demonstrable way to reducing rates of criminal conduct, particularly recidivism. When the demand arises in the context of a corrections crowding task force or a master's search for options that will reduce jail or prison crowding, emphasis again is on improvements in any and all aspects of the correctional enterprise. This time, however, focus shifts to changes that might contribute in some demonstrable way to reducing rates of commitment or length of stay in prisons and jails, presumably without unacceptable increases in levels of criminal conduct, particularly recidivism, and technical violations of supervision conditions.

For government budget officers or, ironically, through the similarly focused lens of libertarian advocates, correctional options that work are often those that contribute significantly to managing offenders at a lower financial cost or in a more parsimonious way, respectively. In either case, the motivating focus on cost or parsimony is tempered by an implicit underlying constraint that any new option should not do appreciably worse in terms of public safety than the one it replaces. If the demand for programs that work originates in a victims' rights forum, focus is likely to be centered around that constituency's particular interests, such as calls for more efficient and effective restitution programming, in which the principal measure of what works will be tied to the collection and disbursement of money owed by the offenders to their victims (Harland & Rosen, 1990).

Although predominantly driven by utilitarian concerns, questions about the optimal nature and scope of correctional options have not escaped the attention of retributivists. Options that work for them need have little to do with consequentialist concerns for public safety; rather, they focus on sanctions that would reduce the measure of community corrections to equitably administered units of pain and suffering, on the same kind of unidimensional, and to its advocates, morally superior tariff of punishment with which imprisonment has come to be equated under desert-based sentencing schemes (see, e.g., Knapp, 1988a, 1988b; Von Hirsch, 1992).

Levels of Choice and Black Box Options

Although the search for options that work can be pursued in relation to almost any facet of the corrections business, the most prevalent image is probably one of an intervention measure or combination or program of such measures designed to reduce the criminal's proclivity or opportunity to reoffend. The search could extend beyond such a programmatic or intervention-specific focus to include improvements in other areas, including policies, technologies, staffing (qualifications, training, remuneration, etc.), facilities, and resource allocation decisions in general. Thus the search encompasses not only options that focus directly on control or reform of offenders but diagnostic and assessment tools that indirectly might play an important role in maximizing the impact of such efforts. Still more broadly, it might include the way in which policies are developed or in which planned change takes place more generally in correctional settings, particularly in the actual design phase of program development. In either case, assessments of whether the options work depend on cost and political feasibility concerns as well as on the degree to which they can be linked ultimately to advancing the kinds of reductive, reparative, and retributive goals outlined earlier.

In a practical sense, the task of choosing correctional options that work most typically occurs at two separate levels of decision making, each involving selection from a menu of coercive or facilitative measures for dealing with offenders. First, it is the task of the sentencing judge and other practitioners who provide case-by-case input to sentencing decisions. Second, it is the task of correctional agency specialists who, as part of a larger process of program development,[1] are expected to incorporate the best available ingredients into the design of programs or interventions for inclusion on the menu.

It is an important challenge for those involved in correctional research and evaluation to make it easier for decision makers in the day-to-day sentencing (or bail or parole) function, and in the program design process, to compare and make more rational decisions about different options. Only with an information base generated in response to this challenge about the differential effectiveness of correctional options is it likely that the ones that are selected will achieve the goals they are expected to accomplish and that correct decisions will be made about interchangeability or equivalence of options according to different decision-making criteria. Such information must be tied to as precise a definition as possible of the options in question and in particular to the specific offender(s) being targeted. Against that backdrop, the task for researchers is to work with case-by-case decision makers and program designers to generate and compile evaluation data in terms of as many as possible of the essential common dimensions that they might find salient in making their choices.

In striving to construct such a body of information, the tasks of assessing an option's likely congruence (fit) with the decision maker's dominant goal(s), and comparing it to other alternatives, will be more complex and susceptible to ambiguity and misunderstanding when the option under consideration is not just a discrete treatment measure or other sanction but, instead, a program in which an amalgam of intervention measures is involved. In the latter situation, comparisons must take into consideration the likelihood of direct and interaction effects of combinations of individual parts of the program on subgroups of participants, as well as effects of the program as a whole. Otherwise, offenders may be subjected to all-or-nothing involvement in the standard regimes of, say, a day treatment center or boot camp, when perhaps only one or more of the program elements is really warranted. Scientifically sound evidence about even the overall impact of many popular correctional programs would be an improvement over the anecdotal and impressionistic basis on which so many decisions to adopt, continue, or refine them have already been made. Making decisions about correctional options in terms of kitchen sink or black box programs rather than in relation to the multiple and often conflicting intervention measures that they comprise, however, can lead to overprogramming and wasteful and possibly counterproductive application of correctional resources.

Structuring the Choice

In the context of program design and individual sentencing decisions, choosing correctional options that work—or more realistically, seem most likely to work—can be viewed as part of a three-stage exercise of constructing the most appropriate disposition for different offenders. It begins with an analysis of the risks, stakes, and needs presented in any particular case to identify the kinds of reparative, preventive, or retributive concerns that may be indicated. The second step is to match compensatory, punitive, treatment, or incapacitative techniques from a general menu of known alternatives. This is followed in Stage 3 of the process by selection from corresponding specific options available in the jurisdiction involved. Table 1.1 summarizes the general range of sanctioning techniques employed by sentencing authorities at Stage 2 of the process. It is in the third stage—in choosing corresponding programs or specific intervention measures from among options available locally, or recommending to program designers that new ones be added—that the need for clear and reliable descriptive and evaluative information about possible alternatives becomes essential.

Table 1.1 summarizes the range of intervention possibilities typically contemplated, if not present, in most jurisdictions, and illustrates the sizable

TABLE 1.1 Summary Listing of Major Correctional Options

WARNING MEASURES (Notice of consequences of subsequent wrongdoing)	Admonishment/cautioning (administrative, judicial) Suspended execution or imposition of sentence	
INJUNCTIVE MEASURES (Banning legal conduct)	Travel (e.g., from jurisdiction, to specific criminogenic spots) Association (e.g., with other offenders) Driving Possession of weapons Use of alcohol Professional activity (e.g., disbarment)	
ECONOMIC MEASURES	Restitution Costs Fees Forfeitures Support payments Fines (standard, day fines)	
WORK-RELATED MEASURES	Community service (individual placement, work crew) Paid-employment requirements	
EDUCATION-RELATED MEASURES	Academic (e.g., basic literacy, GED) Vocational training Life skills training	
PHYSICAL AND MENTAL HEALTH TREATMENT MEASURES	Psychological/psychiatric Chemical (e.g., methadone, psychoactive drugs) Surgical (e.g., acupuncture, drug treatment)	
PHYSICAL CONFINEMENT MEASURES	Partial or intermittent confinement	Home curfew Day treatment center Halfway house Restitution center Weekend detention facility/jail Outpatient treatment facility (e.g., drug/mental health)

number of alternatives that may be in competition for the decision maker's attention in any given case. The table represents the type of menu from which sanctioning authorities will ordinarily be required to select. Once fleshed out to reflect the actual legal and practical circumstances of an individual juris-

TABLE 1.1 (Continued)

PHYSICAL CONFINEMENT MEASURES (cont'd.)	Full/continuous confinement	Full home/house arrest Mental hospital Other residential treatment facility (e.g., drug/alcohol) Boot camp Detention facility Jail Prison
MONITORING/COMPLIANCE MEASURES (May be attached to all other sanctions)	Required of the offender	Mail reporting Electronic monitoring (telephone check-in, active electronic monitoring device) Face-to-face reporting Urine analysis (random, routine)
	Required of the monitoring agent	Criminal records checks Sentence compliance checks (e.g., on payment of $$ sanctions; attendance/performance at treatment, work, or educational sites) Third-party checks (family, employer, surety, service/treatment provider), via mail, telephone, in person Direct surveillance/observation (random/routine visits, and possibly search, at home, work, institution, or elsewhere) Electronic monitoring (regular phone checks and/or passive monitoring device—currently used with home curfew or house arrest, but could track movement more widely as technology develops)

diction concerned about structuring the discretion of key actors at the third stage of the correctional process, this kind of list also could serve as sort of checklist in a "desk manual" for judges, for probation presentence investigators preparing recommendations, or for defense-based advocates preparing client-specific sentencing plans. It should also stand as a summary table of contents to the more detailed descriptive accounts of each substantive sentencing option that such a reference work would also ideally provide.

Ranking and Grading Options

At both the case-specific and program design levels, surprisingly little attention has been paid to the issue of scaling criminal penalties in such a way as to aid decision makers in judging how well penalties are likely to work at all and in relation to each other, in terms of satisfying concerns uppermost in the minds of sanctioning authorities. Recent efforts to respond to the need for guidance with respect to intermediate sanctions have focused heavily on ways to grade them in terms of weight or value on a scale of severity or onerousness (Knapp, 1988a, 1988b; Von Hirsch, 1983, 1992; Von Hirsch, Wasik, & Greene, 1989; cf. Sebba, 1978). Among the most frequently applied attempts along these lines have been the efforts of day fines advocates to assign "units of punishment" to offenses—rather than fixing dollar amounts—so that offenders of different financial means would be assessed the same number of punishment units for similar offenses but would satisfy them in terms of their individual payment abilities—each might be required, for example, to pay a day's income for each unit assessed (Greene, 1988).

Arguments that primacy of scaling and fixing exchange rates for different sanctions should be given to a value of assuring equality of severity or suffering have not gone unchallenged. Instead, it has been suggested that sanctions might be more usefully and realistically scaled, and equivalencies gauged, in terms of their value (or perceived value) in satisfying broader, more functional system goals, rather than simply on their ability to satisfy purely retributive demands for assuring that comparable levels of pain be inflicted on offenders committing similar offenses (McGarry, 1990, p. 4; Morris & Tonry, 1990, p. 104). The decision maker's demand might, for example, be for an ordering that allows ready comparison of the different options in Table 1.1, not only or even principally in terms of how much pain and suffering they each represent; rather, interest might call for a ranking and scaling on the basis of their perceived or demonstrated value as utilitarian techniques for controlling the rate of crime (value as a general deterrent measure) or recidivism (value as a rehabilitative, incapacitative, or specific deterrent measure).

In addition to traditional retributive and utilitarian preventive aims, scaling and comparison could also proceed along a restorative dimension based on the value of different sanctions in their ability to address goals such as reparation to the victim, community, or society. The term *accountability*—in the sense of holding offenders accountable for their crimes—has also been used widely in recent years, especially in juvenile justice restitution circles, as if it were an independent goal of criminal sanctions (Schneider & Warner, 1989). In my view, this is often only an unhelpful code word for retribution. Or to be more charitable to its proponents, it is at best no more than a rephrasing of the equally ambiguous desire to make offenders "pay" for their crimes, which can either mean pay in the sense of suffer (retribution) or pay in the sense of compensate (reparation). In either case, conceptual clarity and intellectual integrity are both better served by using the more specific underlying terms.

As well as comparing sanctions in terms of their value in satisfying the primary goals *of* sentencing (restorative, preventive, and retributive), other dimensions of a continuum of sanctions might involve scaling and grading in terms of various limiting principles or goals *at* sentencing. At a program and policy level, for example, decision makers from budget and oversight agencies may have a more specialized concern in seeing sanctions graded and assessed according to the economic costs that each represents. Still a further possibility is to grade sanctions in terms of their political implications, including their value on a scale of public satisfaction or approval by different criminal justice professionals, victims groups, or other important constituencies.

In sum, correctional options might be scaled according to their relative value in relation to a number of important goals of sanctioning authorities. A simplified graphic illustration of the type of decision tool to which such an undertaking might lead is presented in Table 1.2. Collectively, the resulting ratings would inform judges and other decision makers involved in the correctional process how well each option is considered to fit, or work, on the different dimensions or measures of effectiveness, efficiency, and fairness represented by the goals being measured.

We are a very long way from even beginning the research agenda by which the kinds of scaling values for the cells suggested in Table 1.2 might be supplied (Byrne & Pattavina, 1992; Harland, 1993; U.S. General Accounting Office, 1990). Moreover, even assuming numerical scores could be inserted in the cells for every option and scaling dimension in Table 1.2, selection and interchangeability decisions must further be guided by policies and rules determining the relative weight and priority to be given to each dimension when conflicts (e.g., between punishment and treatment) arise. Assuming

TABLE 1.2 Illustration of Scaling Possibilities for Correctional Options: Type of Option, by Scaling Dimensions and Units of Measurement

TYPE OF OPTION	SCALING DIMENSIONS						
	RETRIBUTIVE SEVERITY	CRIME REDUCTION[a]	RECIDIVISM REDUCTION[b]	REPARATION	ECONOMIC COST	PUBLIC SATISFACTION	ETC.
	UNITS OF MEASUREMENT/ASSESSMENT						
OPTION A	Value	Value	Value	Value	Value	Value	
OPTION B	in	in	in	in	in	in	
OPTION C	terms	terms	terms	terms	terms	terms	
	of	of	of	of	of	of	Etc.
	pain	impact	impact	compensating	cost	public	
OPTION D	and	on	on	aggrieved	efficiency	approval	
	suffering[c]	crime	reoffense	parties[d]		ratings	
ETC.		rate	rate				

SOURCE: Harland (1993).
NOTES: a. General deterrence effects.
b. Specific deterrence, incapacitation, rehabilitation effects.
c. Or in terms of units of onerousness, intrusiveness, or deprivation of autonomy/liberty.
d. Direct victims and possibly indirectly affected individuals, groups, or entities (e.g., family, insurers, taxpayers, community, society).

adequate specification and description of the different options on any list of possibilities from which the system's response to a given case might be crafted, the next question that arises is, Given such a range of choices, is there a consistent, principled order or sequence in which the various measures should be factored into the construction of an appropriate sanctioning response? In any given case or class of cases, how does the sanctioning decision maker know where to start the selection process, where to stop, and how to resolve conflicts that may arise between competing possibilities on the list? All things being equal, for example, should a comprehensive sanctioning scheme afford primacy of attention to compensating victims and other interests of restorative justice? Or must those goals be subordinate to the public safety concerns of prevention advocates? Where does either rank in relation to retributive demands that our primary concern should be to make sure that offenders are made to suffer some appropriate degree of pain and suffering for their crimes, regardless of considerations of social utility? And how should costs (direct, opportunity) and public satisfaction factor into the final analysis?

A Working Tool for Decision Makers

A considerably cruder but more immediately applicable tool for decision makers who must choose among contending correctional options is presented in Table 1.3. Without prejudging what particular correctional options should be chosen, the approach outlined in Table 1.3 is predicated on the assumption that such decisions, especially in the strategic planning and reform context, should be shaped and guided in an environment characterized as much as possible by the principles of *rational decision making.*

Acceptance of this preference or bias may seem at first glance to be a noncontroversial or even trivial point. That it is not becomes painfully evident when the full implications of what rational decision making involves are truly appreciated, when the structural impediments that make the traditional criminal justice system so unconducive to it are acknowledged,[2] and when the deplorably chaotic nature of much traditional criminal justice decision making is understood:

> These decisions are not always highly visible. They are made, ordinarily, within wide areas of discretion. The objectives of the decisions are not always clear; and

TABLE 1.3 Rational Assessment Matrix: Framework for Choosing Among Correctional Options

SECTION I	SECTION II	SECTION III						SECTION IV
GOAL OR IMPACT MEASURE ON WHICH COMPARISON OF OPTIONS IS BEING MADE	RANK ORDER OF IMPORTANCE ASSIGNED TO GOAL [1, 2, 3, 4, ETC.]	COMPARATIVE RATING — OPTION A: ___ vs. OPTION B: ___						ROW SUBTOTAL FOR EACH GOAL LISTED [+2 to −2]
		Option A is much better [A++]	Option A is somewhat better [A+]	A and B are about equal [0]	Option B is somewhat better [B+]	Option B is much better [B++]	Unsure, need more info [D/K]	
Crime reduction (general deterrence)								
Recidivism reduction (rehab./incapacitation/specific deterrence)								
Appropriate level of retribution ("fit" with crime seriousness)								
Reduce disparity/increase equity								
Reduce delay, expedite processing								
Reduce jail population levels (admissions/length of stay)								
Reduce prison population levels (admissions/length of stay)								
Victim benefits (restitution, other)								
Offender benefits (employment, education, other)								
Legality/constitutionality								
Reduce financial costs to system								
Satisfy key constituent opinion (public/professional/political)								
Other _____								
Other _____								

indeed, the principal objectives of these decisions are often the subject of much debate. Usually they are not guided by explicit decision policies. Often the participants are unable to verbalize the basis for the selection of decision alternatives. Adequate information for the decisions usually is unavailable. Rarely can the decisions be demonstrated to be rational. (Gottfredson & Gottfredson, 1988, p. xvii)

The exercise condensed into Table 1.3 is an attempt to begin to remedy the foregoing types of deficiency in the way decisions about justice policies, programs, and cases are typically made by communicating as succinctly as possible an understanding of the nature and importance of a rational decision-making model, highlighting the skills and resources required for its successful use and serving as a specific tool—the Rational Assessment Matrix—that it is hoped may be helpful as an instrument in both the instruction and practical application of rational decision-making principles.

Ingredients of the Rational Assessment Model

Briefly, a rational decision has been defined by Wilkins (1975), borrowing from statistical decision theory, as the choice from among available alternatives that in light of the information available maximizes the achievement of the purpose of the decision. Broken down, this implies a number of steps to the rational decision-making process:

1. Specify decision goals.
2. Define decision options.
3. Develop information to assess the relative merit of each option.
4. Select, according to articulated decision rules, the option(s) thought to be most congruent with the stated goals.[3]

Table 1.3 is intended to offer both a schematic representation of the preceding process and a working tool that can be used by individuals or groups to structure decision making at the individual case level or for program or policy development purposes. It is designed around the premise that most decisions reduce to a matter of choice between a couple of leading contenders, about which the decision maker(s) have at least a general understanding going into the assessment and selection process. The choices usually include a reform or innovation option (styled Option A in Table 1.3) versus the status quo or problem option (Option B in Table 1.3).[4]

To use the instrument in Table 1.3 as a basis for making choices about sanctioning options, participants in the assessment begin by listing, in Section I, the major goals against which they believe the soundness of their decision should be evaluated. In one sense, this list is no more than specifying the immediate problems facing the decision maker(s), such as preventing recidivism or reducing overcrowding of correctional facilities. At another level, it requires reflection on other important, "constraining" goals within which such immediate objectives must be pursued; these may be spelled out in an agency's broader mission statement or derive from similarly general goals of the system as a whole, such as operating within acceptable limits of public safety (crime and recidivism risks), justice for offenders and for victims, cost-conscious management of resources, and so on.

Although not intended to be an exhaustive listing, the criteria included in Section I of Table 1.3 are representative of the most common dimensions of concern expressed in the justice literature. Their generality and importance have been confirmed repeatedly by participants in a variety of training and conference settings over the past several years. Consequently, although different cases, problems, or change situations will obviously generate their own lists of goal statements, as will different decision makers, the criteria will, in all probability, tend toward some variant of the illustrative factors in Table 1.3.

Preliminary discussion should focus on developing a shared sense of the meaning of the goals listed, whether from the examples in the table or from additions entered in the empty rows. Participants may also elect to assess separately any subcomponents of the measures already specified (e.g., rehabilitative vs. incapacitation impact in the "recidivism reduction" row; or employment, education, other gains, in the "offender benefits" row). To the extent possible, each goal should be operationally defined as early as possible, by specifying in advance the most appropriate measurable indicators of its achievement; in practice, this step may occur later in the process, after a clearer definition of the problem and response options has been developed.

Step 2 in the assessment exercise requires consensus building around the rank order of importance attributed to each goal. The results of this discussion are entered in Section II, with the most important criterion assigned a value of 1, the next 2, and so on. Tied rankings are not fatal to the exercise but should be broken wherever possible by further discussion.

Step 3 is perhaps the most deceptive and time-consuming part of the exercise summarized in Table 1.3, requiring a detailed description (definition) of the two options to be compared. This will include the main actors and intervention measures involved, ideally thorough mapping of processing routes, time frames, and attendant resource and cost allocations for each option under assessment. Based on this detailed understanding of what each option entails, Step 4 then involves identifying and applying the best logical and empirical evidence available to make a judgment about which of the two options rates better on each of the criteria listed in Section I.

Starting with the goals ranked highest, participants enter a check mark, row by row, in one of the columns in Section III. If the leading reform candidate (Option A) is judged to look "much better" than existing practice (Option B), in terms of likely impact on jail population, for example, a check mark would be marked in the column headed A++ on the row in which that goal is listed. A check mark under the column A+ would indicate an assessment that Option A was "better" than Option B on that dimension. The "about equal" column would be checked for those criteria on which the conclusion is that one option is likely to be as good or bad as the other. Check B+ if Option B looks "better"; check column B++ if Option B looks "much better"; and very important, enter a check mark in the column headed "Unsure, need more info" if the available theoretical and empirical information simply is not adequate to make a decision on anything other than blind faith or unexplicated instinct.

Next, participants can enter in Section IV the numerical scores corresponding to the check mark on every row (A++ = 2; A+ = 1; About equal = 0; B+ = −1; B++ = −2; and Unsure = D/K). These scores give at a glance an indication of the number of dimensions on which the proposed innovation (Option A) fares better and worse than its competition and a rough indicator for each criterion of how much better or worse. Obviously, if Section IV ends up being filled with positive scores of 2 on every measure, the case for proceeding to adopt the new option appears very strong. If it scores well on many of the criteria but poorly on one or more ranked as being highly important, however, the decision is less clear.

One advantage of this admittedly crude scoring technique is that any negative scores for an innovation that otherwise is judged to fit well with a majority of the goals identified need not be taken as grounds for rejection. Rather, such scores can be used to identify dimensions on which design revisions might be considered at the outset to strengthen the original conception of what the reform option would look like and directly address the weaknesses that caused it to score poorly on a particular measure in the first analysis. Entries in the Unsure column obviously highlight areas in which further information might be collected or where early monitoring and evaluation data ought to be emphasized if a decision is taken to proceed in advance of obtaining such information.

The framework for assessing decision options encapsulated in Table 1.3 is designed to be useful at two levels. First, it is intended to capture succinctly, but comprehensively, the most crucial elements of what is required to satisfy the minimum standards of rational decision making. Second, it is a tool that may be used as a sort of worksheet to guide those engaged in actual decision situations as to whether to adopt, continue, modify, or reject a particular option, whether as a disposition in an individual case or as a matter of choice between one criminal justice program or policy and another. It may be used by decision makers seeking to hold themselves accountable to the intellectual and scientific rigor of such a process and to challenge others who would impose their own options for perhaps more ideological, emotional, or purely political reasons.

In each instance, the instrument serves as a reminder of the major conceptual stages in the decision process and of the complexity of goals, value judgments, and theoretical and empirical information that must be weighed in selecting the most rationally compelling course of action. It highlights the importance of clarifying and prioritizing goals and of identifying and defining target populations and other baseline details of the principal options for achieving them. Insofar as the instrument exposes inconsistencies or lack of fit between important goals and aspects of a program or policy being assessed, it also helps to pinpoint design weaknesses and corresponding areas needing reformulation and improvement. In addition, by explicitly and precisely targeting gaps in our knowledge about the relative ability of either option to deliver on the assumptions and expectations underlying the major goal statements, the instrument exposes deficiencies in available evaluation data and information systems that must be remedied to inspire confidence that a truly informed choice has been made.

Finally, and perhaps most important, by emphasizing the significance of measurably defined objectives and evaluation standards, and the corresponding role of demonstrably relevant performance and outcome information, the instrument demonstrates the vital need for close and ongoing collaboration between the key decision maker(s) and the research scientist under a rational decision-making approach (Harland & Harris, 1984, 1987). This type of collaborative, group process approach to program or policy development and evaluation is generally known as the action research model. Propounded almost half a century ago by Kurt Lewin, it has been described as involving a sequence or circle of problem analysis; fact finding; conceptualization, development, selection, and execution of action responses; more fact finding or evaluation; and then a repetition of this whole circle of activities (Sanford, 1970). Ultimately, it may be the criminal justice system's best and only hope for advancing the cause of correctional options that work.

Notes

1. Program design is only one phase of a much larger process of program development. It is an increasingly voiced belief in the planned change literature that overall program success or failure may be influenced as much or more by how systematically and well each phase of that process is tackled as by any particular strength or weakness in the program concept itself. Aspects of this issue are taken up by Harris and Smith in Chapter 7.

2. Ross (1980) describes the contexts most conducive to rational decision making as being characterized by minimal uncertainty: Feasible courses of action can be defined, the outcomes of alternatives can be predicted, there is agreement on the relative value of outcomes, the decision-making organization is stable and relatively immune to outside influence, and so forth. None of these conditions, of course, typically prevails in the criminal justice policy environment. Numerous writers have suggested that where existing organizational attributes are an obstacle to innovation, a separate decision-making structure should be established to initiate and develop innovations, or, in other words, for strategic planning (see, e.g., Hudzik & Cordner, 1983; Lawrence & Lorsch, 1969; Zaltman & Duncan, 1977).

3. Because a rational decision model assumes that goals may change or the ability of a particular option to achieve a desired goal may change or that new options may be discovered that will do better, a fifth step can be added to the process—reassessing decisions on a periodic basis, based on feedback from prior outcomes (Juvenile Justice Statistics and Systems Development Program, 1991).

4. Even when two or more reform proposals are being compared, the process of choosing between them is often one of deciding which offers the greatest potential for improvement over the status quo or problem situation to which they are expected to respond.

Risk-Needs Assessment and Treatment

James Bonta

One of the major tasks of any correctional agency is to enhance the protection of the public by managing the risk that offenders pose for harmful acts. At a very simple level, this can mean separating offenders from the community through imprisonment. In North America, for most offenders, this approach serves as a temporary measure. Confining individuals indefinitely is reserved for the most serious crimes. The vast majority of offenders receive less restrictive sentences, and they are eventually returned to the community.

Reintegrating offenders into the community, or in the case of probation and parole, maintaining offenders within the community, depends on two important strategies. One strategy involves making sound release decisions, and the second involves effective treatment programming. The first strategy relies on risk assessments and, as typically used in practice, seems to have little relevance to the second strategy, the planning and delivery of effective rehabilitation programs. The purpose of this chapter is to show that risk assessment, along with other forms of assessment, is not only related to rehabilitation but essential for good correctional practices.

AUTHOR'S NOTE: Opinions expressed are those of the author and do not necessarily represent the Ministry of the Solicitor General.

The Assessment of Offenders

The assessment of offenders has long been appreciated as an essential function for those who work with offenders. Many of the early criminologists and students of human behavior recognized the importance of differentiating criminal offenders and developed complex models to assign offenders to different categories. Lombroso described "atavistic" features, Freud outlined differences in personality structure, and sociologists categorized deviance as a function of social values and structure. What is common to all is the view that not all offenders are alike, and their differences are important for assessing their "criminality" and defining the approach for dealing with them.

Burgess's (1928) classic study of parolees provides the origins of efforts to systematically and empirically develop objective offender assessment tools, the so-called risk assessment instruments. I refer to these as "second-generation" offender assessment approaches. The "first generation" of offender assessments has probably been with us since the first man or woman intentionally hurt another human being. First-generation assessments are described by various terms, such as *subjective assessment, professional judgment, intuition,* and *gut-level feelings.* These assessments involve decision rules not easily observable and difficult to replicate. Second-generation assessment instruments publicly identify the factors that contribute to the assessment process.

Using the terms *first generation* and *second generation* does not imply that subjective, professional judgment assessments are no longer practiced or that they are completely undesirable. First-generation assessments are prevalent and can play an important role in offender assessment. I argue, however, that overreliance on these measures is wrought with problems and has played an inhibiting role in furthering knowledge on criminal behavior and effective interventions. This is not to say that second-generation assessments are wholly satisfactory either. They are an improvement over first-generation assessments, but there is a "third" generation, risk-needs assessment, that finally links the assessment process to rehabilitation and advances us still further. Without a doubt, someday there will be a fourth generation. All we can say right now is that advances in offender assessment are proceeding at an exponential rate. It took a millennium to progress to the second generation, 50 years to the third (1928 to 1979), and less than 15 years from the beginning of risk-needs instrumentation, we are on the verge of a fourth generation.

First-Generation Assessment

First-generation assessments involve the collection of information on the offender and his or her situation and then interpreting this information in a meaningful manner (usually with respect to the propensity for criminal behavior and treatment needs). Almost every worker in a social service agency, be it correctional or not, is familiar with this form of assessment. It usually involves an unstructured interview with the client and a review of official documentation followed by some general conclusions and recommendations concerning the client.

The most serious weakness of this approach is that the rules for collecting the information and formulating interpretations of the "data" are subject to considerable personal discretion. The interviewer is free to ask questions and seek information that he or she thinks is important. This information may or may not be relevant to the decisions at hand, or commonly agreed on. Correctional agencies may provide policy manuals and procedures as guides to what information is important and where to place the emphasis, but these guidelines are often vaguely defined. As a result, the correctional worker can easily overlook or overemphasize information based on personal knowledge of criminal behavior (which may or may not be correct) rather than on empirically defensible theories of crime.

A dependency on first-generation assessments makes accountability and fairness difficult. Outside observers find it a challenge to identify the specific reasons why decisions are made and why offenders who appear similar are sometimes treated differently by various professionals. Research on the inter-rater reliability of professional judgments has frequently shown that professionals are just as likely to disagree on the key features of a case as they are to agree (Monahan, 1981; Wardlaw & Millier, 1978).

Finally, the evidence as to how well clinicians and other experts can predict future criminal behavior based on their professional judgment clearly shows that their accuracy is legally, ethically, and practically unacceptable (Andrews & Bonta, 1994; Gottfredson & Gottfredson, 1986; Monahan, 1981). A recent illustration can be found in a study by Menzies and his colleagues (Menzies, Webster, McMain, Staley, & Scaglione, 1994). From behind a one-way mirror, various professionals (nurses, psychologists, psychiatrists, social workers, and correctional officers) observed offenders receiving mental health status examinations. The observers were asked to rate the "dangerousness" of each offender, and their ratings were then correlated with measures of offender reoffending over a 6-year period. The results failed to demonstrate consistent predictions of dangerousness based on the professional judgments of the observers.

This sorry state of affairs has fueled the critics who argue that criminal behavior cannot be predicted. In addition, the antiprediction arguments have created the impression that research into individual differences is a wasteful exercise and that the focus on the person is misguided. Rather, it is argued, social factors are the true roots of crime. Fortunately, some researchers have continued to recognize the importance of individual differences and the measurement of these factors in an objective manner. This attitude has produced the second generation of offender assessments.

Second-Generation Assessment

Objective, empirically based offender risk assessments can be traced back to Burgess's (1928) study of over 3,000 parolees. Burgess identified 21 factors that differentiated parole successes from parole failures and he used these factors to construct a risk scale. The presence of a factor was assigned a score of 1, and the higher the score, the greater the likelihood of failure while on parole. For example, offenders who fell in the highest risk category had a failure rate of 76% and those in the minimum range had a failure rate of 1.5%.

The next major step in the development and use of second-generation offender assessments is seen in Glueck and Glueck's (1950) prediction tables. Variables that differentiated delinquents and nondelinquents formed the basis for empirically derived estimates of the probability of delinquent behavior. The new twist to the objective assessment process was that weights were assigned to the different variables (the Burgess method is simply a 0-1 scoring format). The assignment of weights to different items on risk scales can be achieved in many different ways (see Chapter 3). Today, nearly all objective risk instruments use either the 0-1 scoring method first developed by Burgess (1928) or a variation on the weighting methodology. Regardless of the method used, the predictive power of the tests is approximately comparable (Gottfredson & Gottfredson, 1979, 1985).

In the 1970s, research on risk assessment virtually exploded. On a national scale, we saw the development of the Salient Factor Score (SFS; Hoffman, 1983) in the United States. In Canada, there was the development of the Statistical Index on Recidivism (SIR; Nuffield, 1982). These risk scales were based on sound empirical research, and they performed satisfactorily in differentiating lower-risk offenders from the higher-risk offenders (Hann & Harman, 1992; Hoffman, 1983; Hoffman & Beck, 1985; Hoffman, Stone-Meierhoefer, & Beck, 1978; Nuffield, 1982). Their major weakness, however, was that the instruments provided little direction for treatment. And why? Mainly because the items making up the scales are historical in nature. For example, 6 of the 7 SFS items and 13 of the 15 SIR items deal with historical factors such as criminal history.

Rehabilitation is based on the premise that people can change, and if assessment is to contribute to rehabilitation efforts it must be capable of measuring change. This notion of the measurement of change is what fundamentally separates the second-generation assessment tools from the third generation.

Third-Generation Assessment

Risk-needs assessments form what I call the third generation of assessment. These classification instruments go beyond statistical risk prediction, in which the major purpose is to make decisions about the degree of freedom granted an offender. There is an acceptance of the need to deliver rehabilitation services if we are to manage risk. Furthermore, treatment services cannot be given to everyone because of the costs involved, nor can they be randomly assigned as in a lottery. Treatment must be matched to the "needs" of the offender.

Although psychologists, psychiatrists, social workers, and other social service providers have long noted the need to identify and attend to offender needs, wide-scale application of needs assessment in the criminal justice system is only a recent phenomenon. Early applications of psychologically based classification systems, such as the Megargee MMPI (Megargee & Bohn, 1979), Quay's AIMS (Quay, 1984), and the I-level (Sullivan, Grant, & Grant, 1957), attempted to classify offenders into groups assumed to differ in their treatment needs and therefore requiring different types of intervention. Studies of these classification systems showed some differentiation with respect to treatment responsiveness, but evidence for their predictive validity was scant (Andrews & Bonta, 1994; Andrews, Bonta, & Hoge, 1990; Van Voorhis, 1993, 1994). Thus they claimed to identify needs, but whether or not they predicted criminal behavior was unanswered.

The psychological classification systems reflected a belief that needs assessments were somehow fundamentally different from risk assessments; the two were like apples and oranges. Scholarly discussions of offender needs assessments rarely raised the question of risk prediction (Clements, 1986; Duffee & Duffee, 1981). This tradition is best mirrored in the most widely used offender classification system in the United States: the Wisconsin classification system (Baird, 1981).

Wisconsin's classification system is composed of three parts: risk assessment, needs assessment, and client management classification (CMC). CMC involves its own assessment of offenders and a prescribed treatment strategy. The three parts operate relatively independently. The only overlap between the risk and needs scales is that the offender is assigned to supervision levels depending on which scale he or she receives the highest score. In the available research with the Wisconsin classification instruments, information on predictive validity is available only for the risk scale (Andrews, Kiessling, Mickus, & Robinson, 1985; Baird, 1981; Baird, Heinz, & Bemus, 1979; Motiuk, 1991; Robinson & Porporino, 1989; Wright, Clear, & Dickson, 1984). Save for the Wright et al. study (1984), research on the Wisconsin risk instrument has confirmed its predictive validity.

For the CMC, there are only two reported studies addressing the predictive validity of the classification scheme, and the findings are mixed. Harris (1994) found evidence of predictive validity, whereas Loza (1991) failed to find a relationship between the CMC subtypes and postrelease recidivism. There is no information as to whether the needs items and scale also predict future criminal behavior. It seems nobody thought it was worth investigation, apparently assuming that needs assessment has little to do with criminal behavior.

Recent research has identified a category of needs referred to as *criminogenic* (Andrews & Bonta, 1994; Andrews, Bonta, et al., 1990). Criminogenic needs are linked to criminal behavior. If we alter these needs, then we change the likelihood of criminal behavior. Thus criminogenic needs are actually risk predictors, but they are *dynamic* in nature rather than static.

Demonstrating criminogenic needs requires assessments and reassessments and then relating the changes to future criminal behavior. Often, changes between intake assessments and reassessments have been perceived as indicating instability and unreliability in the measurement instrument. This is an appropriate interpretation when the assessment tool comprises static variables. For offender assessment tools that have a significant number of dynamic items, however, it is possible that the difference in scores between intake and reassessment may actually reflect a change in the person and the person's situation.

TABLE 2.1 Comparison of Selected Items in the Wisconsin and Manitoba Needs
            Assessment

Item	Wisconsin	Manitoba
Family/Marital Relationships	Yes	Yes
Financial Management	Yes	Yes
Alcohol Use Within Family	No	Yes
Emotional Stability of Probationer	Yes	Yes
Mental Ability of Probationer	Yes	Yes
Health	Yes	Yes
Peers/Companions	Yes	Yes
Drug/Alcohol Use	Yes	Separated into two items: (a) Drug and (b) Alcohol
Sexual Behavior	Yes	Yes
School	No	Yes
Employment	Yes	Yes
Academic/Vocational	Yes	Yes

Following the previous discussion, it is reasonable to suspect that perhaps
the Wisconsin needs assessment is tapping criminogenic needs. If so, then use
of the needs scale for treatment purposes would receive an added boost.

In an effort to explore the validity of the Wisconsin needs instrument, my
colleagues and I have embarked on a series of studies using data collected in
the province of Manitoba. Manitoba adopted the Wisconsin risk-needs scales
without any modification and implemented them across the province in 1982
for use in probation services. In 1986, a few items from the instrument were
modified or dropped and several others added. The majority of the items,
however, especially with respect to the needs scale, remained the same (see
Table 2.1). Drawing on data between 1986 and 1991 for over 14,000 probationers, we found, as expected, that the risk scale predicted failure on probation (rs in the low .3 range; Bonta, Parkinson, Pang, & Barkwell, 1994).

More important, we also examined the predictive validity of the needs scale.
First, the item scores on the needs assessment were summated to form one
composite score, and then the summated needs score was correlated with
failure while on probation (both technical violations and new offenses).
Although the magnitude of the relationship was not as large as with the risk

TABLE 2.2 Correlations of Risk and Needs Total Scores With Probation Outcome

Sample Year	N	Risk	Need
1986	1,565	.23	.10
1987	1,501	.24	.18
1988	1,640	.22	.18
1989	2,110	.33	.20
1990	2,347	.33	.20
1991	2,452	.33	.22
1992	3,032	.33	.21

NOTE: Data based on Manitoba's risk-needs classification (from Bonta et al., 1994).

scale (*r*s in the .2 range), the combined scores of the needs assessment nevertheless did predict failure on probation. As shown in Table 2.2, the needs assessment of the Manitoba-Wisconsin classification system showed predictive validity.

Then in a new analysis, we explored the relationship between changes in needs classification between intake and termination of probation and failure while on probation. The results for the year 1990 illustrate our general findings (see Table 2.3). Individuals who increased in their needs level show increased failure rates, whereas those who decreased in needs level show decreased failure rates. It appears that the needs instrument is sensitive to criminogenic needs.

To our knowledge, there are only two offender classification instruments *intentionally* designed to measure criminogenic needs: the Level of Supervision Inventory (LSI; Andrews & Bonta, 1994), presently used in the province of Ontario and the state of Colorado, and the Correctional Service of Canada's Community Risk/Needs Management Scale (Motiuk, 1993). To underscore the belief that criminogenic needs are a subset of risk factors, the needs items are integrated with the more traditional risk items to form one scale instead of two independently scored scales (an example of some of the items is shown in Table 2.4). Furthermore, both scales are systematically readministered to offenders to measure changes that may result from intervention and to realign services to maximize the reduction of criminal behavior.

The LSI includes 54 items ranging from static, criminal history variables to more dynamic items, such as the offender's present employment and

TABLE 2.3 Percentage of Failure on Probation by Changes in Needs Level as Measured by the Manitoba-Wisconsin Needs Assessment

	Retest Needs Level			
Intake Needs Level	Low	Medium	High	Overall
Low	12.9	30.4	56.2	14.3
	(441)	(112)	(16)	(100/569)
Medium	14.4	33.8	57.5	28.2
	(486)	(607)	(113)	(340/1,206)
High	26.1	33.5	60.2	44.4
	(92)	(221)	(259)	(254/572)
Overall	14.8	33.3	59.3	29.6
	(151/1,019)	(313/940)	(230/388)	(694/2,347)

financial situation. Scoring of the instrument follows the Burgess 0 to 1 method where the presence of a risk factor is scored as 1. Scores are then summated to give a total risk-needs score. The LSI can be further analyzed into its subcomponents, many of which reflect dynamic aspects of the offender's situation (e.g., living accommodations). High scores on the subcomponents suggest criminogenic needs or areas to target for intervention. Of course, successful elimination of these criminogenic needs contributes to a total reduction in the risk-needs score.

The Community Risk/Needs Management Scale shares many of the same subcomponents as the LSI. The various needs areas are rated by parole officers as low, medium, and high. The results are combined with an accompanying risk scale, and the results are used to inform decisions regarding service delivery.

Both offender assessment instruments have been shown to predict recidivism across a wide range of offenders (cf. Andrews & Bonta, 1994; Motiuk, 1993). For example, Motiuk and Porporino (1989) found the Community Risk/ Needs Management Scale predicted outcome (suspension or revocation) while on conditional release for a sample of 453 federally sentenced male offenders (in Canada, all sentences of 2 years or more are a federal responsibility).

More extensive evidence is available on the LSI as tapping criminogenic needs. For example, three studies have found subcomponents of the LSI

TABLE 2.4 Examples of Items Composing Risk-Needs Classification for Two
Canadian Classification Systems

	Level of Supervision Inventory	*Community Risk/Needs Management*
Historical Risk Items:		
	Prior convictions	Criminal history
	Violent offense	Sex offense
Dynamic Need Items:		
	Financial management	Marital/family relationships
	Antisocial friends	Living arrangement
	Alcohol/drug abuse	Attitude

predicting correctional outcomes (Andrews, 1982; Bonta & Motiuk, 1985; Motiuk, Bonta, & Andrews, 1990). A more direct test of criminogenic needs assessment in the LSI system is research measuring changes in LSI scores and future criminal behavior. In a study by Andrews and Robinson (1984), 57 probationers were assessed at intake and 12 months later. During this time period, some probationers decreased in risk level (as measured by the LSI), some increased, and some stayed the same. A minimum 6-month *post*probation follow-up (recall that the Manitoba test-retest project involved failure only while on probation) found that these changes were associated with criminal behavior: Those who showed reductions in risk level also showed reductions in criminal behavior, those who increased in risk level showed increases in recidivism, and those who did not change in LSI scores showed no change in future criminal behavior (see Table 2.5).

Similarly, Motiuk (1991) administered the LSI to 54 inmates on release from prison and once again when they were in the community under probation supervision. One-year *post*probation recidivism data were collected and the findings replicated the earlier Andrews and Robinson (1984) results (see Table 2.6).

The importance of criminogenic needs or dynamic risk factors lies in the fact that they may serve as targets for correctional intervention. They form the treatment goals for staff who counsel offenders, run treatment programs, and in general, attempt to reduce the risk of future criminal behavior. Thus third-generation offender assessments are inextricably linked to rehabilitation

TABLE 2.5 Percentage Recidivated by Changes in Risk Level as Measured by the LSI

At Intake	At Reassessment				
	Low	Moderate	High	Very High	Overall
Very High	—	—	50	100	75 (4)
High	—	0	27	100	41 (22)
Moderate	0	33	40	—	27 (11)
Low	0	0	0	100	5 (20)
Overall	0	10	32	100	28
	(19)	(10)	(19)	(9)	(57)

SOURCE: Andrews and Robinson (1984).

and control efforts. These assessments are concerned not only with questions such as who should be paroled or how closely an offender should be monitored but also with what must be changed about the offender or the offender's situation to minimize the risk for reoffending.

It is important at this point to insert a note of caution: We should not abandon risk assessments. Risk assessments are important from a treatment perspective in assigning intensive intervention programming to higher-risk offenders and minimal interventions to low-risk offenders (Gendreau, Cullen, & Bonta, 1994). This matching of risk level to treatment services, called the *risk principle,* appears to be an important factor in reducing recidivism (Andrews, Bonta, et al., 1990). For example, in reviews of the offender rehabilitation literature (Andrews & Bonta, 1994; Andrews, Zinger, et al., 1990; Chapter 5, this volume), providing intensive services to low-risk offenders is rarely, if ever, found to be associated with reduced recidivism. Sometimes, matching intensive services with low-risk offenders is found to produce *increased* recidivism. More typically, intensive treatment services produce lower recidivism rates when they are matched with higher-risk offenders. But once risk level is assessed and a decision is made as to how much treatment to provide, the assessment of criminogenic needs tells us *what* needs to be changed.

In summary, third-generation assessments recognize types of offender needs that are related to criminal behavior. In this regard, criminogenic needs are also risk predictors, but they are dynamic risk predictors.

TABLE 2.6 Percentage Recidivated by Changes in Risk Level as Measured by the LSI

	Retest Risk Level		
Intake Risk Level	*Low*	*High*	*Overall*
High	20.0	52.2	46.4
	(1/5)	(12/23)	(13/28)
Low	18.2	25.0	19.2
	(4/22)	(1/4)	(5/26)
Overall	18.5	48.1	33.3
	(5/27)	(13/27)	(18/54)

SOURCE: Motiuk (1991).

What Is Effective Rehabilitation?

I will not review in detail the major characteristics of effective correctional rehabilitation programming. More comprehensive reviews follow in Chapters 5 and 6. I also cannot assume, however, that the "assessment" function of the correctional process is complete. As noted in the previous paragraph, risk-needs assessment is directly linked to correctional treatment. For this reason, a few further comments need to be voiced.

Correctional rehabilitation can be defined as an intervention to reduce recidivism. Criminogenic needs are the intermediary links to recidivism. For the correctional interventionist, programs that target criminogenic needs form one of the basic approaches to reducing crime (other factors such as risk and responsivity are also important and discussed in more detail in Andrews & Bonta, 1994; Andrews, Bonta, et al., 1990). In other words, if criminogenic needs are not targeted, then reductions in recidivism are unlikely.

Evidence for the importance of targeting criminogenic needs for effective rehabilitation has been documented by meta-analyses of the rehabilitation literature (Andrews, Zinger, et al., 1990; Chapter 5, this volume). I will not comment on this literature. I do wish to emphasize, however, the general failure of criminal sanctioning to reduce recidivism (Gendreau, Paparozzi, Little, & Goddard, 1993; Chapter 4, this volume). The main reason for this failure is, quite simply, sanctions do not target criminogenic needs. For the most part, offenders are not assigned to different sanctions based on their criminogenic needs. Such assignments are usually based on offense rather offender characteristics. Can electronic monitoring programs, boot camps, or intensive supervision programs really change, for example, the substance abuse of some offenders or their antisocial attitudes? Beyond some general selection parameters (usually involving low-risk offenders), how specific are the assignments? Not very. Sanctions provide only the setting for service delivery, and it is the intervention within the setting that has the actual power to produce offender change (Andrews & Bonta, 1994; Gendreau et al., 1994).

Conclusions and Future Directions

Students of history like to say that the pendulum always swings back. It appears that we are returning to the rehabilitation days that were predominant in the 1960s and 1970s. It is no longer embarrassing to say the word *treatment* in public; interest in delivering rehabilitation programs, especially from front-line workers, is on the rise. But are we simply witnessing history repeating itself? Twenty years from now, will the pendulum swing back to punishment?

If this emerging prorehabilitation climate is to be more than a blip on history's radar screen, then researchers, practitioners, and policymakers must capitalize on the present climate by abandoning old models of criminal behavior and embracing new approaches that are *empirically based.* I empha-size empirically based because the field of criminology has been notoriously antiempirical (Andrews & Bonta, 1994). Research that failed to support favored theories on the causes of criminal behavior has been ignored, whereas weak evidence that supported traditional theory was promoted (Andrews & Wormith, 1989). With such disrespect for evidence, is it little wonder that many past assessment and rehabilitation methodologies showed weak effects?

To build on the present research and in consideration of other implementa-tion issues (see Chapter 7), I recommend the following steps:

1. Administer to offenders the best validated risk-needs assessment instruments. As we approach the 21st century, it is becoming incomprehensible that so many jurisdictions still depend almost entirely on "professional judgment," first-generation offender assessments for decisions affecting individual liberties.

2. Some agencies already may use well-validated risk instruments. These assess-ments may be quite appropriate for release and supervision decisions, but they can also be helpful for planning interventions that *reduce* risk. Following the risk

principle, programs must match the intensity of services to the risk level of the offender.

3. The "needs" in risk-needs assessments must include *criminogenic* needs. One of the major goals of corrections is to protect the public. In the short term, this is accomplished through intensive monitoring and restrictions of liberty. In the long term, however, we can reach this goal by reducing the risk for recidivism through treatment. Otherwise, sanctions by themselves are likely to have little impact on recidivism. Effective treatment depends on targeting those needs of offenders that are related to their offending behavior, and the assessment of those criminogenic needs in a systematic and objective manner is highly desired.

4. Monitor changes in offenders and their situation by conducting reassessments of their criminogenic needs. This serves two purposes. First, reassessments assist the correctional agency in protecting the public by alerting the agency to changes in the offender's situation that may signal increased risk and a responsibility to intervene. Second, reassessments facilitate evaluations of the agency's effectiveness. For example, demonstrable reductions in criminogenic needs at reassessment indicate that something is going right.

5. Following from the fourth point, once we attend to measuring changes in offenders we are naturally led to inquiring into the practices that bring change. If we see reduced or increased risk in our clients, then we ask what is it exactly that we are doing to produce such changes? The answer to this question is important in a time of fiscal constraint for choosing which rehabilitation programs to keep, which to modify, and which to discard. Even if we see *no* changes in our offender clientele, we are further ahead, for the alternative is to continue what we are doing in blissful and misleading ignorance.

6. In this chapter, I have emphasized the assessment of risk and criminogenic needs. There is a third aspect of assessment that is not understood as well but that may play an important role in maximizing the effectiveness of a treatment program. This third aspect is what has been referred to as the *responsivity principle* (Andrews & Bonta, 1994; Andrews, Bonta, et al., 1990).

The responsivity principle derives from the fact that offenders differ in motivation, personality, and emotional and cognitive abilities, and these characteristics can influence the offender's responsiveness to various therapists and treatment modalities. Matching on risk and targeting the appropriate criminogenic needs are fundamental to effective rehabilitation, but attention to responsivity factors can serve as a catalyst for treatment. For example, an agency may deal with high-risk offenders who have the same criminogenic needs (substance abuse), but within that group there are individuals differing along such dimensions as anxiety, intelligence, self-esteem, and so on. These factors affect how well the client responds to the style and modes of therapy and necessitate a matching of client characteristics with treatment. It is quite possible that withdrawn and shy clients may respond best when treatment is given on an individual basis, whereas extroverted, self-confident clients may respond well to a group therapy format. The assessment of possible responsivity factors can guide these decisions (this is perhaps fourth-generation assessment?).

All of the previous six points are held together by a healthy respect for evidence. Correctional personnel must continue to ask if research supports their assessment methodology and intervention practices. Assessing risk, needs, and responsivity must be rooted in research. Invoking reassessments and investigating the practices that promote offender change is truly research in action. It is also research that has tremendous practical significance, as it carries correctional agencies beyond merely controlling offenders in the immediate situation to risk reduction continuing beyond the judicially mandated period.

Risk Prediction
in Criminal Justice

Peter R. Jones

Risk prediction studies have burgeoned within the past decade largely because of several interrelated trends. The first trend has been the need for criminal justice agencies to adjust shrinking budgets to meet increasing demands for service. The prison overcrowding crisis and the search for effective intermediate sanctions have produced a demand for techniques that permit better identification of serious and persistent offenders. Second, the research community has responded with a range of criminological studies on career criminals and "high-rate" offenders, firmly establishing the notion that a small number of offenders contribute disproportionately to the crime rate. Third, in the past decade we have seen shifts in sentencing and correctional philosophy to call for improvements in the "equity" and "appropriateness" of decision making throughout the system. All these trends have implications for risk prediction. Prediction research and the use of prediction in criminal justice, however, is by no means a recent phenomenon. Prediction is a conventional aim of criminal justice, and it is almost axiomatic to state that effective control of criminal behavior requires an ability to predict such behavior. Within this broader context, risk prediction offers a means to summarize previous experiences in a way that will guide future decisions.

There is another, very pragmatic reason why risk prediction—particularly statistical risk prediction—has become a central issue within criminal justice decision making. The 1980s ushered in a computer revolution that dramatically changed the way institutions maintain and analyze information. Most criminal justice agencies—public and private—now have electronic databases that can be accessed very quickly and economically. Coincident with these advances in information technology has been a dramatic growth in the availability of statistical packages capable of performing sophisticated analyses. The result of these concurrent trends is that risk prediction—once a rather esoteric interest of academics and researchers that required large amounts of data and even larger amounts of money—is now firmly in the lexicon and the agenda of even the smallest of agencies.

As might be expected, the increased demand for risk prediction combined with greater facilitation of research on risk has produced a large but qualitatively uneven literature. Several excellent books (Farrington & Tarling, 1985; Gabor, 1986; Gottfredson & Tonry, 1987; Maltz, 1984; Schmidt & Witte, 1988) and many articles describing rigorously designed studies have been published in recent years. But the risk prediction literature—especially the applied literature—contains many studies that suffer from serious methodological problems, data weaknesses, inadequate sample sizes, design faults, measurement errors, and inappropriate applications. The fact that recommendations from research on risk prediction are increasingly being implemented in the decision-making process of criminal justice agencies underscores the need for improved understanding of the methodological, ethical, and political issues involved in such work.

The "problem of prediction" does not just concern design, methodological, or statistical issues. Such problems are identifiable and can be corrected. A more intangible problem lies in the approach to, and use of, risk devices. Risk prediction instruments are undoubtedly in vogue during the early 1990s, "guiding" important criminal justice decisions through the identification of "dangerous," "high-risk," and "violent" offenders (juvenile and adult). Intervention and penal policies are largely shaped by risk instruments that administrators view as being value-free, objective tools that emerge from a very mechanical, statistical process that brooks no "biased" human intervention. The fact that risk instruments inevitably reflect a series of policy and value decisions—including the choice of variables, cutoff points, and relative values given to false positives versus false negatives—is often unrecognized or ignored. Consequently, important decisions are left to researchers or, worse, to the default options of the computer package being used!

The goal of the present chapter is to address all these issues—from the important design to methodological and statistical issues surrounding risk prediction to those broad contextual political and ethical issues that we need to recognize. The intent is not to discuss the strengths and weaknesses of particular studies but to outline best practice in the field so as to construct a basic, practical guide for establishing sound prediction research designs. I will not address prediction topics involving univariate or multivariate forecasting, estimation of length of criminal careers, time-series analysis, or simulation models.

What Type of Prediction?

Predictions occur daily throughout the criminal justice system—a victim's decision to report a crime may hinge on predicting whether the police can or will do anything; the police in turn decide how to intervene (ignore, issue summons, or take into custody) based on the officer's prediction of the outcomes of the decision; pretrial decisions are made based on predictive issues about flight and crime; and prosecutors' decisions to charge frequently reflect a prediction about the outcome of the legal proceedings. Although these predictive decisions can range along a continuum from highly systematic to highly unsystematic, the literature generally recognizes two basic forms of prediction—clinical or statistical. Clinical predictions may well be systematic but include more subjective factors in assessment and provide more general and, at times, ambiguous prognoses. Ideally, the clinical assessment will be based on well-specified models of human behavior and will be undertaken by people with clinical training sensitive to factors potentially biasing their assessments. In practice, this is rarely the case. In a study of parole decisions in England, Bottomly (1973) found that factors such as the prisoner's personality and attitudes had greater weight than those relating to prior record, family situation, or employment prospects. Clearly, such emphasis on subjective factors, such as demeanor, perpetuates disparities in the disposition of offenders with objectively similar characteristics.

Statistical prediction is based on more "objectively" discernible criteria than those used in clinical prediction. The aim is to provide statistical statements regarding the predictive criteria that can be readily subjected to validation. All the available evidence strongly points to the superiority of systematically derived empirical tools over unsystematic or even trained clinical decision makers (Gottfredson & Gottfredson, 1979; Meehl 1954; Monahan, 1981, 1984; Morris & Miller, 1985; Sawyer, 1966).[1] Indeed,

Gottfredson and Gottfredson (1986) report that "in virtually every decision-making situation for which the issue has been studied, it has been found that statistically developed predictive devices outperform human judgments" (p. 247).

Prediction Studies in Criminal Justice

Attempts to predict criminality permeate all aspects of criminal justice and have a surprisingly long history. Much of the early prediction work focused on juvenile delinquency and parole. As early as 1928, Burgess completed one of the most famous prediction studies in the area of parole. Each person was assigned a score of 0 or 1 on each predictor, depending on whether the parole violation rate of persons in the same category was less than or greater than average. Subsequent work by Ohlin (1951) and Gottfredson, Wilkins, and Hoffman (1978) provided significant methodological improvements and gave prediction methods a major role in policy making. The predictive device developed by Gottfredson et al.—the Salient Factor Score—formed the basis for later work on the creation of parole guidelines. Indeed, prediction research has been applied to parole decision making in Great Britain (Nuttall et al., 1977), Australia (Challinger, 1974), and Canada (Nuffield, 1982). In the past decade, this work has grown to encompass the expansive literature on guideline development and application within other fields of criminal justice, including the sizable research literature on parole guidelines (Gottfredson et al., 1978), sentencing guidelines (Blumstein, Cohen, Martin, & Tonry, 1983; Coffee & Tonry, 1983; Fisher & Kadane, 1983), and pretrial release guidelines (Goldkamp & Gottfredson, 1985; Jones & Goldkamp, 1991a, 1991b).

A second important strand of early prediction research dealt with delinquency. The work of Glueck and Glueck (1950) comparing 500 institutionalized male delinquents with 500 unconvicted boys in ordinary schools is one of the best-known prediction studies in the history of criminology. Farrington and Tarling (1985) relate how President Nixon was advised that the Glueck Social Prediction Table enabled "9 out of 10 delinquents [to be] correctly identified at the age of 6" (p. 8). Such claims inevitably attracted microscopic evaluation of the Gluecks' work and some severe criticism. Anderson (1951) identified a number of serious problems:

- The delinquents and nondelinquents in the study were extreme groups and generalizations from the research were invalid.
- The high delinquent base rate (50%) in the study population made it far easier to predict delinquency than is true in the general population.
- The interviewers knew who was delinquent, thus introducing the possibility of bias.
- Predictive relationships for boys at age 14 to 15 may not be valid at age 6.
- There was no validation sample.

Even though the Glueck Social Prediction Table was implemented and validated in different settings (Craig & Glick, 1963; Havighurst, Bowman, Liddle, Mathews, & Pierce, 1962; Trevvett, 1965; Veverka, 1971), widespread criticism of the Gluecks's work tended to discredit prediction research in general and the prediction of delinquency in particular. Consequently, most delinquency prediction research during the past two to three decades has been undertaken by psychologists. The Minnesota Multiphasic Personality Inventory (Hathaway & Monachesi, 1957; Hathaway, Monachesi, & Young, 1960), the Eysenck Personality Questionnaire (Putnins, 1982), the Jesness Inventory (Graham, 1981), and in Great Britain, the Bristol Social Adjustment Guide (Stott, 1960) represent the best-known products of this field of work. Farrington and Tarling (1985) suggest that severe and continued criticism of delinquency prediction studies has made work in this field almost a taboo area. Indeed, Wilkins (1985) writes, "I have conducted research into the prediction of recidivism and see no moral objection to this, but I have not, and would not, carry out research aimed at predicting probable delinquency" (p. 35).

Although parole and delinquency represent the context for much of the early work in prediction research, more recent researchers have shifted their focus to a broader range of substantive areas. In the forefront of this expansion has been the application of prediction research to dangerousness and selective incapacitation. Research on the prediction of dangerousness has served more to undermine the credibility of clinical techniques (Monahan, 1981) than to develop a dangerousness or violent behavior prediction device based on sophisticated multivariate techniques. There is a surprising paucity of statistical prediction research in this field, although a major study is currently being undertaken in New York City to develop an instrument to predict "violent reoffending" among probationers. The research, discussed in more detail below, forms part of a comprehensive restructuring of adult probation in the city, and the final prediction instrument will be used as a guide to determining the level of intervention (from low-level "kiosk" responses to high-level intensive supervision) received by probationers.

One of the better-known applications of prediction research in recent years is in the field of selective incapacitation. Generally, researchers in this area aim to estimate the number of crimes prevented by sentences of incarceration (Haapanen, 1988; Petersilia & Greenwood, 1978; Van Dine, Dinitz, & Conrad, 1977). The work of Greenwood (1982) has been particularly influential. Following a decade or so of pessimism over the rehabilitative efficacy of incapacitative strategies (Martinson, 1974; Sechrest, White, & Brown, 1979), interest in selective incapacitation developed alongside research on criminal careers. Greenwood's (1982) research identified a reoffending prediction score based on seven items:

- Incarceration for more than half the 2-year period preceding the most recent arrest
- A prior conviction for the crime type that is being predicted (burglary or robbery)
- A juvenile conviction prior to age 16
- Commitment to a state or federal juvenile facility
- Heroin or barbiturate use in the 2-year period preceding the current arrest
- Heroin or barbiturate use as a juvenile
- Employment for less than half of the 2-year period preceding the current arrest

Employing a Burgess scoring scheme (0 or 1), Greenwood (1982) was able to discriminate between recidivists to such an extent that the low-risk group (0 or 1 point on a 7-point scale) had a median annual offense rate of 1.4% compared with a rate of 92.9% for the high-risk group (4 or more points). The apparent efficiency of Greenwood's (1982) risk instrument coupled with his forceful argument for its implementation as a basis for a selective incapacitation policy made this work enormously attractive to legislators, judges, and correctional administrators. Unfortunately, the study was thought by some to be superficial. Farrington and Tarling (1985), for example, describe a number of major methodological failings of the study—not least of which is the absence of a validation sample.

During the past two decades, the application of predictive research has expanded beyond the four main substantive areas discussed earlier. In both the adult and juvenile systems, there has been a significant growth in the use of formal assessment instruments to aid decision making related to caseload management and supervision as well as to appropriate community placement. The use of risk classification has also become increasingly important in quasi-experimental evaluation studies (Farrington, 1983; Jones, 1991). So expansive is the recent literature on risk prediction that a review even of the major studies is not possible within the context of this chapter. Before considering any methodological, ethical, or implementation issues, however, it is important to illustrate the range of applications of risk research within criminal justice today.

The Edgecombe Day Treatment Center, New York City

The New York City Department of Probation has traditionally employed a four-level risk classification scheme for probationers. In the past few years, however, the department has used risk prediction in some different ways. The first involves the role of risk prediction as a screening device in the planning of the Edgecombe Day Treatment Center (DTC). The DTC targets probationers against whom the department had initiated revocation proceedings (Jones, 1993b). The department's revocation process was slow (normally 6 months or more from initial revocation to final hearing), and almost 30% of probationers awaiting the final revocation hearing were being arrested during this 6-month period. The department designed the DTC to provide an alternative means of dealing with this recidivist group. A risk instrument was needed to identify, at the point of initial revocation, those probationers who were most likely to reoffend during the time to final hearing. These probationers were then offered the opportunity to enter the DTC. The final model of risk following revocation was composed of four variables:

- Reported drug abuse at the time of the violation
- Recent incarcerations
- Selected conviction offense
- Age at first arrest

The model correctly predicted 79% of cases for the estimation sample and 72% for the validation sample (Jones, 1993a). The predictive efficiency of the model (measured by relative improvement over chance [RIOC]) was 69% for the estimation and 43% for the validation models. The model was composed of low-, medium-, and high-risk groups; rearrest rates within 6 months of revocation were 12%, 26%, and 57%, respectively. The value of the risk instrument is that it enables the department to identify those probationers most likely to reoffend during the prerevocation hearing period and, consequently, be highly likely to receive an incarcerative sentence. Given the program's explicit goal of reducing pressure on New York City jails, this type of screening device is critical to the program's success.

Adult Probation Restructuring, New York City

In 1993, the New York City Department of Probation was forced to face the dilemma of planning to supervise an ever-increasing number of probationers with a significantly lower level of funding. The response was to significantly restructure the philosophy and implementation of adult probation within the city. At the core of the change was a decision to focus disproportionately resources on those probationers who were felt to pose the most significant problem—the "violent" offender.[2] Research is currently under way to develop a risk instrument to effectively predict "violence" during the postsentence probation period, enabling the department to target those offenders posing the greatest threat to public safety.

Pretrial Drug Testing

Drug use has been a potential predictor in criminological studies for several decades. Gottfredson and Ballard (1964) included a history of opiate use as an unfavorable indicator of parole outcome; the salient factor score used by the U.S. Parole Commission includes drug use variables (Gottfredson, Wilkins, & Hoffman, 1978), and more recently, Greenwood (1982) included heroin or barbiturate use in the 2 years prior to incarceration or as a juvenile in his predictive device for selective incapacitation. Indeed, drug use is well established as a decision-making criterion at all stages of the criminal justice system (D. M. Gottfredson, 1987).

Based partly on the hypothesized value of drug use information to predictions of pretrial flight and crime and the encouraging results of some early studies (Toborg, Yezer, & Bellassai, 1987; Yezer, Trost, & Toborg, 1987), the Bureau of Justice Assistance funded research to learn whether drug use information gathered through pretrial urine tests would be valuable to judges as a predictor of pretrial failure (flight and crime). Goldkamp, Gottfredson, and Jones (1988) tested this hypothesis in Dade County (Miami) and concluded that "once prior record measures were controlled most of the slight relationship disappeared" (p. 80).[3]

The Goldkamp et al. study highlights an important principle in prediction research and decision making. Burnham (1990) argues that decision makers feel uncomfortable with only a limited set of data items and require a range of information, most of which they do not take into account. He differentiates between *information* and *noise,* and points out that the noise had to be there for some sort of psychological support. Decision makers, he suggests, wanted the reassurance that they had rejected certain items of information to arrive at an original judgment. Set in this context, the contribution of pretrial urine test results to decision making lies firmly in the category of noise rather than information.

Pretrial Guidelines

One of the most important contributions of the movement to reform bail in the United States was the emphasis placed on the range of information that ought to be considered by judges in bail determinations. For example, the Vera Institute's championing of own recognizance (OR) release in New York was premised on the need for judges to consider defendants' community and family ties in addition to the more traditional criteria of offense seriousness. The Vera Institute study (1972), however, exemplifies the need to test hypotheses about expected relations. Although the community ties information provided to judges by the Vera Institute seemed plausibly to be related to pretrial success, Gottfredson (1974) showed that the relations, when examined empirically, were very weak.

Goldkamp and Gottfredson (1985) undertook a large-scale study of the correlates of pretrial misconduct as part of their development of policy guidelines for the Philadelphia judiciary. This study provides an excellent example of how prediction can apply not only to defendant behavior but to the decision-making process itself. The first stage of the guidelines research involved a careful analysis of the correlates of the decision to release. Current charge was the dominant variable, with knowledge of the defendant's prior arrests, prior felony convictions, prior failures to appear, pending charges, employment, and living arrangements playing a secondary role. By modeling the decision-making process Goldkamp and Gottfredson (1985) were able to make implicit decision-making practices explicit, opening them to debate and discussion.

After describing the decision-making process, Goldkamp and Gottfredson (1985) turned to an analysis of pretrial failure. They showed that considerable disparity existed between the predictors of judicial decisions (i.e., the information used by decision makers) and the predictors of defendants' performance during pretrial release. Through an iterative process of discussion about the type of information that was, and should be, used in the pretrial decision, Goldkamp and Gottfredson (1985) were able to develop a guidelines instrument to aid decision making. Interestingly, the judges rejected the notion of an entirely actuarial model of bail decision making and preferred to adopt a two-dimensional guidelines framework based on risk and offense seriousness (which was not a predictor of pretrial failure). The inclusion of a "stakes" dimension reflected judicial recognition of the differential costs associated with prediction error—that is, the cost of a false negative differs for a shoplifter and a rapist.

The empirical approach to modeling risk that was central to Goldkamp and Gottfredson's (1985) Philadelphia study has subsequently been adopted in several jurisdictions (Goldkamp, Gottfredson, & Jones, 1994). This body of applied prediction research, particularly through its close relationship to policy development, has produced some very practical insights into the benefits and difficulties associated with utilitarian predictive research. Most important, it points to (a) the need to test empirically theoretical assumptions about relations between plausible predictors and an outcome, (b) the importance of validation to the quality of prediction research, and (c) the need to recognize and make explicit all the limitations of predictive devices prior to implementation. As Goldkamp (1987) cautions, prediction devices help in the decision-making process, but they produce errors that must be addressed through careful review and other due process measures.

Intervention Strategies for High-Risk Youths

A large number of studies have reported on community-based alternatives for juvenile offenders during the past two decades (see Armstrong, 1991). The history of such programs has been rather dismal, frequently resulting in net widening rather than diversion (Krisberg & Austin, 1982; Blomberg, 1980). Selection of the appropriate target population is perhaps the most important component of program design and implementation. After identification of the target population, it is critical that the process remain free from the manipulation of judges and administrators who may wish to use the program in inappropriate cases. Recent research on two cohorts of first-time juvenile petitioners in Orange County, California, found that a very small group—approximately 10%—accounted for over half of subsequent offenses (Kurz & Moore, 1993). Based on these findings, the Orange County Probation Department is developing a risk-based intervention strategy that emphasizes risk rather than crime seriousness. Preliminary findings identified a profile of the "high-risk" juvenile petitioner as someone aged 15 or less at initial system referral and displaying two or more of the following attributes:

- School behavior or performance problems (truancy, recent suspensions or expulsions, detentions, functioning significantly below grade level, "flunking" or significant learning problems)
- Family problems (death, financial problems, recent divorce/separation, child abuse/neglect, criminal family members)
- Substance abuse problems
- Delinquency factors (includes runaway or stealing behavior, gang membership)

The preliminary prediction work conducted in Orange County is an example of juvenile intervention strategies being adopted in many jurisdictions (often with program development assistance from agencies such as the National Institute of Corrections). Similar research is currently under way or planned in the juvenile justice systems of Los Angeles, New York City, and Philadelphia. The critical issue, of course, is that it be done correctly.

Methodological Issues

A number of excellent reviews have been published on methodological issues in risk prediction (S. Gottfredson, 1987; Simon, 1971; Tarling & Perry, 1985). Interestingly, they all reach an important, if surprising, general conclusion: "No method is consistently better than any other in validation samples" (Tarling & Perry, 1985, p. 264). The implications of this finding are far-reaching. Two in particular are worth noting even before beginning to discuss methodology. It is clear that data limitations in risk prediction research significantly constrain the potential of sophisticated and more appropriate statistical approaches to analysis. Without better and different data, we simply cannot improve on the rather basic analytic approaches of the past. Second, because the lack of differentiation is more apparent during the validation than the construction of the instrument, it is clear that development of risk instruments without validation is an extremely risky enterprise.

Although the advantages of one method over another appear to be marginal, it would be wrong to infer that the choice of approach is of no significance (see discussion of combining predictors below). There are a number of factors that significantly affect the accuracy and validity of predictions. Each of these is discussed below.

What Sample Should Be Used?

There are two basic sampling issues—how many cases should be sampled and what sample should be used. Prediction models require data on a large sample of persons, and the sample should be as representative as possible of the population for whom predictions are to be made. Clearly, the optimal size of a sample is difficult to specify. Given that risk prediction ideally requires two subsamples (estimation and validation—see below), a useful working minimum would be approximately 500 cases. If total sample size is below 500, validation becomes problematic.

Inappropriately selected samples affect the base rate (i.e., the proportion of successes and failures in the sample); inappropriately sized samples affect the accuracy of the prediction instrument. Even if a sample is large and appropriately drawn, serious problems may emerge. Sampling theory shows that patterns found in one sample can lead to overestimating the patterns that might exist in other samples. Consequently, the "power" of a predictive device combines two components—predicted relationships found in a particular sample that exist in any other sample drawn from the same population and predicted relationships that are unique to the particular sample and unlikely to be replicated in other samples. The primary purpose of validation in prediction research is to test the extent to which empirically derived relationships persist across samples. A prediction device that consists of a large unique component is unstable and inaccurate when applied to other samples.

Despite theoretical exhortations to develop a representative sample, there are many significant practical reasons why this is hard to do. Often, one simply does not know for whom the predictions will be made. Alternatively, one might know exactly for whom the prediction device will be used, but it is impossible to select a representative sample. For example, if one wants to develop a risk instrument predicting reoffending among juveniles on probation (perhaps for use within a new diversion program), it will be possible only to identify a sample composed of those juveniles actually released on probation in the past. The prediction instrument developed on the selective sample will then be applied to a population containing a wider range of risk than those originally studied.[4] Under such circumstances, the best policy is to identify a random sample that is as closely related as possible to the population of interest. When the risk instrument is developed, it may be possible to examine differences between the original sample and the population of interest.

How Should We Measure the Criterion Variable?

Almost all criminological prediction studies use some form of official record of offending as the criterion variable, usually arrest, conviction, or incarceration.[5] This has significant theoretical implications, as one can never disentangle the extent to which official measures confound actual criminal behavior with the labeling of criminality in the criminal justice system. Thus, if arrest is the criterion measure and police agencies are biased or selective in their arrest procedures—by race or social status, for example—then the study will likely identify those factors associated with the police selection process as "predictors" of criminality. It is important to recognize that official measures confound the behavior of the individual with the behavior of system, especially when the prediction instrument being developed is to be implemented in the policy-making process. For example, a probation department might discriminate between high-risk and low-risk probationers for supervision purposes. A risk instrument is developed based on official measures of arrest that disproportionately include young, male, minority offenders. The instrument is used to identify high-risk offenders prospectively, and as expected, the high-risk group disproportionately included young, male, minority probationers. Based on the risk classification, this group is assigned to intensive supervision probation in which the conditions and the level of control are more stringent. The higher "failure" rate of the intensely supervised as compared to regular probationers serves to fulfill the prognosis of the classification. We are left, however, to ponder how much of the original prediction reflected innate criminological tendencies rather than differential system response and how much the policy decision to place individuals under intense supervision compounds the initial discrimination. The problems inherent in choosing arrest as a criterion are compounded when we select measures such as conviction or incarceration. Charge bargaining can produce very different impressions of the seriousness or dangerousness of an arrest record depending on whether one uses initial charge or conviction charge to measure the underlying behavior.[6]

There are several possible responses to this dilemma. One is to employ an alternative measure of criminality, such as self-report. Delinquency research has long used such measures of offending, although these are also of questionable validity. Weis (1986) reports that black respondents underreport criminal activity more than whites. The predicted relationship between race and criminal behavior therefore confounds the "true" effect and the differential propensity to self-report (i.e., an error or bias term). Farrington (1985) has argued that because official and self-report are two reasonably valid measures of criminal behavior, with each subject to different biases, any factor that predicts both is likely to be predictive of actual offending rather than either willingness to self-report or likelihood of selection for official processing. In a study comparing official and self-report delinquency, Farrington (1985) found that he could predict official delinquency better than self-report and that the predictors related solely to official measures of delinquency all involved social background variables—criminal parents, social handicap, low income, and low vocabulary.

It is sometimes thought that one approach to the definitional problem is to use official measures of criminal behavior as the criterion but to exclude possible biasing factors—such as race—from the list of possible predictor variables. As explained below (see section on combining predictors), this would be a serious mistake.

Aside from definitional issues, there are two other important decisions to be made concerning the criterion variable. The first is the length of the follow-up period for the predicted behavior to occur. Often, one is forced to adopt a relatively short follow-up period (studies predicting pretrial misconduct rarely include follow-up periods of more than 6 months; Jones & Goldkamp, 1991a). A general rule of thumb is that follow-up periods should not be less than 2 years, if at all possible.

The second criterion decision is level of measurement. Usually, the criterion is dichotomous—delinquent/nondelinquent, recidivist/nonrecidivist. Although this is easier to analyze, more efficient or elaborate definitions are possible—including the frequency of recidivism, the seriousness of the recidivism, the time to first offense, and the rate of offending per unit time at risk (Blumstein, Cohen, Roth, & Visher, 1986; Farrington & Tarling, 1985; Maltz,

1984; Schmidt & Witte, 1988). Given the theoretical and statistical inefficiencies of adopting a broadly defined, binary criterion measure, it is important that future prediction researchers attempt to specify more precisely the nature of the behavior they wish to examine. Most researchers would argue that the prediction of the timing or nature of recidivism is a critical adjunct to the standard approach of predicting whether or not someone will recidivate within a given time frame.[7]

How Should We Select and Measure the Predictors?

Prediction models can be developed without any individual characteristics—we can simply model the distribution of time until recidivism (Maltz, 1984). More commonly, we estimate models that include individual and environmental variables as predictors, although there is a significant discrepancy between the way these predictor variables should be identified and the way they usually are identified. Ideally, the pool of possible predictors is theoretically derived, with one variable representing each theoretical construct and each of these selected variables tested for validity and reliability. In practice, prediction research is constrained by poorly defined theory and limited data. Most data available to the researcher are unsystematic, incomplete, unreliable, and excessively subjective. At a time when we are making major methodological advancements, prediction research is being severely limited by poor-quality data.

I cannot describe in this chapter the range of possible predictors or even outcome measures that might be considered in various settings. Excellent published reviews listing salient predictors for a range of possible outcomes are available (Baird, 1973, 1991; Gabor, 1986; S. Gottfredson, 1987; Tarling, 1993). For each type of criterion considered, there are similarities among the risk scales produced, irrespective of the setting. Thus, for a juvenile parolee population Baird, Storrs, and Connolly (1984) identified the following general predictors of continued criminal involvement:

- Age at first adjudication
- Prior delinquent behavior
- Number of prior commitments to juvenile facilities
- Drug or chemical abuse
- Family relationships

- School problems
- Peer relationships

Beyond these "staples," the research points to a number of other potential predictors of crime for juveniles and adults:

- Early problem behavior—for example, troublesomeness (Mitchell & Rosa, 1981)
- Parenting and family management techniques (Riley & Shaw, 1985)
- Family disruption—for example, separation or divorce (Wadsworth, 1979)
- Family size and structure (West, 1981)
- Parental or sibling criminality (Farrington, 1983)
- Delinquent peers (Reiss, 1986)
- Alcohol use (Gottfredson, 1984)
- Gender (Hindelang, Hirschi, & Weis, 1981)
- Personality (McCord & McCord, 1964)

Alternatively, one can consider predictors of various criminal justice outcomes, either in the context of descriptive studies (identifying which variables predict the decision itself) or in normative studies (identifying which variables predict the outcome of interest). S. Gottfredson (1987, pp. 34-35) presents a table listing important salient predictors for a range of criminal justice outcomes, reproduced in Table 3.1.

What Should We Do About Missing Data?

Invariably, prediction studies face a significant problem of data missing on potential predictor variables. Often, this problem is unrecognized by researchers. Or it may be acknowledged but not addressed. The main effect of missing data is to reduce the size of the effective sample at the stage of multivariate analysis. How best to deal with this situation depends in part on how much data is missing, how important the particular variables involved are thought to be as predictors, and what mechanism gave rise to the missing values. If there are few missing values and the data are missing completely at random, then we should base our analysis on those cases with a complete set of variable values. Other than the reduced effective sample, this complete-case approach poses no problems.

TABLE 3.1 Parole Predictors

Descriptive Studies	*Normative Studies*
Seriousness of offense	Prior record
Subjective risk assessment	Offense type
Attributions regarding offender and offense	Age (particularly age at onset)
	Employment
Institutional behavior	Marital status
Alcohol history	Alcohol or drug use
Age	Education
Prior record	Institutional behavior
	Criminal associates

SOURCE: S. Gottfredson (1987, pp. 34-35).

An alternative approach, which makes more use of the available information, is to include all cases that have values for a group of variables. This available-cases approach has the significant disadvantage that statistics such as means and variances are based on different samples. A third approach— mean substitution—involves the estimation of missing values based on those data that are available (Little & Rubin, 1987).

The optimal decision about missing data is largely dependent on the scale and the nature of the problem. Because missing values rarely occur randomly in official records, we have to recognize that the inclusion of potential predictors with significant numbers of missing values creates bias in the attrition of the original sample and produces an effective sample whose relationship to the original is largely unknown (though sample comparisons on nonmissing factors can be undertaken). As a general statement of good practice, it is preferable to exclude cases with a large number of missing data on predictor variables and to monitor carefully the effects of this sample attrition on the distribution of the effective sample.

How Should We Combine the Predictors?

The goal of most prediction studies is to combine a small number of predictors into a simple, parsimonious composite model that maximizes predictive efficiency in terms of validity, cost, and usefulness. In theory, the type of analytic method selected should have a significant impact on the accuracy of the prediction device. In criminal justice, for a variety of reasons, this does not appear to be the case. Simon (1971) compared seven different statistical techniques only to conclude that they all worked equally well. Subsequent criticism of Simon's (1971) analysis prompted Tarling and Perry (1985) to extend the examination of alternate methods by submitting the same data to analysis by two more sophisticated and appropriate prediction methods—automatic interaction detection (AID) and logistic regression.[8] They concluded that these methods performed equally well but not significantly better than any of Simon's (1971) approaches. Gottfredson and Gottfredson (1979) completed a similar comparative study involving several analytic methods—linear additive models (OLS multiple regression and unweighted Burgess method), clustering models (principal attributes analysis and association analysis), and multidimensional contingency table analysis. They concluded that "simpler and more easily understood and implemented statistical prediction devices may work as well as those based on more complex techniques" (Gottfredson & Gottfredson, 1985, p. 75).

It is tempting to conclude from these comparative studies that the choice of statistical technique is of little importance. This would be wrong. It is important that the method employed is appropriate for the data being studied and the application being considered. If the prediction research requires a simple and fairly rough measure of risk, then a Burgess-type approach may be adequate. If one wants to examine the relative strength of the predictors and their interrelationships,[9] however, then more sophisticated analytic approaches are sensible.

A large number of analytic methods are available to the researcher, though there has been a discernible shift in the methods of choice over the past few decades. The most basic form of combining predictors is the Burgess method, which assumes a linear, additive relationship between the predictor and criterion variables. Burgess (1928) simply scored respondents as 0 or 1 on 21 factors related to successful parole outcome.[10] In this method, each variable in the model is scored as a point when present, and the total points score represents each individual's predicted likelihood to succeed or fail. The Burgess method represents an unweighted approach because it gives each predictor equal weight even if they are unequal in their predictive importance. Furthermore, it is insensitive to possible redundancies in variables due to interactions. For these reasons, the Burgess approach is generally thought to be not only inappropriate but "intolerably crude and inadequate" (Wilkins & MacNaughton-Smith, 1964, p. 18).

By the mid-1950s, criticism of Burgess-type approaches combined with advances in statistical techniques led to the increased use of regression-based approaches to prediction (Mannheim & Wilkins, 1955). Although this technique is generally very robust and has repeatedly been shown to outperform clinical prediction (Dawes, 1975; Meehl, 1954), there are several inherent problems with its use on criminological data (Palmer & Carlson, 1976). The most serious problems involve the use of a dichotomous dependent variable (violating a basic statistical assumption of OLS), the inclusion of a relatively large number of potential predictors (because of the potential for unidentified interaction terms), and the presence of correlated explanatory variables (multicollinearity).

In response to criticism of multiple regression approaches, researchers turned to alternative multivariate methods, particularly clustering techniques, such as configural analysis, predictive attribute analysis, and automatic interaction detector analysis (Brennan, 1987). The goal of each technique is to classify populations into increasingly homogeneous subgroups on the basis of the criterion measure. Although these methods are statistically appropriate for criminological data and are excellent vehicles for exploratory data analysis, they are notoriously arbitrary and difficult to replicate (Everitt, 1993). The implications of this instability are a matter of debate, with some critics arguing that an inability to replicate cluster solutions effectively negates the value of the approach to prediction. Gottfredson and Gottfredson (1985) disagree, suggesting that replication is less important than validation. They posit that as long as the predictive efficiency of a cluster-based device can be demonstrated, then it should not matter that the cluster structure cannot be successfully replicated.

In the midst of the debate over multiple regression and clustering approaches to prediction, log-linear and logistic regression techniques were introduced to the criminology literature (Goldkamp & Gottfredson, 1985; Gottfredson & Gottfredson, 1979; Payne, McCabe, & Walker, 1974; Solomon, 1976). The log-linear technique is statistically far more appropriate for the types of data generally available within criminal justice, though there is little evidence that it significantly outperforms even the simplest Burgess method of prediction (Gottfredson & Gottfredson, 1979; Tarling & Perry, 1985).

Optimally, the choice of analytic technique is determined by the nature of the data. In criminal justice, the criterion variable is most commonly categorical (usually dichotomous) and the predictor variables a mix of categorical and continuous measures. Under such circumstances, the choice is essentially between the clustering and log-linear approaches. Indeed, at this point the key to a successful prediction instrument lies not so much in the selection of a particular technique as in the use of a valid and reliable database and a careful, theoretically guided selection of potential predictor variables. An optimal approach would be to combine the methods, taking advantage of the different benefits of each technique. For example, log-linear and logistic regression techniques (as well as multiple regression) allow some estimate of variable weights and interaction terms, and they enable identification of an optimal model. One difficulty with these approaches, however, is the initial identification of a reasonably sized pool of potential predictors. Clustering techniques provide a solution. Because these approaches are excellent vehicles for exploratory data analysis, they are ideal as a preliminary guide to general data structure and potential interactions between predictor variables.

Prescribing a particular analytic approach to prediction studies is difficult, but some suggestions can be made. There can be no substitute for the development of a carefully constructed theoretical model of potential factors affecting the criterion of interest. Accordingly, the starting point of any prediction research has to be a thorough review of the existing literature, particularly that involving causal or predictive models. Defining a pool of possible predictors is the first stage of the overall analysis. This initial pool represents a rhetorical model of risk—those factors that we believe should be considered if data availability were not an issue. The next stage is to define those factors that can be validly measured. This is a critical stage, as there is a temptation to restrict analysis to that subset of variables that is readily available. After eliminating all variables that cannot or will not be measured, we are left with the "evaluable" model.[11]

If the number of potential predictors in the evaluable model remains large, it is appropriate to screen out those demonstrating the weakest relationship with the criterion. A simple, bivariate approach to screening is to cross-tabulate each predictor with the criterion and examine the strength of the relationship. At this stage of analysis, we need to consider two important issues—the distribution of missing values across the predictor variables and the possibility of collapsing predictors across different cells. If any variable has missing values for more than 10% of cases, one should seriously consider excluding it from further analysis. Also, the predictor variables (e.g., "age group" with 10 categories) should be considered for respecification (by collapsing across age groups) wherever possible. This initial screen of the variables composing the evaluable model removes all potential predictors that have weak associations with the predictor or unacceptably high numbers of missing values.

The next stage is exploratory data analysis using clustering techniques. Although the most commonly used cluster technique in criminological settings has been principal attributes analysis (PAA), Tarling and Perry (1985) present strong evidence to suggest that this is inferior to automatic interaction detector analysis (AID). For PAA, the predictor and the criterion variables must be dichotomous; where no natural dichotomy occurs in the data (as frequently happens in criminological settings), one has to be imposed. As Tarling and Perry (1985) indicate, this not only injects a subjective element into the analysis, it can lead also to a significant loss of information. AID comes in different forms, with one particular algorithm—CHAID (Kass, 1980)—applicable when the criterion and predictors are categorical, though not necessarily dichotomous.[12] In addition, CHAID offers the researcher an ability to handle missing values, and it controls for Type I error at each split in the tree (although not overall).[13]

The main value of the exploratory stage of analysis is that CHAID (or an alternative clustering technique) enables the researcher to identify possible interactions in the data and to develop some feel for the relative importance of predictor variables in terms of their relationship to the criterion.

The next stage of the analysis involves the use of multiple regression or logistic regression (depending on the nature of the criterion) as confirmatory techniques.[14] The OLS and logistic models developed from this stage of the analysis identify the most significant predictor variables and provide estimates of the relative importance of each predictor (independently or through an interaction term) to the criterion. These weights can then be transformed into a points score for implementation of a risk scale.[15]

How Good Is the Prediction Device?—
Assessing Predictive Power

For a prediction device to be useful, it must discriminate between high- and low-risk cases, with individual failure rates as close to either 0 or 1 as possible. The predictive power of any device can be conceptualized as the degree to which the predicted probability of failure (scored from 0 to 1) correlates with the observed probability of failure (0 or 1). Predictive power, however, is partly dependent on the distribution of the criterion (the base rate) and the cutoff point at which it is determined that someone is predicted to "succeed" or "fail" (the selection ratio).

Generally, prediction of any event becomes more difficult the further the base rate departs from 0.5 (S. Gottfredson, 1987; Meehl & Rosen, 1955; Quinsey, 1981)—that is, the more frequent or infrequent the criterion the greater the chance of errors in prediction. Consequently, it is to be expected that attempts to predict a rare event—such as violent crime—will be far more difficult than attempts to predict a more common criterion measure such as general criminality. Furthermore, if one attempts to predict a relatively rare outcome such as pretrial crime (estimated to approximate 0.15; Jones & Goldkamp, 1991a, 1993), then a blanket prediction of "no crime" will be correct 85% of the time and will prove superior to a carefully constructed statistical prediction model that predicts no pretrial crime in 80% of cases. S. Gottfredson (1987) notes that the base rate provides one marginal distribution for an expectancy table; the selection ratio (the point on the prediction scale where a person changes from a likely success to a likely failure) provides the other. Taken together, the two marginal distributions determine the chance expectancies for the table. Thus manipulation of the cutting score can have direct consequences on prediction.

Unfortunately, attempts to consider the influence of base rates and selection ratios on prediction results are rather rare in prediction research. In part, this stems from the fact that there is no widely accepted method of measuring predictive power. This inevitably obstructs any attempt to compare the relative power of different prediction studies.

The easiest and most common approach to measuring predictive power is to count the proportion of predictions that are correct—a method that we have seen to be largely dependent on the base rate and selection ratio. Attempts to overcome the base rate problem include Ohlin and Duncan's (1949) proportionate reduction in error index;[16] the phi statistic;[17] the point-biserial correlation coefficient (Simon, 1971); Duncan, Ohlin, Reiss, and Stanton's (1953) mean cost rating (MCR);[18] and Loeber and Dishion's (1983) RIOC index.[19] RIOC appears to be increasingly employed in the literature and is perhaps the best measure of predictive power available (Taylor, 1993). Its computation is briefly demonstrated below.

Imagine a prediction study that produces the data shown in Table 3.2a. The base rate of arrests is 0.7 (700/1,000) and the selection ratio is 0.5 (500/1,000). The prediction instrument was correct in 90% of the cases in which it predicted arrest (450/500)—the valid positives (VP)—and in 50% of the cases predicted

TABLE 3.2 Estimating the Relative Improvement Over Chance (RIOC) of a Prediction Instrument

TABLE 3.2a A Hypothetical Distribution

	Actual Outcome			
Predicted Outcome	No Arrest	Arrest	Total	%
No Arrest	250 (VN)	250 (FN)	500	(50)
Arrest	50 (FP)	450 (VP)	500	(50)
Total	300	700 (FP)	1,000	
	(30%)	(70%)	(100%)	

NOTE: VN = valid negatives; FN = false negatives; FP = false positives; VP = valid positives.

TABLE 3.2b Expected Distribution Based on Random Chance

	Actual Outcome			
Predicted Outcome	No Arrest	Arrest	Total	%
No Arrest	150 (VN)	350 (FN)	500	(50)
Arrest	150 (FP)	350 (VP)	500	(50)
Total	300	700 (FP)	1,000	
	(30%)	(70%)	(100%)	

NOTE: VN = valid negatives; FN = false negatives; FP = false positives; VP = valid positives.

to have no arrests (250/500)—the valid negatives (VN). The prediction instrument failed therefore in 300 cases. Of these, 50 were predicted to be arrested but were not (false positives), and 250 were predicted to be arrest free but were arrested (false negatives). To calculate how the instrument's predictions are compared to chance, we need to calculate the numbers that would have appeared, by chance alone, in each of the four cells of the table (Table 3.2b). Note that the cell totals are simply a product of the base rate and the selection ratio.[20] Essentially, this random or chance distribution illustrates what the distribution of cases would have been like if the prediction instrument was totally unrelated to arrest. Examination of Table 3.2b shows that by chance alone, we could have simply "guessed" the outcome in each case and obtained 150 valid negatives and 350 valid positives. Comparing Tables 3.2a and 3.2b, we can see that the prediction instrument improved our valid

TABLE 3.2c Optimal Distribution Based on Best-Possible Predictions

Predicted Outcome	Actual Outcome			
	No Arrest	Arrest	Total	%
No Arrest	300 (VN)	200 (FN)	500	(50)
Arrest	0 (FP)	500 (VP)	500	(50)
Total	300	700	1,000	
	(30%)	(70%)	(100%)	

NOTE: VN = valid negatives; FN = false negatives; FP = false positives; VP = valid positives.

positive score from 350 to 450, and overall, we had 200 more cases correctly predicted using the instrument. To assess the efficiency of the instrument, an additional piece of information is necessary—what are the best possible predictions we could make if we knew the marginal distributions in the data (i.e., the base rate and selection ratio)? To estimate best practice, we begin with the valid positives—that is, we assume that all cases predicted as arrests will be correct (Table 3.2c). Once we fix the value for this cell, we also fix the values for the remaining cells. The best we could have done, knowing the marginal distributions, is 800 correct predictions (500 VP and 300 VN).

We now have three ways of assessing predictions—those correct by chance (random correct [RC]), those correct using the instrument (actual correct [AC]), and the maximum possible correct given the marginal distributions (maximum correct [MC]). To calculate the simple improvement over chance (IOC) we compare RC and AC and find that the latter improved over the former by 20%. This measure, however, ignores both the base rate and the selection ratio. To incorporate these, we calculate RIOC using the following equation:

$$\text{RIOC} = \frac{\%\text{IOC}}{\%\text{MC} - \%\text{RC}} \times 100$$

Applying this formula to the hypothetical data in Table 3.2a would produce the following result:

$$\text{RIOC} = \frac{\%20}{\%80 - \%50} \times 100 = 66.7\%$$

The RIOC statistic enables comparison among prediction studies with different base rates and selection ratios. Interpretation is straightforward: The larger the statistic, the lower the combined number of false negatives and false positives in the data. It should be noted that the RIOC statistic does not differentiate between false positives and false negatives, although these may have very different ethical or financial costs.

Is the Instrument Valid?

Prediction instruments must be validated. Variables that prove to be highly predictive in one setting at one time may not realize the same predictive power at a different time or in a different setting. Gottfredson and Gottfredson (1979) warn that

> the greatest limitation of prediction methods is that the devices are developed and validated with respect to specific criteria, using available data, in a specific jurisdiction, during a specific time period. Thus any generalizations to other outcomes of interest, or after modifications of the item definitions used, or to other jurisdictions or populations, or to other time periods, are to be questioned. (p. 10)

Ideally, prediction instruments should be constructed on one sample (the construction sample) and validated prospectively on another (the validation sample). During construction, the statistical analysis identifies those predictors that have high correlations with the criterion for that specific sample. It is unlikely, however, that such correlations could be replicated in the population. Consequently, it is vital to obtain an unbiased estimate of the population predictive efficiency, and the simplest method is through validation of the instrument on a different sample of people. When the prediction model is applied to a validation sample, it is invariably less powerful than it originally seemed. This reduction in power is termed *shrinkage*. Copas (1985) argues that the more complicated the model being fitted (i.e., a large number of predictors or interaction effects), the more influence random fluctuations in the data have on the coefficients of that model and the greater the shrinkage.[21]

Splitting the sample into two parts—construction and validation samples— necessarily reduces effective sample size and reduces the reliability and perhaps the validity of the prediction instrument (especially when original samples are relatively small). Furthermore, some authors argue that a single estimate of shrinkage is of limited value and suggest instead the use of "bootstrapping" or "jackknifing" methods in which one or more cases are removed from the sample in a number of iterations to provide multiple measures of shrinkage. Clearly, this is a time-consuming and potentially expensive approach. Yet another approach is to use the complete data set as a construction sample, leaving validation to a subsequent time period.[22]

Will the Risk Score Ever Change?—
Static and Dynamic Prediction

Many applications of risk prediction involve one-off assessments of a person's chance of criminal behavior or some other outcome. The application of risk instruments to probation or parole settings, or even as part of a program evaluation strategy, however, calls for repeated examination of risk (e.g., the New York City Department of Probation reclassifies a probationer's risk level every 6 months). In situations where risk is assessed at more than one point in time, it is important that the reassessment tool move away from a reliance on variables that remain constant over time. Static indicators can be historical (e.g., parental criminality) or ascribed (e.g., gender or race). As Gabor (1986) indicates, individuals exercise no control over these variables, and, therefore, the variables are insensitive to changes over time. Indeed, the repeated use of these same variables for a population—for example, juvenile offenders—can result in individuals being censured over and over for the same attributes. Psychiatric measures; personality measures; response to supervision or institutionalization; and if the time period is long enough, age, employment, and family situation are dynamic factors. An example of a risk reassessment involving dynamic factors is offered by Baird (1984). His initial risk instrument involves the factors presented in Table 3.3.

The reassessment instrument in Table 3.3 retains the more significant initial predictors—age at first adjudication, prior criminal behavior, and institutional placements of 30 days or more. Although some other variables appear unchanged—parental control, school discipline, and drug/alcohol abuse (combined in the reassessment instrument)—the period over which the assessment is to be made has now become the time since the last assessment. Finally, the peer relationships variable has been replaced by two new variables—response to supervision and use of community resources.

Inclusion of dynamic factors in risk instruments raises a number of difficult ethical and methodological concerns. First, what is the relative weight that should be given these short-term factors compared with the longer-term

TABLE 3.3 Risk Assessment and Reassessment Instruments

INITIAL ASSESSMENT OF RISK

Select the *highest point total* applicable for each category.

AGE AT FIRST ADJUDICATION

>   0 = 16 or older
>   3 = 14 or 15
>   5 = 13 or younger

PRIOR CRIMINAL BEHAVIOR

>   0 = No prior arrests
>   2 = Prior arrest record, no formal sanctions
>   3 = Prior delinquency petitions sustained;
>   no offenses classified as assaultive
>   5 = Prior delinquency petitions sustained;
>   at least one assaultive offense recorded

INSTITUTIONAL COMMITMENTS OR PLACEMENTS OF 30 DAYS PLUS

>   0 = None
>   2 = One
>   4 = Two or more

DRUG/CHEMICAL ABUSE

>   0 = No known use or no interference with functioning
>   2 = Some disruption of functioning
>   5 = Chronic abuse or dependency

ALCOHOL ABUSE

>   0 = No known use or no interference with functioning
>   2 = Occasional abuse, some disruption of functioning
>   5 = Chronic abuse, serious disruption of functioning

PARENTAL CONTROL

>   0 = Generally effective
>   2 = Inconsistent and/or ineffective
>   4 = Little or none

SCHOOL DISCIPLINARY PROBLEMS

>   0 = Attending, graduated, GED equivalence
>   0 = Productively used
>   2 = Needed but not available
>   2 = Used but not beneficial
>   5 = Available but rejected
>   5 = Major compliance problems, totally uncooperative

PEER RELATIONSHIPS

>   0 = Good support and influence
>   2 = Negative influence, companions involved in delinquent behavior
>   4 = Gang member

(continued)

TABLE 3.3 (Continued)

REASSESSMENT OF RISK

Select the *highest point total* applicable for each category.
AGE AT FIRST ADJUDICATION

> 0 = 16 or older
> 2 = 14 or 15
> 3 = 13 or younger

PRIOR CRIMINAL BEHAVIOR

> 0 = No prior arrests
> 1 = Prior arrest record, no formal sanctions
> 2 = Prior delinquency petitions sustained;
>> no offenses classified as assaultive
> 4 = Prior delinquency petitions sustained;
>> at least one assaultive offense recorded

INSTITUTIONAL COMMITMENTS OR PLACEMENTS OF 30 DAYS PLUS

> 0 = None
> 1 = One
> 3 = Two or more

Rate the following based on experience since last assessment:
DRUG/ALCOHOL ABUSE

> 0 = No known use or no interference with functioning
> 2 = Some disruption of functioning
> 5 = Chronic abuse or dependency

PARENTAL CONTROL (Include foster or group home experience)

> 0 = Generally effective
> 2 = Inconsistent and/or ineffective
> 5 = Little or none

SCHOOL DISCIPLINARY PROBLEMS

> 0 = Attending, graduated, GED equivalence
> 1 = Problems handled at school level
> 3 = Severe truancy or behavioral problems
> 5 = Expelled/not attending

RESPONSE TO SUPERVISION REQUIREMENTS

> 0 = No problems of consequence
> 2 = Moderate compliance problems (e.g., missed
>> appointments, some resistance to authority)
> 5 = Major compliance problems, totally uncooperative

USE OF COMMUNITY RESOURCES/TREATMENT PROGRAMS

> 0 = Not needed
> 0 = Productively used
> 2 = Needed but not available
> 2 = Used but not beneficial
> 5 = Available but rejected
> 5 = Major compliance problems, totally uncooperative

SOURCE: Baird (1984).

measures that underpinned the original risk classification? Second, dynamic factors are often subjective—attitudinal, intuitive, or clinical—and they introduce a certain degree of discretion into the classification process. As Underwood (1979) cautions, the inclusion of subjectively scored factors, whether or not the scores are reliably reproduced by various decision makers, provides the opportunity for the decision maker to cloak personal biases in the mantle of scientific judgment.

How Well Should We Be Able to Predict?

Few people would question the proposition that statistical prediction outperforms intuitive or clinical prediction. But the repeated failure of sophisticated statistical approaches to improve significantly on the "intolerably crude and inadequate" (Wilkins & MacNaughton-Smith, 1964) early models of Burgess (1928) has resulted in some pessimism over the possibility of predicting criminal behavior at all. Schmidt and Witte (1988) argue that we must recognize the constraints on prediction in criminal justice. They note that in disciplines with well-developed, specific theories and relatively accurate data, prediction instruments struggle to "explain" more than half the variation in the criterion. In criminology, the generally poor quality of data combined with the highly random nature of criminal behavior ensures that prediction research rarely explains more than 15% to 20% of the outcome variance (S. Gottfredson, 1987) and may never do much better than 30%.

The gloomy figures should not induce excessive pessimism. With large samples, a prediction model explaining just 10% of variance can produce statistically significant results. We clearly need to monitor the explanatory power of our statistical models, but we need to do it against realistic rather than unachievable targets.

The Ethics of Prediction

Excellent discussions of the ethical and legal issues involved in prediction are available in the literature (Goldkamp, 1987; Petersilia & Turner, 1987; Tonry, 1987; Underwood, 1979; Wilkins, 1985). Here, the focus is on some specific issues that have very practical implications for how to perform or use prediction research.

Some critics argue that it is unnatural to use statistical models to predict behavior. Statistical prediction methods fail to respect individual autonomy by reducing autonomous persons to predictable objects. Critics, however, generally accept the empirical superiority of statistical over clinical prediction and the significant advantage of making explicit the precise criteria by which decisions are made (Underwood, 1979). Wilkins (1985) argues, "The ultimate test of predictive methods is neither the scientific nor the statistical nature of the exercises, but their honesty, rigor and moral underpinnings" (p. 50). Thus the ethical questions surrounding prediction are not so much with the methods of prediction as with the uses to which predictions are put. Clinical prediction clearly renders the decision process more obscure and provides the danger that the decision maker may rely on illegal or unethical criteria such as race. Despite the generally explicit nature of statistical prediction methods, several issues require close and careful scrutiny.

One such issue concerns prediction error—earlier classified as false positives and false negatives. Wilkins (1985) argues that the former category represents risks to the individual and the latter category risks to the community. How we treat either category—involving equal or differentially weighted social costs—is a moral rather than statistical question. Irrespective of how much we try to minimize the overall proportion of prediction failures, there will always be a trade-off between false positives and false negatives. Farrington and Tarling (1985) correctly note that any determination of the adequacy or desirability of a prediction model must consider not only overall predictive efficiency but the real costs and benefits associated with the different possible outcomes. One significant advantage of statistical over clinical predictions is that they permit such determinations to be made.

A second issue is the range of information that might legitimately be included in prediction research. Much of the discussion in the literature focuses on one variable—ethnicity or race—although there is a good case to be made for similar concern over other variables, particularly ascribed and environmental variables that are generally beyond the control of the subjects being studied. The ethical concern centers on whether one should consider variables such as race for inclusion in prediction research and, if so, what to do if they prove to be significant predictors (Blumstein et al., 1986; Goldkamp, 1987; Morris & Miller, 1985; Tonry, 1987). One approach is to simply remove the race variable from consideration. This will not, however, remove the race effect from the model. Any variable—such as housing, education, income—that is strongly correlated with race will if included in the model produce a coefficient that partly reflects the true effect of that variable and partly the indirect effects of race (Fisher & Kadane, 1983; Goldkamp, 1987). The statistical laundering of the race effect through other correlates may make the prediction instrument ethically acceptable at a superficial level, but it remains no less discriminatory than a model that explicitly includes race.

The correct way to remove the effects of status—gender, race, religion, and so forth—from prediction requires that we view prediction research as a two-step process involving (a) the independent stages of estimation and validation of a model and (b) the implementation of a model to predict future behavior. At the estimation and validation stage, all available information should be used, including race, gender, age, and religion. After identifying the optimal model (at least in statistical terms), we must ask the difficult ethical and political questions about the kinds of information being used. Goldkamp (1987) describes how the resolution of these ethical questions inevitably requires explicit policy decision.[23] The key point is that by including all variables in the initial estimation and validation analysis, we can assess the effect of different policies with regard to status variables on the classification of subjects. Attempts to undertake such analysis have generally found that removal of status variables, such as race, gender, and employment, do not seriously damage the predictive efficiency of an instrument (Petersilia & Turner, 1987; Schmidt & Witte, 1988).

A slightly different twist to the variable inclusion issue revolves around the way one handles predictor variables with values within the control of agency personnel. For example, if information on past drug abuse was found to be an important predictor and the source of this information was probation officer file entries, then it becomes possible for the officer to affect a subject's risk classification through his or her reporting of this information. Again, although the use of such variables in initial model construction and validation is appropriate, researchers should think very carefully about the use of such variables in applied risk instruments (particularly risk reassessments involving more subjective predictions).

How Well Can We Improve Prediction?

The most significant obstacle to improved implementation of prediction research does not lie with design issues or statistical techniques or even with poor-quality data. It lies in the commonly held belief that prediction research is a very mechanical, technical procedure that brooks no policy input. This view is mistaken, and it is important that future prediction research is not conducted in a policy vacuum. Wilkins (1985) argues forcefully that a team approach is essential to good predictive research and that there should be an openness and honesty in all communications between the users and producers. Unfortunately, a team approach rarely exists, and it is far more likely that researchers produce an instrument for administrators who generally know (or care) little about the design, statistical, or ethical decisions that were made. Researchers, for their part, do not engage administrators in the prediction exercise; key decision points are treated as if they were somehow value free and outside the policy realm. In fact, all prediction instruments inevitably reflect the behavior not only of the people studied but also of the people who created the instruments. Researchers and administrators alike have a moral responsibility to understand this fact and to ensure that the decisions that shaped a particular instrument are explicit and public. Such accountability provides a significant improvement over decisions based on intuitive or clinical prediction because the decision maker relies on something other than public trust to defend her or his determinations.

To achieve more of a team effort in prediction studies, it is necessary that users and producers have a clearer understanding of what makes up good practice. The goal is to raise the level of discourse about risk prediction beyond issues of time and cost. In this chapter, I have discussed many factors that affect the quality of prediction research. In conclusion, a brief review of the key points seems appropriate.

Data

We need to improve the reliability and validity of both the predictor and criterion variables we use in criminal justice. The value of variables such as employment history, family composition, and even prior criminal record is notoriously poor. Researchers have a professional obligation to assess the quality of the data with which they work. If we learn that employment status and living arrangements variables exist on a database and that only 5% have missing values, we have learned only about that information's availability. We need to talk to the producers of that information—probation officers, agency personnel, and so on—about the quality of the data. Alternative definitions of the variables, involving perhaps some scaling of prior and current offense seriousness (Gottfredson & Taylor, 1986) and consideration of time to failure or time at risk (Schmidt & Witte, 1988) would significantly improve prediction research.

Statistical Approach

Despite the discouraging results of comparative studies, it is important that researchers use the most appropriate rather than most amenable analytic methods. For example, there would need to be some compelling reason why principal attributes analysis (PAA) was selected over automatic interaction detector (CHAID). In general, it is useful to approach the analysis through the use of first exploratory and then confirmatory techniques.

Where's the Theory?

Risk prediction research has a tendency to be highly atheoretical. Although predictive research does not aim to develop causal or explanatory insights, it remains true that theory rather than data availability should drive the initial identification of possible predictor variables. In this sense, computerization should be seen as both friend and foe, making information handling and analysis quick and easy but tempting the practitioner or researcher to constrain conceptual and operational development to the information that is electronically available. Prediction researchers need to broaden their vision rather than restrict themselves to those fields of information routinely collected in criminal justice agencies.

Risk Instrument Franchising

The construction of a risk instrument is a relatively expensive and time-consuming enterprise. Not surprisingly, agencies often decide to select an "off the peg" rather than custom-made instrument. Consequently, a risk instrument originally developed for a specific population in Wisconsin ends up being used, often in modified form if the data called for are not available, for a different population in a very different setting. This is a worrying trend, and at a minimum, administrators should recognize the inherent problems in the wholesale adoption of risk instruments from other agencies.

Validation

Whether constructed or borrowed, all risk instruments must be validated. Ideally, this should be done through a split construction and validation sample approach when analysis begins. This approach, however, is often impractical, especially when the researcher is faced with small sample size. Alternative strategies are available, including initial estimation on the entire sample and subsequent validation on a later sample or validation through repeated testing of the risk instrument on randomly selected subsamples from the initial (estimation) sample—a procedure termed bootstrapping.

Dynamic Risk Prediction

In settings where risk instrument are to be used repeatedly on the same subject, it is important to build in an opportunity for change to occur. The identification of short-term change measures, the nature of their measurement, and the relative weight attached to these compared with the longer-term variables are all issues that need to be addressed.

One Size Fits All

We tend to assume that prediction instruments should be developed for a single population. But one can use cluster techniques to identify relatively homogeneous subgroups within the population and then construct statistical prediction models for each. These models can be combined into an expectancy table for the full sample.

We Can Do It!

Practitioners do not need to become statistical or research design experts to become involved in prediction research. They should, however, encourage a team effort and require that they be informed of the key points in the process where policy preferences implicitly or explicitly enter the process. For their part, researchers have a moral and professional responsibility to ensure that administrators recognize that such decision points exist and have to be answered, with or without the administrators' input. We laud the explicit nature of statistical risk prediction, arguing that it describes the precise criteria by which decisions are made. The means by which the risk instrument were developed should be held to the same standard of visibility and accountability.

Notes

1. See Underwood (1979) for a critical view of statistical prediction.

2. The term *violent* is somewhat misleading, as the target group includes serious nonpersonal crimes such as burglary.

3. Similar results were reported by Goldkamp and Jones (1992) for analyses conducted as part of an evaluation of pretrial drug testing programs in Prince George's County (Maryland) and Milwaukee (Wisconsin).

4. For a discussion of the sample selection problem see Berk (1983).

5. Selection of the criterion is particularly important for survival models because the prediction focuses on time to an event. If date of incarceration or conviction is chosen as the criterion measure, then one seriously confounds the temporal aspects of criminal behavior with official case-processing times.

6. The New York City Department of Probation is currently developing a prediction instrument for violent reoffending while on probation. The issue of whether violence (past or present) should be measured by initial or conviction charge is clearly a matter of great import.

7. Survival models specifically focus on time to reoffending. Such models represent a significant increase in statistical sophistication and are by no means as widely available as standard prediction methods. Excellent treatments of survival approaches to prediction in criminal justice are offered in Schmidt and Witte (1988) and Tarling (1993).

8. Simon (1971) used principal attributes analysis (PAA) and OLS multiple regression in her work.

9. Ideally, predictor variables will be strongly correlated with the criterion but completely independent of each other. Under such circumstances, each predictor contributes uniquely to the overall, additive, risk score. In practice, predictors are often highly intercorrelated—a condition termed multicollinearity—and their inclusion in a predictive model involves redundancy. Thus, if bivariate analyses showed that drug use and prior arrests were strongly correlated not only with recidivism but also with each other, the inclusion of both in a prediction device would be inefficient and misleading.

10. The score of 0 or 1 was awarded depending on whether the parole violation rate of persons in the same category was less than or greater than the average. This scoring method was subsequently modified by Ohlin (1951) so that each person scored −1, 0, or +1 depending on whether the value of the predictor was associated with an above-average, average, or below-average success rate. Ohlin (1951) also reduced the number of factors on which an individual was classified to those most closely associated with the criterion.

11. The evaluable model is a subset of the rhetorical model in the sense that it represents that portion of the theoretically derived variables that is subjected to empirical verification.

12. CHAID is now available as an option in the statistical package SPSS for Windows.

13. AID methods have been used in criminological studies (Fergusson, Donnell, Slater, & Fifield, 1975; Schumacher, 1973) but have generally failed to significantly outperform comparative multiple regression or Burgess methods.

14. Logistic regression is a flexible version of the general linear model in that it permits the use of both categorical and continuous predictor variables.

15. There are various means by which regression coefficients are transformed into "points." One approach would be to set the smallest significant coefficient to 1—a base coefficient—and assign points to other predictors according to the relative size of their coefficients compared to the base coefficient. An alternative would be to multiply all coefficients by a standard number to produce integer weights. It is important to note that the sign of the coefficient should not change.

16. In a sample with 50% of failures, we might develop a risk instrument that was wrong in 25% of cases. The proportionate reduction in error for the instrument is 0.5—(50–25) divided by 50. Note that the index does not differentiate between false positives and false negatives.

17. This statistic is derived from the chi-square statistic, but it does not increase linearly with sample size. It is employed in situations in which both the predictor and criterion variables are dichotomous

18. The MCR compares two variables—"cost" (the proportion of Type II errors) and "utility" (the proportion of correctly predicted failures). The cost-utility curve relates costs to utilities for all possible selection ratios (cutoff points). The MCR is proportional to the area between the curve and a diagonal (cost = utility) line produced when we assume chance expectations. Unfortunately, the conceptual simplicity of the MCR has to be balanced against the fact that it has an unknown sampling distribution, making tests of statistical significance impossible.

19. Copas and Tarling (1984) have discovered some problems with the RIOC measure—it does increase as the selection ratio increases, and it fails to differentially weight Type I and Type II errors—but overall, it seems to offer a useful method for assessing predictive efficiency.

20. The cell value is computed as follows:

$$\text{Random cell value} = \frac{\text{Row marginal for cell} \times \text{Column marginal for cell}}{\text{Total } N}$$

21. Copas (1985) notes a second type of shrinkage, this time affecting the correlation coefficient between observed and predicted values. He suggests that a halving of the original correlation is not uncommon.

22. Horst (1966) has argued that this is methodologically sound but ethically somewhat problematic, especially if decision making is affected by the instrument, thereby constraining the validation sample subsequently derived.

23. Goldkamp (1987) suggests that one fix the values of the questionable variables by selecting just one value for them—that is, for gender we would have to make the policy decision to treat all subjects as females or males irrespective of actual gender prospectively.

Control in the Community

The Limits of Reform?

Francis T. Cullen
John Paul Wright
Brandon K. Applegate

The U.S. correctional system is in crisis—most commentaries on corrections, whether by academic researchers, members of the media, or policymakers, begin or end with this statement. There is the risk, of course, that the sweeping use of the term *crisis* distorts as much as it captures. It ignores, for example, the many devoted correctional workers surmounting difficult circumstances to gain small and at times large successes in their everyday interactions with offenders. It ignores as well the wide variation across and within jurisdictions in how adequately agencies are administered—a finding that suggests that crisis does not lead ineluctably to organizational breakdown (DiIulio, 1987, 1991).

Still, there is a part of reality that the idea of crisis does capture: the sense that we cannot continue doing what we have been doing. Throughout much of the 1900s, incarceration rates did not vary much; indeed, these rates seemed so entrenched that criminologists advanced the "stability thesis" of punishment (Blumstein & Cohen, 1973; see also Zimring & Hawkins, 1991). Over the past two decades, however, all this changed.

The correctional system has been at the nexus of two incompatible and powerful forces: first, the unrelenting rise in offender populations within prisons and, we might add, under community supervision; and second, the increasing fiscal constraints facing state and local governments. In virtually all jurisdictions, corrections has become the Pac-Man of government budgets, gobbling up resources as legislators seek to finance competing needs with shrinking tax revenues (Pierce, 1991). Exacerbating matters, this expensive, two-decade experiment with imprisoning the United States out of its crime problem has not seemed to work; meaningful reductions in the crime rate have not been achieved (Clear, 1994; Currie, 1985, 1989; Irwin & Austin, 1994; Petersilia, 1992; Steffensmeier & Harer, 1993; Visher, 1987).

Crisis, even a sense of failure, is not without a silver lining, if it can serve as a catalyst to change directions, to choose a different future (Sherman & Hawkins, 1981). It is not clear that the correctional crisis has yet precipitated such a fundamental soul searching; the chorus calling for more of the same—more prisons, more punishment—hardly has been silenced. Even so, the events of the past two decades have created enough doubt that space exists for other voices to be heard.

Of those voices, we as a nation have listened closest to those arguing for "intermediate punishments," sanctions that exist "between prison and probation" (Morris & Tonry, 1990; see also Harland, 1993). If prisons are expensive and ineffective and traditional community supervision is too lax and jeopardizes public safety ("not really punishment"), it was claimed, then we need initiatives that avoid the cost of imprisonment and the risk of community release. Intermediate sanctions seemed the logical solution: By closely supervising, monitoring, testing—in short, controlling—offenders, it would be possible to sanction effectively and comparatively inexpensively in the community.

But does community control work? Will intermediate sanctions solve, or even substantially alleviate, the current correctional crisis? Is this movement to exert control in the community a panacea or a reform with unavoidable limits? Our intent is to provide some provisional answers to these questions.

We begin by placing the matter of community control in a broader context. Before reviewing the data on program effectiveness, it first seemed prudent to review the origins of the community control movement, to discuss how far it has progressed, and to assess what it is meant to accomplish. With this context established, we then present the methods used in the study. Next, we review evaluation studies on four major intermediate sanctions: intensive supervision, electronic monitoring and house arrest, drug testing, and boot camps or shock incarceration. Finally, we attempt to draw conclusions on community control from the existing evidence.

Community Control in Context

The Appeal of Intermediate Sanctions

The intersection of the prison population boom and fiscal constraints, as we have noted, has created conditions ripe for change. In virtually every discussion of the origins of intermediate sanctions and community controls, participants cite as the major impetus for reform the need to deal with this crisis (Petersilia & Turner, 1993c). "Our interviews with 150 criminal justice officials," conclude DeJong and Franzeen (1993), "revealed that support for the expansion of intensive supervision, boot camps, house arrest, and other intermediate sanctions is being driven by the continued problem of prison crowding and the lure of possible cost savings from a reduced reliance on incarceration" (pp. 67-68).

Undoubtedly, these observations are accurate but only in a sense. If we were to put ourselves in a different time and place—say, the 1960s—we might see that a crisis of crowded cells and too little money might engender a very different range of options. We might have debated, for example, not the merits of electronic monitoring versus boot camps but, rather, the comparative cost savings and reductions in recidivism achievable through deinstitutionaliza-tion, shorter prison terms, prison furloughs, programs to reintegrate offenders into the community, the provision of equal employment opportunities, and the like (see Stojkovic, 1994). It is illuminating that by the 1980s, these sorts of alternatives did not warrant even token consideration.

The point, of course, is that intermediate *punishments* or community *controls* "made sense" because the rhetoric of this reform resonated with the prevailing politics of crime. By the 1980s, the legacy of the Great Society programs and of "doing good" in corrections was in disrepute, and it was a rare politician—liberal or conservative—who did not blame lenient punish-ments for the U.S. crime problem and promise if elected to toughen up criminal sentences. In this context, intermediate punishments drew their appeal from the often-repeated belief that whether exercised in the prison or in the community, threats of punishment and enhanced surveillance were the keys to deterring criminality. It made little difference that when first proposed, there was little theoretical or empirical basis in the criminological literature for believing that these programs would be effective (Finckenauer, 1982).

The popularity of intermediate punishments—indeed, the reason they did not face stiff opposition—also can be traced to their ability to give something to everyone. Although not enamored with the control rhetoric, liberals took solace in what they saw as perhaps the first viable opportunity in a decade to limit the use of incarceration. And conservatives took solace in the promise of control at a reduced cost. Not a bad bargain for either side.

Within the criminal justice system itself, a few prosecutors might resist substituting community punishment for a prison term, and some probation officers might dislike the attention and resources given to colleagues relieved of high caseloads in order to carry out the intermediate punishments (DeJong & Franzeen, 1993). Overall, however, the reform satisfied a key principle of correctional success: It appeared to advance the interests of those working in the criminal justice system (Rothman, 1980; Walker, 1989). "Conscience and convenience," in Rothman's (1980) terms, were not at odds but in harmony. Commenting on the intensive supervision program in Georgia, Tonry (1990) captures this situation nicely:

> Georgia probation officials have created the opposite of a zero-sum game: everyone wins. Offenders are spared imprisonment. Judges have to handle a new, believable intermediate punishment. Prison crowding is reduced. The state saves money. The probation department is seen to have achieved all these things and, at the same time, increased the department's size and funding. (p. 185)

The public, moreover, had little reason to protest the use of intermediate sanctions. Again, the promise of equal control at a lower cost made sense. When a sample of Alabama residents was asked to rate various solutions to prison crowding, 84% favored finding "new ways to punish offenders that are less expensive than prison, but harsher than probation." After receiving information on the correctional crowding crisis, 9 in 10 respondents agreed that "some people" on probation and in prison "should really be put into alternative programs like Strict Probation, House Arrest, and Boot Camp" (Doble & Klein, 1989, pp. 27, 46; see also Williams, Johnson, & McGrath, 1991).

More generally, public opinion about corrections is much mischaracterized. To be sure, Americans are punitive, and surveys can easily show high support for sending almost any criminal to prison (Durham, 1993; Zimmerman, Van

Alstyne, & Dunn, 1988). But another truth about public attitudes is invariably misunderstood: Public views are complex and "mushy" (Durham, 1993). Citizen attitudes are complex in the sense that people are not purely punitive. There now is an extensive body of research showing that the public favors offenders being not only punished but also rehabilitated (Cullen, Skovron, Scott, & Burton, 1990; Innes, 1993; McCorkle, 1993; Thomson & Ragona, 1987). The attitudes are mushy in the sense that citizen views are not rigid or stable but can be manipulated toward greater or lesser punitiveness (Durham, 1993; Scheingold, 1984).

This does not mean that the public will passively endure *any* policy initiative, especially if a direct interest is threatened (e.g., placing offenders in one's neighborhood) (Innes, 1993). But these findings do suggest that people are potentially open to a broader range of correctional alternatives than believed by policymakers, who typically overestimate the public's punitiveness (Gottfredson & Taylor, 1983). Accordingly, a backlash against intermediate sanctions appears unlikely, particularly if community leaders take visible stands favoring such initiatives.

In summary, the community control movement is not the only correctional response that might have been made to the prevailing crisis in the system. Rather, this movement must be seen as the product of a particular social and political context that limited permissible options, making some potential reforms seem foolish and others sensible. Intermediate sanctions shared the rhetoric of punishment but offered to accomplish crime control at a reduced cost. It would do all this, moreover, in a way that neither incited public furor nor threatened the occupational and organizational interests of those who would implement the programs in the criminal justice system. No wonder it was a reform whose time had come.

Substantive or Symbolic Reform?

The intermediate punishment movement was, with few exceptions, a child of the 1980s, taking hold and growing as the decade progressed. Today, various programs can be found across the United States, as these figures illustrate:

- Over 70% of states use intensive probation supervision, with a total caseload of almost 60,000 offenders (Camp & Camp, 1993b, pp. 20-21).
- Over 60% of states use intensive parole supervision, with a caseload of over 63,000 offenders (Camp & Camp, 1993b, pp. 48-49).

- Approximately half the states use electronic monitoring for probationers or parolees, with the number of offenders being monitored at any one time totaling about 10,000 (Camp & Camp, 1993b, pp. 20-21, 48-49).
- In 48 states and the federal system, probationers are tested for drug use, with the annual average number of tests per jurisdiction in excess of 50,000—up from 16,130 in 1988 (Camp & Camp, 1993b, pp. 28-29). A study of adult felons on probation indicated that 31% had received drug testing (Langan, 1994, p. 791).
- In 45 jurisdictions and the federal system, parolees are tested for drug use, with the average number of tests per jurisdiction in excess of 77,000 (Camp & Camp, 1993b, p. 58).
- Over half the states have at least one boot camp program, and five additional states have plans to implement a program (Camp & Camp, 1993a, p. 60; Lillis, 1993, p. 8).

It remains to be seen how far jurisdictions will proceed in implementing intermediate sanctions. At present, the movement does not seem to have run its course. More and more states are starting more and more programs. The prison crowding-resource shortage problem has not receded and, indeed, is likely to be exacerbated as legislators continue to pass "get tough" laws (e.g., "three strikes and you're out") that drive up, but do not provide the resources needed to house, inmate populations. Accordingly, the ostensible impetus for intermediate sanctions remains.

The critical issue is whether the movement ultimately will be substantive or symbolic (see Cullen, Maakestad, & Cavender, 1987). Substantive reform involves true institutional change. Programs would not be an appendage to a correctional agency—an isolated unit dealing with a limited number of cases—but integrated systematically into the agency and into the sentencing process. In contrast, symbolic reform is more for show, with programs emerging as popular, indeed political, responses to crises to show that government is doing something about the crime problem. Such programs ultimately wane as the political context changes and the means to express symbolic responses change with it.

At this stage, it is difficult, perhaps premature, to judge the movement's quality. In some jurisdictions, such as Florida with its "community control program," the reform has been institutionalized and affects thousands of offenders (Baird & Wagner, 1990; see also Camp & Camp, 1993b, p. 20). In many other jurisdictions, the programs cover a limited number of offenders (Camp & Camp, 1993b, p. 20) and probably function more as symbolic responses to the local or state "correctional crisis." There also are likely to be differences by type of intermediate sanctions. Intensive probation supervision seems more entrenched organizationally and across jurisdictions; boot camps, in contrast, are a ready means for politicians to increase their political capital, and thus the future expansion of boot camp programs may hinge more on the winds of electoral change (DeJong & Franzeen, 1993, p. 64).

In any case, one lesson from the history of correctional reform is clear: Whether reforms are large or small, lasting or temporary, substantive or symbolic, has less to do with whether they work than with how they mesh with organizational and political interests (Cullen & Gendreau, 1989; Cullen & Gilbert, 1982; Finckenauer, 1982; Rothman, 1980; Walker, 1989). This view may seem overly jaundiced until one realizes that the current movement toward intermediate sanctions was based more on hunch and ideology than on criminological data. Similarly, it remains unclear whether emerging program evaluation studies will be used as a basis for revising, and perhaps discontinuing, programs, or when uncomfortable findings emerge, whether these studies will be dismissed as another example of the principle that there are "lies, damn lies, and statistics" (DeJong & Franzeen, 1993, p. 64; Finckenauer, 1982).

We are not fully pessimistic on this point. In our survey of state departments of corrections, we discovered a number of evaluation studies completed, in progress, or in the planning stage. Furthermore, conference programs—such as the one at which this chapter was originally presented—suggest that correctional professionals are far more open than in previous generations to incorporating empirical data into their decision making. As with the intermediate sanctions themselves, it remains to be seen whether the current interest in evaluation data is symbolic or substantive.

Finding Out What Works

Part of the problem, of course, is not that correctional practitioners are deaf to the data but that researchers cannot always provide unequivocal advice on what works in corrections. Particularly when reforms are new and studies are few, responsible researchers present conclusions cautiously. Equally telling is that finding out what works in corrections is a difficult job. Of the host of obstacles that need to be surmounted, we discuss three main factors that make it difficult to provide definitive answers on program effectiveness.

First, in general, there is a *lack of evaluation studies using an experimental design* (Petersilia & Turner, 1993c; see also Sherman, 1992). Random assignment into the experimental versus the control group has the important advantage of avoiding *selection bias*—a flaw that if not addressed makes an evaluation study misleading if not useless. Such bias may occur when offenders are assigned to an experimental group not randomly, but based on some other factor or factors that may be related systematically to recidivism. For example, if offenders are allowed to volunteer for an experimental program (e.g., a boot camp), the program may show lower recidivism rates not because it works but because compared with those who refused to participate, the offenders who volunteered for the program were less likely to return to crime in the first place. In short, random assignment allows researchers investigating the effects of an intervention program on experimental and control groups to compare apples with apples, whereas selection bias creates a situation in which apples are compared to oranges.

The difficulty with random assignment is that its use shifts decision making from the hands of criminal justice officials to the researcher's design: Offenders are placed in an experimental program randomly and not based on whether an official, such as a judge, believes that this placement is appropriate for a given lawbreaker. Forfeiting such decision-making power is less problematic when offenders are subject to more rather than less control, such as when the experimental condition is an intermediate sanction and the control or comparison group is "regular probation." In contrast, it is riskier for officials to allow the experimental condition to be less severe, such as an intermediate sanction rather than a prison term (Petersilia & Turner, 1993c). As a result, researchers often are better able to answer some questions than others, such as how offenders in intermediate sanction programs fare versus probationers as opposed to prison inmates (Petersilia & Turner, 1993c).

Second, *outcome measures on criminal involvement can be interpreted in different ways.* Typically, success in an intervention program is assessed through offender recidivism. But how are we to measure recidivism? Most often, researchers use "official statistics," such as being arrested or having probation or parole revoked for a technical violation. Other outcome measures are possible (e.g., having offenders self-report on their criminal involvement), but official statistics have the advantage of being more readily available. The difficulty with these statistics is that they are open to two interpretations: First, that they are accurate measures of offender behavior; second, that they are, at least in part, measures of how vigilant officials are in catching offenders (a "program effect").

As might be anticipated, this problem is especially relevant in evaluating the effects of intermediate sanctions. The very nature of these programs is that they subject offenders to greater and more certain surveillance. If these offenders have more arrests and violations, is this because the intermediate sanction did not work or because being in the program increased the chances that offenders' misbehavior would be detected?

Third, when programs do not appear to work—for example, rates of recidivism are the same for offenders on regular probation versus intensive supervision—this does not necessarily mean that the intervention is mis-guided: *Failure could be due to a lack of program integrity* (Gendreau & Ross, 1979). In other words, an intervention may fail not because it cannot work but, rather, because it is implemented incorrectly.

Researchers often do not measure the "black box" of what goes on between offenders' assignment to an experimental or control group and the outcome of the program 6 months or a year later. Even when researchers attempt to measure the quality or integrity of the intervention, they typically are able to use only crude indicators, such as the number of contacts per month with offenders (not what went on during these contacts) or whether an offender was in a drug treatment program (not the nature or quality of the treatment). As a result, in many evaluations, the question remains whether the program might have worked "if only it had been done the right way."

In listing these obstacles to finding out what works, we do not mean to imply that researchers have little to tell practitioners and other audiences about the effectiveness of existing correctional interventions, including intermediate sanctions. Rather, these research limitations are shared both to provide an appreciation for why provisional conclusions are at times more appropriate than definitive conclusions and as information that should be considered when assessing the worth of existing studies and what questions remain to be answered by future investigations.

Indeed, whatever its inherent limitations, evaluation research moves us beyond the point of implementing programs based on hunches, common sense, the latest fad, political convenience, and the like. It allows us to make more informed choices about what programs are most likely to be effective. This is especially the case as the body of research evidence begins to mount. For as consistent findings, particularly among studies with more rigorous methodology, appear across programs and contexts, we can have more confidence that research results are not hopelessly biased by methodological artifacts but present a good picture of what works and what doesn't work.

Goals in Conflict

As Clear and Hardyman (1990, pp. 47-48) note, intermediate punishment programs have been "sold" as accomplishing a great deal: crime control, reduced prison populations, cost savings. Undoubtedly, programs making more modest promises—for example, reduced prison populations at no cost savings—would have little appeal and never be implemented. So it is understandable why advocates are not, in the words of Clear and Hardyman (1990), "humble in the claims they make for their programs" (p. 47).

As we move from the selling phase of a project to its implementation and evaluation, however, it is critical to distinguish what priority is given to the different outcome goals of a program. Because intermediate punishments often promise so much, it is not always clear that advocates appreciate fully that these goals are complex and potentially contradictory. The lack of clarity of goals, moreover, makes it difficult for evaluators to say whether the program has been successful and, if it has, relative to what goal (Byrne, 1990).

Take, for example, the goal of crime control. The strongest argument—and the one evaluated most often in the literature—is that community control programs deter offenders from getting into trouble. With greater supervision—by officers, electronic devices, urine tests—offenders fear detection and conform to society's mandates. In this instance, success means low recidivism rates and few technical violations.

But crime control can be conceived in a very different way, as a matter of catching those offenders under community supervision who commit crimes or show signs that they are "up to no good." With greater supervision, officers would be in a better position to catch and selectively incapacitate at-risk offenders and thus to protect public safety. In this instance, success would mean high recidivism rates and many revocations for technical violations (Petersilia & Turner, 1993c; Sontheimer & Goodstein, 1993; more generally, see Feeley & Simon, 1992).

The goal of cost savings, which is a major impetus for the current community control movement (DeJong & Franzeen, 1993), introduces another layer of complexity (Morris & Tonry, 1990; Petersilia & Turner, 1993c). Reducing costs hinges on reducing prison populations. Programs that fail to divert meaningful numbers of offenders from incarceration—for example, that in effect use intermediate punishments as an add-on sanction for regular probationers—would, of course, not achieve financial savings.

Equally problematic are programs in which crime control is sought through selective incapacitation or that turn to this means by default when deterrence proves ineffective and offenders recidivate or violate supervision conditions in large numbers. As officers are more successful in detecting offenders' crimes and violations, and thus in shipping offenders to prison, the cost savings of *community* control are commensurately eroded. In short, attempts to protect public safety and to reduce public expenditures are likely to be incompatible.

Conclusions

As noted, our main purpose is to review the empirical evidence on the effectiveness of intermediate sanctions intended to place offenders under greater control in the community. We have seen that the community control movement emerged in the absence of compelling criminological evidence that it would work—that its origins lie in the prevailing correctional crisis and in the sociopolitical context that made only certain policy initiatives feasible. Now that community control programs are in place and are being evaluated, the opportunity exists to take stock of the movement's contributions and limitations. Doing so, however, is complicated by challenging methodological obstacles and by the need to keep clear what goals of the program are being assessed.

Methods

In this review, we concentrate on four intermediate punishments: intensive supervision of probationers and parolees, home confinement and electronic monitoring, drug testing of offenders under community supervision, and boot camps or shock incarceration. These sanctions were chosen because they are used extensively and because they have been evaluated enough to allow for a provisional assessment of their effectiveness.

Intensive supervision, home confinement and electronic monitoring, and drug testing are efforts to impose greater and more certain controls over offenders in the community. In contrast, boot camps are not based in the community per se. We review the evaluations of these programs, however, because like the three community control interventions, boot camp programs are part of the movement to develop sanctions for offenders in the interstitial area between traditional probation and traditional imprisonment.

The main outcome measure of this review is offender *recidivism;* that is, do community control programs (and boot camps) reduce the involvement of offenders in crime compared either to regular forms of community supervision and/or to imprisonment? When appropriate, however, the impact of programs on other outcome measures will be incorporated into the discussion.

In undertaking this review, we attempted to be as exhaustive as possible. To secure evaluation studies, we took the following five steps: First, a review was made of the major criminological journals. Second, we reviewed recent edited volumes containing research studies on intermediate punishments (e.g., Byrne, Lurigio, & Petersilia, 1992; Smykla & Selke, 1995). Third, leading criminologists who had conducted research in this area were asked to supply reprints of their studies and of any other studies on community control programs known to them. Fourth, the National Criminal Justice Reference Center and the U.S. Government Accounting Office were contacted. Fifth, we wrote to all state departments of corrections to ask officials to furnish copies of program evaluation studies made in their office or in other correctional agencies in the state.

We make no claims that the literature review is complete. The lack of access to studies by local correctional agencies, nonresponses to our inquiries, and our own oversight have likely resulted in more than a few omissions. New evaluation studies are being undertaken and may result in the need to revise our conclusions. Even so, we have a measure of confidence that we have secured much of the available evaluation literature and can provide useful insights on the effectiveness of the community control movement.

Intensive Supervision Programs

The Nature of Intensive Supervision

In this section and in the subsequent three sections, we review evaluation studies on intermediate sanctions. We begin each section with a discussion of the nature of the intervention and then assess its effectiveness. Compared with regular probation and parole services, the intensive supervision programs (ISPs) we reviewed provided increased levels of offender surveillance. Based on the number of direct contacts made per client, for example, ISPs deliver on their promise of increased officer-client contact. This surveillance is accomplished through multiple methods. Most programs couple increased officer contact with electronic monitoring and/or home confinement (see, e.g., New Jersey or Oregon). Other indirect methods of observation have been widely incorporated, such as drug testing (Georgia) and regular employment verification (New Jersey). Taken together these direct and indirect means of observation provide unprecedented levels of control within the sphere of probation and parole.

Although ISPs increase levels of surveillance, exactly what constitutes intensive supervision differs by jurisdiction. Contact with offenders varies greatly across programs, and the label *intensive* is applied to disparate numbers of officer-offender contacts. For example, intensive in Ohio is defined as four officer contacts per month over the course of 1 or more years, whereas in Georgia it is five contacts per week for 6 weeks, with reductions in contacts commensurate with approved behavior. The term *intensive* thus includes not only a surveillance component (number of contacts) but a time component (duration of supervision). The length of time an offender serves in an ISP and the levels of supervision accorded remain largely uncorrelated.

Programs also vary in the type of offender served. Typically, ISPs are tailored to three distinct types of clients: probationers (e.g., Massachusetts), parolees (e.g., Oklahoma), and individuals with specialized needs (e.g., Oregon). Still, programs do exist that cover an assortment of client types (e.g., Ohio).

The decision to target a particular offender population is rooted largely in the goals of the program administrators. If the goal is to divert offenders from traditional forms of incarceration, program administrators have historically opted for a front-end approach targeting probationers (i.e., before offenders enter prison). Conversely, if the goal is to reduce prison overcrowding, then a backdoor approach can target parolees (i.e., after offenders enter prison). As will be discussed later, the data suggest that by themselves the addition of these programs does not ensure that probationers will be diverted or prison ranks reduced.

Clearly, enough variation exists between programs to preclude any firm definition of intensive supervision. The best that we can do is to characterize ISP as an approach that functions to increase supervision and control standards. Although the length, nature, and levels of surveillance vary greatly from program to program, virtually all of the ISPs we reviewed provided significantly more surveillance and control than traditional forms of probation or parole.

Early Experiments and Optimistic Outcomes

State-run ISPs grew dramatically in the 1980s. By the end of the decade, virtually every state in the nation had developed some type of ISP (Petersilia & Turner, 1993c). The initial enthusiasm was generated mainly from early reports of success in Georgia and New Jersey. Programs in these two states reflected both prison diversion and prison reduction strategies that kept offenders in the community under stringent controls.

Georgia

The Georgia model is perhaps the most frequently duplicated program in the nation (Petersilia, 1987). Imbued with a punishment philosophy, the Georgia program emphasizes very high levels of contact with the offender by a team of officers, mandatory community service, mandatory curfew, employment, weekly arrest checks, payment of fines, and alcohol and drug testing.

The initial evaluation reported that offenders in the ISP had reincarceration rates of only 16% and that the program achieved a 10% reduction in the number of felons sentenced to incarceration (Erwin, 1986). These findings were hailed by the press and politicians and triggered a wave of optimism within community corrections (Byrne, Lurigio, & Baird, 1989; Petersilia & Turner, 1993c, pp. 282-283). After further review, however, several authors criticized the Georgia findings and brought to light a number of methodological limitations that made the results less than unambiguous or generalizable (Byrne et al., 1989, pp. 24-27). Most important, Tonry and Will (1988) cautioned against drawing conclusions from research in which the experimental (ISP) and control groups were not comparable (i.e., an "apples vs. oranges" comparison):

> Noncomparability between the prison and ISP comparison groups was stark. This is particularly regrettable because the Georgia ISP probationers are supposed primarily to have been diverted from otherwise certain prison terms. The prison group is much smaller (173 vs. 542). Prison comparison group members are twice as likely as ISP probationers to be black, three times as likely to be female, and half again as likely to have been convicted of crimes against persons or to have a "high" or "maximum" risk classification. In other words, the ISP and prison comparison groups are not very comparable at all. (p. 13)

Even if the results were not methodological artifacts, they still may not apply to other states. As Petersilia and Turner (1993b) note, Georgia's high incarceration rate means that the pool of offenders normally sent to prison, and thus eligible for an ISP program, includes a disproportionate number of low-risk, easily managed offenders. Accordingly, the generalizability of the results to other jurisdictions with lower incarceration rates and a different mix of offenders in prison is questionable.

In conclusion, contrary to popular sentiment and the claims made in the evaluation research, the data simply did not support the initial unqualified conclusions that the ISP could reduce crime and prison populations (Byrne et al., 1989; Tonry & Will, 1988). Nonetheless, ISPs began to spread.

New Jersey

The New Jersey program represents one of the first large-scale attempts to use ISP to reduce prison overcrowding. Offenders sentenced to prison must serve at least 30 days of their term but not more than 60 days and are then eligible to apply for placement within the ISP. The criteria for selection into the ISP are rather rigorous. Only 18% of those who apply are accepted (Administrative Office of the Courts, 1992). Generally, applicants must present a personal living plan that details their goals, needs, methods for meeting financial obligations, and living arrangements. After approval by an ISP officer, the application moves to a three-judge resentencing panel. If the panel approves the application, the inmate is placed on a 6-month trial period. If the inmate is successful during the trial period, a resentencing hearing is held to alter the original sentence. Overall, this selection process is one of the most rigorous in the nation and all but ensures the exclusion from ISP of high-risk offenders.

The conditions of the program are just as stringent. A team of officers maintains a minimum of 20 contacts per month for the first 14 months. In addition to high levels of surveillance, the ISP includes mandatory curfews, drug and alcohol testing, compulsory treatment for individual needs, employment, community service, and electronic monitoring.

Initial outcome measures indicated that after a 2-year follow-up, 24.7% of the ISP sample had been rearrested compared to 34.6% of the control group (Pearson, 1987b). These findings seemed to affirm what was found in Georgia: High levels of surveillance can reduce recidivism. Again, however, the initial optimism outpaced critical review.

Many of the methodological problems found in the Georgia study were duplicated in the New Jersey study. The quasi-experimental nature of the evaluation hindered the ability of researchers to discount potentially competing explanations of the results. In particular, the control group, a "matched sample," differed significantly from the experimental group—so much so that the evaluator had to take a subsample of the control group to try to minimize between-group differences. Even so, significant differences between groups could not be eliminated fully (Pearson, 1987b).

Pearson (1987b) also notes that when rearrest and revocations for technical violations are combined, 40% of the ISP participants were returned to prison within the first year, compared to 32% for the control group. Of those returned to prison, 75% were reincarcerated for technical violations, predominantly for failing drug tests. Again, such a strong surveillance component, which promotes quick removal of the offender from the community for rule infractions, may enhance societal protection (although this conclusion is arguable). In any case, the costs are continued overcrowding and increased fiscal obligations.

Because the Georgia and the New Jersey studies were limited methodologically, the full meaning of the results was not clear. The inability to use an experimental design had three severely limiting effects: First, researchers found it difficult to develop adequate control groups (Pearson, 1987b). Second, other threats to validity precluded reaching unambiguous conclusions about the meaning of the data (Petersilia & Turner, 1993c). And third, researchers could not separate the confounding effects, such as incarceration, on ISP clients and their respective control group(s) (Byrne et al., 1989).

The RAND Experiment: Recognizing the Limitations of ISPs

Recognizing these serious limitations but also the enormous benefits if the results from Georgia and New Jersey could be confirmed under more rigorous conditions, the National Institute of Justice funded RAND to evaluate, using an experimental design, 14 ISPs located in nine states. The study involved over 2,000 offenders. The RAND experiment represents the largest randomized social science experiment ever conducted in the United States (Petersilia & Turner, 1993c). The results have been summarized by the project's lead researchers, Joan Petersilia and Susan Turner (1993b, 1993c); the text that follows is based on their reports.

Programs were allowed to develop so as to meet site-specific needs. Only two criteria existed that regulated the type of offender served: First, the offender had to be an adult. Second, the offender could not be convicted of a violent crime, such as murder or rape. Other conditions, however, were placed on participating programs. The programs had to use the Georgia model of surveillance, program managers had to attend specialized training sessions, and program officials had to agree to the random assignment of offenders to ISP and control groups. Two programs chose to develop prison diversion programs; the remaining programs chose to enhance their regular probation and parole efforts.

The experimental design employed in the RAND study eliminated many past methodological problems. Adequate control groups were developed by randomizing offender sentences to either ISP, probation, parole, or prison. This represents a marked improvement over past research and allows more confidence in the results.

The RAND study provides criminal justice academicians and practitioners with the rare opportunity to evaluate experimentally obtained results (cf. Sherman, 1992). The consistency of results across sites further enables researchers to draw firmer and more valid conclusions as to the effectiveness of ISPs. We review the study's results in reference to four program outcomes: surveillance, prison diversion, recidivism, and rehabilitation.

Surveillance. The ISP samples were subject to higher levels of surveillance in 10 of the 12 jurisdictions. (Two of the jurisdictions are eliminated from consideration due to inadequate control groups.) The consistency of the findings reveals that probation and parole department officials can organize their staff and time in such a fashion as to elevate significantly their level of surveillance over the offenders. Again, however, what constitutes intensive supervision varied greatly across sites. In Contra Costa County, California, for example, the ISP averaged 2.7 contacts per month over a 1-year period; the average in Waycross, Georgia, was 22.8 contacts per month over the same time. In any case, the level of supervision (i.e., number of contacts) was not significantly related to recidivism.

Prison Diversion. The data on prison diversion were disappointing. Only two jurisdictions attempted to develop prison diversion programs—Marion County, Oregon, and Milwaukee, Wisconsin—and both had severe implementation problems. Taken together, these facts suggest that the potential to use ISPs to reduce prison crowding is limited (Petersilia & Turner, 1993c, p. 303).

The RAND researchers documented the difficulty associated with developing ISPs to divert offenders from prison. For example, program administrators in Marion County, Oregon, faced stiff resistance from judges and made program requirements so stringent—probably due to their fear of liability associated with the possibility of an offender seriously recidivating—that the offender pool virtually evaporated before the program's inception. In Milwaukee, Wisconsin, judges and probation and parole officers routinely overrode random assignment guidelines and demonstrated a continued reliance on incarceration and regular probation. Again, these findings point to the obstacles to using an ISP as a true alternative to incarceration as opposed to being an add-on to regular probation.

Recidivism. Recidivism was measured using statistics on arrests and technical violations. The obvious limitation to the use of arrest as an indicator is that it may reflect a system's response capability. Jurisdictions with a proactive law enforcement agency may experience higher levels of offender recidivism as a result of differential policing tactics. The same criticisms can be applied to the use of technical violations as an indicator. To a large degree, jurisdictions vary in response to technical infractions. The rate of technical violations thus reflects not only offender behavior but also program orientation, such as officials' strict application of the rules.

The critical evaluation criterion is whether ISPs are effective in reducing recidivism. The RAND results are not promising. "At no site," conclude Petersilia and Turner (1993c, pp. 310-311) "did ISP participants experience arrest less often, have a longer time to failure, or experience arrests for less serious offenses"; in fact, after 1 year of following offenders, arrests were higher among the ISP offenders (37%) than among the control group (33%). As Petersilia and Turner (1993c) note, "this is a strong finding, given the wide range of programs, geographical variation, and clientele represented" (p. 311) in the project.

When technical violation rates are considered, the program results are even less promising. The average ISP violation rate was 65%, compared to 38% for the controls, a significant difference (Petersilia & Turner, 1993c). Twelve of the 14 sites had violation rates above 50%, with 4 of the sites maintaining rates above 80%.

As noted, interpreting technical violation data is difficult, because high rates of infractions could be due to the increased scrutiny that offenders receive in ISPs. Furthermore, it is possible that technical violations reduce crime, because it means that offenders who are showing signs of irresponsibility and may be about to recidivate are subjected to control. The RAND study, however, did not support this latter possibility. Because arrests and technical violations were not correlated, there was "no support for the argument that violating offenders on technical conditions suppressed new criminal arrests" (Petersilia & Turner, 1993c, p. 312).

Rehabilitation. Although no significant relationship exists between levels of surveillance and recidivism, the RAND researchers did detect significant reductions in rearrest for those who had participated in treatment programs. RAND investigators noted that ISP participants in California and Texas who had been involved in treatment programs experienced a 10% to 20% decrease in recidivism (Petersilia & Turner, 1993c, pp. 313-315).

Conclusions

Given the consistency of the RAND results across jurisdictions and the methodological rigor of the research design, it is possible to offer, with some confidence, several conclusions on the effectiveness of ISPs as a crime-reduction strategy. First, the RAND data show that most ISPs succeeded in increasing the surveillance of offenders. Recall that the theory underlying ISPs holds that such increased control should deter individuals from committing criminal acts; but this theory appears to be incorrect.

This observation leads to our second conclusion from the RAND study: *Surveillance and control appear to have little impact on offender recidivism.* This assessment receives support from the existing evaluation research. In a review of 18 studies, Byrne and Pattavina (1992) note that the "majority of ISP program evaluations do *not* support the notion that 'intensive' supervision significantly reduces the risk of offender recidivism" (p. 296). Our own review of studies reached similar results. Although occasional reductions in recidivism were observed, recidivism rates were not improved significantly in most ISPs (Byrne & Kelly, 1989; Fallen, Apperson, Hall-Milligan, & Aos, 1977; Latessa, 1991, 1992, 1993a, 1993b; Mitchell, Zehr, & Butter, 1985a, 1985b; Molof, 1991; Moon & Latessa, 1993; National Council on Crime and Delinquency [NCCD], 1991; Van Ness, 1992). Accordingly, continued reliance on surveillance as a crime control mechanism should be reevaluated in light of its limited ability to effect offender change.

Third, rates of technical violations will generally increase in ISPs and are not related to reduced criminal recidivism. The risk of using ISPs is thus that they may precipitate the very conditions they were designed to help alleviate: further prison overcrowding and increased fiscal outlays. To avoid these outcomes, program managers should consider, as an alternative to revoking the sentence of community supervision, responding to technical violations with other intermediate sanctions, such as withdrawing offender privileges or imposing short stays in jail (1-2 days).

Fourth, when comparing ISPs to one another, the evidence does not show a significant relationship between levels of surveillance (e.g., number of contacts) and reductions in recidivism. This finding suggests that trying to get tougher with ISP offenders is unlikely to be the magic bullet that makes these programs work. Indeed, it is important to note that many ISPs already incorporate numerous strategies to impose control and supervision, such as supervising offenders 24 hours a day (Pearson, 1987b), and are experienced by offenders as punitive (see Petersilia & Deschenes, 1994).

Finally, the RAND study contains a salient suggestion: ISPs that are treatment oriented appear to reduce recidivism. Notably, these results are consistent with evaluations of other ISPs.

In Massachusetts, for example, Byrne and Kelly (1989) reported that "58% of the offenders who demonstrated improvement in the area of substance abuse successfully completed the 1-year at risk, as compared with only 38% of those who did not improve" (p. 37). Overall, the researchers found "strong support for crime control through treatment" (p. 37) and called into question the domination of the surveillance and control components of most ISPs to the exclusion of treatment services.

Data from Oregon shed further light on the potential value of treatment within a community control program (Jolin & Stipack, 1991). Fully 50% of the high-risk drug clients experienced revocation for technical violations. Treatment, however, appeared to play a significant role in lowering the amount of offenders' drug use (from 95% at entry to 32% at program completion). Multivariate analysis revealed that the program actually reduced participants' probability of rearrest below that of both an electronic-monitoring group and a work-release group.

Furthermore, in a series of evaluations conducted in Ohio, Latessa (1991, 1992, 1993a, 1993b) found that in an ISP with a treatment component, high-risk clients did no worse, and in some cases did better, than random samples of regular probationers. Similarly, Gendreau, Paparozzi, Little, and

Goddard (1993) report the results of an ISP in New Jersey that targeted high-risk offenders. Compared to a matched sample of regular probationers, the ISP group achieved a lower rate of recidivism (21% vs. 29%), a finding the researchers attributed to the ISP offenders receiving "significantly more treatment services" (Gendreau et al., 1993, p. 34).

The data thus suggest that treatment is potentially an essential and complementary component within community crime control programs. The continued emphasis on surveillance and control, at the expense of rehabilitative efforts, merits reevaluation. Indeed, Gendreau, Cullen, and Bonta (1994) argue that "intensive rehabilitation programs" should be the "next generation" of community corrections programs (see also Gendreau et al., 1993; Gendreau & Ross, 1987).

Home Confinement and Electronic Monitoring

The Nature of HC/EM

The terms *electronic monitoring* (EM) and *home confinement* (HC) are often used interchangeably. We should note, however, that electronic monitoring is a *means* of monitoring a home confinement sentence; electronic monitoring programs cannot work independent of a home confinement sentence, although the opposite is not the case. This distinction is important because, as will be discussed later, home confinement may have effects on offenders independent of electronic monitoring.

Both electronic monitoring and home confinement are designed to restrict the offender to his or her place of residence. They can also serve as elements within other community-based programs, such as intensive supervision (see, e.g., Oklahoma). In these instances, the goal is the same: to regulate and restrict the freedom of the offender within the community.

In response to the crowding crisis and the push for intermediate sanctions, home confinement seemed to offer the best of all worlds: The state saves the costs associated with detention in a secure facility; the offender remains free from the possible abuses that can occur within the confines of the institution; community resources can be directed toward the offender's specific needs; the offender keeps family ties intact and may be allowed to remain employed; and the stigma associated with traditional incarceration is avoided (Mainprize, 1993). Large-scale use of home confinement began to appear as a feasible alternative for many offenders. But without omnipresent state control over offenders, home confinement lacked the legitimacy necessary to be considered an effective sentence—a problem that electronic monitoring seemed ideal to solve.

Adding electronic monitors made the idea of home confinement more acceptable by ostensibly ensuring that offenders would stay in their residences and not jeopardize public safety. Without monitoring technology, supervising officials would only know whether offenders failed to be at home and thus "confined" through manually checking (e.g., telephone call, visit). Electronic monitors could alert officials located at a central office whenever offenders left their residences. By increasing the certainty of detection, such monitoring might be expected to deter house arrestees from violating their confinement and, in any case, would allow officials to react quickly when offenders were at large in the community.

Even so, initial programs targeted low-risk offenders, particularly those convicted of alcohol-related traffic incidents (Lilly, Ball, Curry, & McMullen, 1993). Program officials actively worked toward achieving a level of acceptance within the criminal justice system by selecting only those clients most likely to succeed (Lilly, Ball, & Wright, 1987). Given the unproven nature of the technology, this cautious orientation in targeting offenders was understandable. Indeed, initial reports indicated that there were numerous problems with monitoring equipment and its implementation (Neville, 1989).

What we have witnessed with home confinement is the coalescence of the state's need to handle more offenders with a technology that seemed to offer the means to address this need. It is doubtful that the large-scale use of home incarceration would have been politically feasible had monitoring technology not provided a method of enforcing compliance. The rapid expansion of HC/EM illustrates this point well (Renzema & Skelton, 1989).

Target Groups for HC/EM

Most HC/EM programs historically have targeted low-risk offenders, with a heavy concentration on driving while intoxicated (DWI) offenders (Lilly et al., 1993; Petersilia, 1986). There is growing evidence, however, that programs are beginning to relax admittance criteria (Rogers & Jolin, 1991). Since 1987, such programs have admitted more persons involved in property, sex, and person-to-person crimes; drug offenders; and parolees as opposed to probationers (Beck & Klein-Saffran, 1989; Renzema, 1992a; Renzema & Skelton, 1989; Schmidt, 1989a, 1989b). Because the admission of serious offenders into home confinement programs is rather recent, the existing research generally has not evaluated how HC/EM works with this offender population. Only a few of the studies we reviewed evaluated programs that included high-risk offenders (Austin & Hardyman, 1991; Brown & Roy, 1995; Jolin & Stipack, 1992).

Methodological Limitations

For our review of HC/EM generally, we were able to assess a growing body of evaluation studies (Austin & Hardyman, 1991; Ball, Huff, & Lilly, 1988; Baumer, Maxfield, & Mendelsohn, 1993; Baumer & Mendelsohn, 1991; Beck & Klein-Saffran, 1989; Brown & Roy, 1995; Davis, 1986a, 1986b, 1987; Jolin, 1988; Jolin & Stipack, 1992; Lilly et al., 1993; Lilly et al., 1987; Loveless, 1990; Maxfield & Baumer, 1991; Ministry of Correctional Services, 1991; NCCD, 1991; Neville, 1989; Quinn & Holman, 1991; Rush, 1988; Sandhu, Dodder, & Mathur, 1993; Smith, 1990; Smith & Akers, 1993; Tuthill, 1986). Even so, insights into the effectiveness of HC/EM programs are less well developed than those into ISPs, because the HC/EM area has no investigation comparable to the RAND multiple-site experimental study of intensive supervision. Indeed, the research on HC/EM programs has generally been limited by one or a combination of three factors: the low-risk nature of most samples, too few experimental evaluations, and the confounding effects of inadequate program integrity (Bonta, 1993).

First, as noted, most programs evaluated thus far have served low-risk offenders. Because these offenders are nonviolent and easily managed, they likely would do well in any type of program (Petersilia, 1988). This selection bias makes it difficult to ascertain the broader effectiveness of the programs with higher-risk clients. Thus far, data from Oklahoma and Oregon suggest that higher-risk clients can be maintained within the community, even without the use of electronic monitoring (Austin & Hardyman, 1991; Jolin & Stipack, 1992). Still, much more research needs to be done in this area.

Second, evaluation researchers on HC/EM have had difficulties securing control groups adequate for interpreting whether programs are effective. Eight of the studies we reviewed failed to use any type of control group. When comparison groups have been employed, they often have been less than ideal. Many HC/EM experimental groups have been matched with groups from jail (Lilly et al., 1987) and halfway houses (Sandhu et al., 1993) and by use of nonrandom selection practices (Tuthill, 1986). In these instances, and especially in the absence of multivariate analysis to control for differences among samples, it is difficult to discount potentially confounding influences, such as incarceration experiences.

Three studies reviewed, however, did involve random assignment (Austin & Hardyman, 1991; Baumer et al., 1993; Baumer & Mendelsohn, 1991). Especially in light of their consistent findings, these three studies can be viewed with more confidence than could be placed in past research efforts. We detail their conclusions in the next section.

Third, beyond limitations involving design and sampling, only a few studies have assessed the issue of program integrity (Gendreau & Ross, 1987)—whether programs are being implemented as intended (see, e.g., Austin & Hardyman, 1991; Baumer & Mendelsohn, 1991). As Baumer and Mendelsohn (1993) illustrate, the ability of program personnel to follow through on organizational objectives affects the integrity of the program; in turn, the integrity of the program may bias research outcomes. Baumer and Mendelsohn (1991) describe how an HC/EM program for juvenile burglars appeared to be functioning quite well based on official recidivism and revocation measures. Yet the program was fraught with problems: It was not accepted by the staff, the police did not meet surveillance obligations, and above all, the offenders were not controlled. Merely examining the outcome measures would have been misleading.

Data from an Indiana survey also illustrate a level of confusion as to the use of home confinement and electronic monitoring (Automotive Transportation Center, 1990). Based on the responses of judges, prosecutors, and program managers, the survey demonstrated that an element of organizational confusion existed as to the proper use of HC/EM, the legality of sentencing to HC/EM, and the ability of program officials to respond to infractions. The authors conclude that many HC/EM programs in Indiana are more form than substance.

We mention the limitations of HC/EM research to illustrate two points. First, research has evolved from descriptive efforts designed to elucidate the potential effectiveness of HC/EM to the use more recently of experimental designs employed to test the actual effectiveness of HC/EM. Second, the current state of research into HC/EM largely inhibits making a definite assessment of this intervention's utility. Although more current, and more rigorous, efforts have yielded relatively consistent results, we simply do not have enough evidence for more than provisional conclusions.

The Effectiveness of HC/EM

Prison Diversion

Prison diversion has long been a goal in many community-based programs, including many HC/EM programs. In 1983, for example, the state of Florida developed what is today the largest prison diversion program in the nation. As of 1992, the Florida Community Control Program (FCCP) had over 11,500 offenders under supervision. Offenders are subjected to a range of intermediate sanctions, including intensive supervision (28 contacts with an officer each month) and drug tests. Most salient here, offenders also are confined to their residences unless engaged in a permitted activity, such as work or education (Smith & Akers, 1993; Wagner & Baird, 1993). Today, the program has the capability to monitor electronically 840 offenders or 7% of the current offender population (Office of the Auditor General, 1993).

Such a large program should divert a substantial number of individuals from incarceration. An evaluation of the program indicated that only 50% of the offenders were bona fide diversions (NCCD, 1991). Although some may argue that this number is low, the evaluators judged the program as an effective diversion tool, largely because few other community-based programs have achieved a comparable rate of diversion. It appears, however, that the availability of the program to divert offenders was undermined by sentencing guideline changes. When Florida instituted the FCCP program, the legislature simultaneously increased the number of offenses eligible for incarceration and elevated the severity of traditional sentences. As a result, although diversion occurred, prison populations continued to rise precipitously.

The Florida program far exceeds the size of most programs across the United States. Most programs can accept only a limited number of individuals. Data from Indiana, for example, indicate that at any given time county programs range in size from 1 to 163 offenders (Automotive Transportation Center, 1990). State data from New Jersey show that the mean number of persons on EM at any one time is 80 (Vaughn, 1992). Furthermore, diversion is not always accomplished. In an initial experiment to reduce jail crowding by use of home confinement, Loveless (1990) found a positive relationship between the use of home incarceration and jail overcrowding.

We can draw two conclusions regarding the effectiveness of HC/EM as a prison diversion program. First, because most programs are small in size, they cannot divert a large enough number of offenders to make a significant dent in jail or prison overcrowding. Second, events external to a program may operate to undermine its capacity to reduce prison crowding. Stringent sentencing legislation, such as in Florida, can offset gains in diversion achieved by a program; similarly, a reluctance to use HC/EM with certain categories of offenders (e.g., felony/serious) can reduce the potential of a program to apply to, and thus to divert, a large proportion of prison-bound offenders.

Recidivism

As noted, because research is still in its beginning stages, assessing the effectiveness of HC/EM programs is difficult. Several broad conclusions from the available literature, however, seem possible.

First, almost all programs achieve low recidivism rates. Petersilia (1988) reports that recidivism rates for HC/EM programs typically fall below 25%, whereas Brown and Roy (1995) conclude that existing "evaluation studies indicate that 70 to 94 percent of offenders successfully complete house arrest programs" (p. 2). Our analysis of research through 1993 revealed similar results. Although exceptions exist (Smith & Akers, 1993), recidivism rates generally fell below 30%. Given the low-risk nature of most offenders monitored by HC/EM programs—either by design or due to the selection bias of officials making offender program assignments—these low recidivism rates are unsurprising (Ministry of Justice, 1988; Rogers & Jolin, 1991).

Second, recidivism rates also vary considerably across HC/EM programs— a finding that may reflect differences not only in the type of offenders who are supervised but also in program integrity. Using an experimental design, Baumer et al. (1993) found significant variation in recidivism among programs even though they were within the same jurisdiction, employed virtually the same equipment, and imposed similar rules on offenders. Although noting that these differences may be due to the type of offenders under surveillance (pretrial vs. postconviction), the authors also suggest the potential effects of the quality of program implementation.

Third, rates of revocations for technical violations ranged from 0 to 50% in the studies reviewed. Compared to control groups, HC/EM groups sometimes had higher and sometimes had lower revocation rates (Baumer et al., 1993; Jolin & Stipack, 1992; Loveless, 1990; Quinn & Holman, 1991; Sandhu et al., 1993). In light of these inconsistent findings, it is not clear that HC/EM interventions are able to reduce technical violations more than other forms of correctional supervision.

Finally, the ability of HC/EM programs to achieve low recidivism rates for more serious predatory offenders—precisely those offenders sent to prison in large numbers for longer terms—remains in question. On the positive side, Renzema and Skelton (1989) report that although home confinement programs increasingly enroll more felony offenders, seriousness of offense does not seem to be related to successful program completion. In an evaluation of an HC/EM program in Oneida County, New York, Brown and Roy (1995) found that program completion was inversely related to seriousness of criminal history and (for HC offenders supervised manually but not electronically) to the seriousness of the offenders' most current offense.

Smith and Akers's (1993) research on the Florida Community Control Program (FCCP)—which they term the "nation's largest intermediate sanction (home confinement) program for felons" (p. 267)—is instructive. Examining recidivism for a 5-year period, Smith and Akers (1993) compared a sample of felons in the FCCP to a matched sample of prison inmates (although the inmates had more serious felony records). They found virtually no differences between the groups: About four in five offenders in each group recidivated within 5 years. According to Smith and Akers (1993), these findings suggest "a rethinking of the emphasis on punishment, rather than treatment" (p. 288). They observe that

> a more effective home confinement program may require that elements of rehabilitation and treatment specifically be added as an additional goal of the program. That is, a more persuasive model might move back in the direction of community reintegration and propose that occupational skill enhancement, education, substance abuse treatment, behavior modification, and other practices be added to the principle of closely supervising home confinement. (p. 289; see also Gendreau et al., 1994; Ministry of Justice, 1988)

Is Electronic Monitoring Necessary?

The HC/EM literature suggests an additional conclusion: Electronic monitoring does not guarantee the increased deterrence, and thus conformity, of offenders under home confinement. The data available generally indicate no substantial differences in recidivism outcomes when controlling for whether offenders are supervised manually by probation officers or electronically by monitors. Indeed, a program that delivers consistent supervision manually—for example, in the form of telephone calls and home visits by supervising officers—seems likely to be as effective as a program that relies on electronic monitoring.

In a study of house arrestees, Baumer and Mendelsohn (1991) tested the comparative effects of EM and manual supervision on recidivism and technical violation outcomes. Using an experimental design, the authors found no significant differences in rearrest rates after a 1-year follow-up. There also were no significant differences in revocation rates (20.5% for EM and 18.3% for manual), even though the EM group received significantly more contacts from the EM equipment than the manual group did from program officers. Overall, 42% of both groups had unauthorized absences from the home. The researchers thus concluded that EM does not guarantee increased levels of control beyond what can be accomplished through manual contacts.

Research from Oklahoma also calls into question the need for electronic monitoring. In another study using an experimental design, Austin and Hardyman (1991) found that among offenders on intensive supervision, recidivism did not differ significantly between those receiving and not receiving EM; they concluded that "inmates could be intensively supervised in the community *without* EM at minimal costs to public safety" (p. 114).

Brown and Roy (1995) introduce yet another level of complexity into the analysis. Comparing HC offenders under manual and electronic supervision, they found in contrast to the studies just reviewed that the EM group was more likely than the manual supervision group to complete a home confinement sentence without revocation for a new offense or technical violation. But the difference in failures—18% to 22%—was not substantial.

More important, Brown and Roy (1995) discovered that the effectiveness of the type of monitoring varied according to the offenders being supervised. In particular, EM appeared to be a better alternative (fewer program failures) for offenders who were unemployed and unmarried, which the authors interpreted as indicating "that the level of supervision existing in the manual supervision program is insufficient to control the behavior of those with weak or no social bonds" (p. 51). Although a beginning finding, Brown and Roy's (1995) work suggests the need for researchers to explore systematically the intersection between HC/EM program characteristics and offender characteristics (see also Sherman, 1992).

As noted, many correctional interventions succeed or fail due to their implementation. What makes EM programs stand out is reliance on technology. Corbett and Marx (1992) have warned of "technofallacies"—the unfounded perceptions that technology is a panacea for complex human problems. Numerous authors have described electronic monitoring as labor intensive and have argued that it requires specialized training, altered organizational structures, and high levels of coordination between the officer in the field and the person or company responsible for notification of an infraction (Baumer & Mendelsohn, 1991; Quinn & Holman, 1991; Vaughn, 1992; but see Lilly et al., 1993; Rogers & Jolin, 1991). As Baumer, Mendelsohn, and Rhine (1990) caution, EM is likely to involve for agencies not only benefits but also unanticipated costs:

> Home detention programs, however monitored, are neither a panacea nor a "magic bullet" for criminal justice agencies. They require considerable time, effort, and organization. If the program is to utilize electronic monitors, the realities of the situation are even further removed from such expectations. While electronic equipment does automate contact with clients, and therefore, tends to provide a more balanced, consistent, and randomized set of contacts, it also may create other hurdles. These include: technology shock, information overload, unanticipated computer "programming" time, and extra time tracing and verifying "negative" contacts. In sum, the electronic monitors do relieve some of the burden of field contact, but in turn, create a large amount of technically oriented office work. It is likely that an agency without a computer knowledge base . . . will encounter difficulties in integrating and exploiting the technology of electronic monitoring systems. (p. 35)

Although the limits of HC/EM should be appreciated, this intervention may have value when implemented in well-organized agencies to address problems caused by specific offender populations. This conclusion gains support from Lilly et al.'s (1993) evaluation of an HC/EM program in Palm Beach County, Florida, that had been in existence for 7 years.

The program was not designed for a diverse group of offenders but focused almost exclusively on those convicted for drunk driving (DWI) and for driving on a suspended license (DUS). Faced with a jail-crowding problem at a time of increasing public demands to "get tough" with DWI offenders, the county contracted with a private company to administer an HC/EM program in exchange for fees collected from offenders. Lilly et al.'s (1993) evaluation revealed that the program was cost-effective, diverted DWI/DUS offenders from jail, and achieved high rates of program completion. Given that other research shows the ineffectiveness of jail sanctions with DWI offenders (e.g., Ross, 1992), they further contended that the HC/EM program was unlikely to have jeopardized public safety.

Conclusions

At this stage in the research process, it is not clear that HC/EM programs are more effective in reducing recidivism and technical violations than less intrusive interventions, such as intensive supervision programs or regular probation, or than more intrusive interventions, such as jail and prison sentences. Their greatest value, as Smith and Akers (1993) suggest, may be in providing a community-based program within which treatment services may be delivered (see also Gendreau et al., 1994).

The success of HC/EM as a means of reducing institutional crowding also remains problematic. Some success in diverting offenders has been achieved (Baird & Wagner, 1990; Lilly et al., 1993). Duplicating this success in other jurisdictions depends on agencies having the organizational talent to administer large, well-designed programs and on agencies having an external environment that does not produce such a large flow of offenders as to make their attempts at reducing inmate populations a meaningless enterprise.

Drug Testing

The Nature of Drug Testing

Drug testing has been used for decades in treatment programs to monitor client performance (Visher, 1992). A few states and the federal government have been testing probationers and parolees for drug use for over 10 years. In the past several years, however, this practice has become increasingly common. Although tests often are conducted at the discretion of the probation or parole officer, in many jurisdictions clients are tested regularly (Visher, 1987). Testing also has begun to be used for individuals released before trial (Visher, 1992). With drug testing now occurring in virtually every state, the number of tests conducted annually exceeds 1.3 million (Camp & Camp, 1993b, p. 28). A national study of adult felons on state-level probation found that 31% of offenders were subjected to drug testing (Langan, 1994).

The schedule of testing varies widely across programs. Although many reports simply state that testing is conducted "periodically," typically clients are tested between once per month and once per week. This schedule may be random or fixed, with the client providing a specimen on a predetermined day. Most programs assess drug use by testing a sample of urine either for the drug itself or for metabolites created by the body when a particular drug has been used. Visher (1991) has reviewed the major urinalysis technologies and reports that they are fairly accurate and reliable measures of drug use. Because of potential sanctions for individuals providing "dirty" specimens, however, positive tests should be confirmed using a different technology.

At least five goals of drug testing have been identified in the literature. First, drug testing should provide a reliable method of determining recent drug use (Toborg, Bellassai, Yezer, & Trost, 1989). Traditionally, interviews were conducted with offenders or the circumstances of the crime were examined to assess drug use. Unfortunately, drug abusers often underreport or deny their use. Also, they are often arrested for crimes that do not directly indicate a drug problem. Drug testing provides an alternative to these traditional methods for identifying drug use. The information provided by these tests can then be used to determine supervision and drug treatment requirements (Vito, Wilson, & Holmes, 1993).

As a second goal, urine tests or hair analysis may be used to identify chronic drug users (Wish & Gropper, 1990). A single urinalysis can indicate only whether drugs have been used within the past 24 to 72 hours, but repeated testing can identify patterns of abuse. Conversely, a single test with a 2- to 3-inch sample of hair, which uses emerging technology, can assess drug use for the preceding 4 to 6 months (Baer, Baumgartner, Hill, & Blahd, 1991; Mieczkowski, Landress, Newel, & Coletti, 1993).

Third, drug testing may help estimate national and local trends in criminal drug use (Wish & Gropper, 1990). Fourth, the results of a drug test can provide judges with additional information that may help assess risk and determine the conditions of pretrial release (Belenko & Mara-Drita, 1988; Belenko, Mara-Drita, & McElroy, 1992; Dembo, Williams, Wish, & Schmeidler, 1990; Goldkamp, Gottfredson, & Weiland, 1990; Smith, Wish, & Jarjoura, 1989; Toborg et al., 1989; Visher, 1990).

Finally, it is argued that testing for illegal substances may deter continued drug use and associated criminal activity (Haapenen, 1993; Toborg et al., 1989; Wish & Gropper, 1990). Theoretically, drug testing might be expected to work because it meets one of the core requirements of deterrence: high certainty of detection. The existing evidence on the ability of drug testing to achieve deterrence, however, paints a more complicated picture.

The Effectiveness of Drug Testing

Much of the research on drug testing with offenders does not focus exclusively on whether this procedure reduces recidivism. Instead, these studies have been designed to assess such related issues as the extent of drug use (Dembo et al., 1990; Vito, Holmes, Keil, & Wilson, 1992; Vito et al., 1993; Vito, Wilson, & Keil, 1990), the ability of drug tests to predict the risk that defendants will recidivate while on pretrial release (Belenko & Mara-Drita, 1988; Belenko et al., 1992; Dembo et al., 1990; Goldkamp et al., 1990; Smith et al., 1989; Visher, 1990), and the use of drug testing to identify offenders who are in need of treatment (Vito et al., 1990; Vito et al., 1992; Vito et al., 1993).

Studies have been conducted, however, that provide evidence on the deterrent effects of drug testing. Some of this research suggests that under certain conditions, such testing may reduce offender misconduct. For example, a Coos County, Oregon, study indicates that the effectiveness of testing may depend on the response that is taken when an offender tests positive for drug use. Coos County officials have developed a unique system that incorporates swift, certain punishment into a drug-testing program (Oregon Department of Corrections, n.d., 1993).

Previously in the county, positive tests elicited "no formal court action until an individual was deeply immersed in the abusive use of illegal drugs. Then, with a lack of alternatives and an increase in community frustration, a jail sentence was imposed" (Oregon Department of Corrections, n.d., p. 2). To change this situation, Coos County implemented the Drug Reduction of Probationers (DROP) Program. Positive tests now evoke an immediate arrest and a graduated schedule of sanctions: 2 days in jail for the first violation, 5 days for the second violation, and 30 days for the third violation.

After nearly 2 years in operation, the percentage of positive drug tests has dropped for both probationers (from 43% to 19%) and for parolees (from 47% to 29%). Subsequent research indicates that similar levels in positive tests can be achieved by using a nongraduated sanction schedule, with a 5-day jail term for each failed drug test (Oregon Department of Corrections, 1993). Although definitive conclusions on the DROP program cannot be drawn in the absence of more rigorous empirical analyses (e.g., multivariate analysis), these results suggest that relatively short, but swift and certain, punishments can increase the deterrent powers of drug testing.

Vito et al.'s (1993) study in Jefferson County, Kentucky, also provides evidence that drug testing may have deterrent effects. Vito et al. (1993) report that since the county implemented a drug testing program in 1988, the percentage of probationers and parolees testing positive on initial drug tests has decreased consistently. During the first year of the program, 59% of clients who were referred for testing had a positive urine sample. This percentage dropped to 41% by the program's second year and to 35% by the third year (there was no further change in the fourth year). Although the research design could not rule out the possibility that other factors may have influenced levels of drug use among the probationers and parolees, Vito et al. (1993) conclude "that random drug testing has a general deterrent effect on this population" (p. 353).

Other research suggests, however, that the deterrent effects of drug testing on offenders may be limited (Britt, Gottfredson, & Goldkamp, 1992; Goldkamp & Jones, 1992; Visher, 1992). Perhaps the best experimental studies have been conducted on how drug testing affects the rates of misconduct among offenders released and awaiting trial (Britt et al., 1992; Goldkamp & Jones, 1992).

In experimental studies conducted in two Arizona counties, Maricopa and Pima, Britt et al. (1992) examined rates of rearrest and failure to appear for trial among pretrial releasees who were periodically tested for drug use. According to Britt et al. (1992), the specific deterrent effect of drug testing "appears to be limited. . . . Our results show that monitoring the drug use of offenders on pretrial release has neither a substantively significant nor a statistically significant effect at reducing the level of pretrial misconduct" (pp. 75, 76). These results are especially disconcerting given that the average annual cost of the drug testing program in each county was between $400,000 and $500,000 (Britt et al., 1992, p. 77).

Goldkamp and Jones (1992) report similar results for pretrial drug testing programs in Milwaukee, Wisconsin, and in Prince George's County, Maryland. Their experimental evaluation assessed the proposition that "pretrial drug monitoring during pretrial release would deter defendants from crime and flight better than release without drug monitoring" (p. 430). This thesis received little support: Compared to similar offenders, drug-tested defendants did not have lower rates of rearrest or of failure to appear at court hearings.

The researchers note that the programs' failure to deter offenders may have been due to implementation problems (Goldkamp & Jones, 1992; Jones &

Goldkamp, 1993). Although the specific sanctions differed, offenders who failed or did not appear for drug tests were to be subjected to a graduated schedule of sanctions, ranging from counseling by staff or increased drug testing for an initial violation to a bench warrant or short jail term (e.g., 3-5 days) for a fourth violation. In neither site, however, were the sanctions imposed as designed: To sanction noncompliant defendants, especially with jail terms, would have required hearings that would have consumed considerable court time—an expenditure that officials were "unable or unprepared to accept" (Jones & Goldkamp, 1993, p. 216). Jones and Goldkamp (1993) reveal an added complication: "Should such court time be available and the sanctions enforced, the demand on jail resources would be significant" (p. 216). These results suggest that even if the theory underlying drug testing has merit, the obstacles to achieving program integrity may be too severe in many jurisdictions to make meaningful levels of deterrence obtainable (see also Toborg et al., 1989, p. 14; Visher, 1992, p. 3).

Conclusions

The overall effectiveness of drug testing remains equivocal: Some evaluations provide evidence of successful deterrence; others do not. A critical factor in program effectiveness may be program integrity: Are offenders drug-tested systematically and sanctioned swiftly and certainly when violations are detected? It remains to be determined how many jurisdictions have the organizational capacity to implement well-designed drug-testing programs and, even if they do, whether the deterrence achieved will be large enough to balance the potentially high costs of administering the tests and sanctioning offender noncompliance.

Boot Camps (Shock Incarceration)

The Nature of Boot Camps

According to MacKenzie, Shaw, and Gowdy (1993), since 1983, "41 boot camp prisons have been opened in 26 state correctional jurisdictions, in addition to many programs developed and being considered in cities and counties, and for juveniles" (p. 1). Such programs typically have several components that distinguish them from traditional incarceration (MacKenzie,

1990; Osler, 1991). First, they are highly structured and include military components of drill and physical training. Second, they are designed for nonserious, youthful offenders. Third, offenders stay in the program 3 to 6 months, with an average stay nationally of 4.3 months (Camp & Camp, 1993a, p. 61). Because the time spent in confinement is relatively short, placement in a boot camp is often termed "shock incarceration."

Although boot camp or shock incarceration programs may be defined by an adherence to a military model of discipline, they vary widely in other aspects. MacKenzie and Ballow's (1989) description of 11 state programs demonstrates that across sites, programs vary in size, number of days served, placement authority, whether program entry and exit are voluntary, location, and type of release supervision. Some boot camps incorporate counseling and educational components in proportions equal to, if not greater than, military training; other programs are based on hard work and discipline (see, e.g., New York Department of Correctional Services and New York Division of Parole [NYDCS & NYDP], 1990; Texas Department of Criminal Justice, 1991).

Thus, no single program can be identified as the "model" boot camp. These programs typically share certain core features but may be quite different in other program components—a consideration that may influence variations in program effectiveness.

The Effectiveness of Boot Camp Programs

Although programs exist in over half the states, the federal correctional system, and some local jurisdictions, we were able to identify evaluations of boot camp programs in only a limited number of states. Officials from several more states reported to us that their boot camps were implemented quite recently and evaluations are currently under way. As a result, the conclusions presented here, which largely question the portrayal of boot camps as correctional panaceas (see also Dickey, 1994; U.S. General Accounting Office [U.S. GAO], 1993), may be in need of revision as additional data on varying types of programs become available.

Because shock incarceration differs widely across programs, we begin by examining each state separately. We also explore briefly the impact of boot camps on criminogenic attitudes. Following this review, we present overall conclusions on intervention effectiveness based on cross-program comparisons.

Oklahoma

Holley and Connelly (1993) provide preliminary evaluation information on Oklahoma's Regimented Inmate Discipline (RID) program. According to design, inmates spend 120 days in military-like training combined with educational and treatment-oriented activities. This evaluation found, however, that boot camp participants often were idle because the program was understaffed. After release from the boot camp, no community supervision is imposed on offenders. Holley and Connelly (1993) cite two studies of RID offender postrelease performance that indicate reincarceration rates of 23% to 53%. Although systematic data are not presented, it is suggested that these rates exceed those found among comparison groups.

Massachusetts

Although only descriptive data are available, the results for Massachusetts's 10-month-old boot camp program, which houses male and female adult offenders for 120 days, are pessimistic (Loey, 1994). Based on Department of Correction statistics, 51% of boot camp graduates were reincarcerated within 1 year of release. The reincarceration rate was lower for inmates released from the state's minimum- and medium-security prisons (33% and 35%, respectively) and only slightly higher for releasees from the maximum-security prison (53%).

Virginia

The Virginia Department of Corrections (1992) furnishes a beginning evaluation of its Southampton Intensive Treatment Center (SITC), a boot camp program implemented in 1991. This 90-day program provides young, nonviolent, male offenders with the typical boot camp regimen, supplemented by academic instruction, drug education, and access to counseling. Following graduation from the program, offenders are placed on intensive supervision probation.

At the time the Virginia report was prepared, 239 inmates had graduated from SITC and had been in the community 1 to 15 months. Overall, the recidivism rate for this group was 15.5%. Although this rate is encouraging, the author cautions that it may reflect the short time offenders were in the community. It also is difficult to interpret these data without a comparison group of inmates who did not participate in SITC.

Texas

Program and recidivism information on the Texas Special Alternative Incarceration Program (SAIP) is provided by the Texas Department of Criminal Justice (1991). The program typically lasts 75 to 90 days. Offenders may be placed on probation by the sentencing judge at any time during their incarceration; however, those not given probation by their 91st day in the boot camp are converted to regular incarceration. This program currently is "very much oriented toward work, discipline, and drills," which the Texas Department of Criminal Justice (1991, p. 14) reports leaves little time for treatment activities.

Preliminary recidivism data indicate a reincarceration rate of 32% for boot camp graduates, 19% for parolees, 23% for those on intensive supervision probation, and 32% for offenders sentenced to restitution centers. In short, it does not appear that boot camps are more effective than alternative correctional interventions. The author cautions, however, that because the boot camp and control groups in the evaluation differ greatly, direct comparisons across the groups are not warranted.

South Carolina

Souryal and MacKenzie (1995) report on South Carolina's boot camp experience. This program has undergone two recent changes as control shifted from the parole department to the corrections department and the emphasis on education, release preparation, and crisis counseling was increased.

In the evaluation study, old shock graduates (i.e., those participating in the program prior to these changes) and new shock graduates are compared with parolees, split probationers, and regular probationers. Statistical controls for group differences were introduced, and the samples were compared on four outcome measures: arrest, any revocation, revocation for a new crime, and revocation for a technical violation. The results indicate that old shock graduates failed significantly more often on every measure of recidivism than new shock graduates. New shock graduates also were significantly less likely to have their probation status revoked than regular probationers and were less likely to experience revocation for a technical violation or arrest than split probationers. Boot camp graduates did not differ significantly from parolees on any outcome measure.

Georgia

Two evaluations are available for Georgia's Special Alternative Incarceration (SAI) program (Flowers, Carr, & Ruback, 1991; Souryal & MacKenzie, 1995; see also U.S. GAO, 1993). The SAI program has two phases. Offenders first serve 90 days in a militaristic boot camp setting; in the second phase, most offenders are released to regular probation.

Flowers et al. (1991) compared the adjusted reincarceration rates for boot camp graduates to the rates for parolees with varying criminal histories, offenders sentenced to an ISP, offenders sentenced to a diversion program, and offenders sentenced to regular probation. Although offenders were tracked for up to 60 months, the authors conducted significance tests only for the follow-up period of 36 months. They found that the boot camp graduates had a significantly lower reincarceration rate than all comparison groups except for the offenders sentenced to the diversion program and to regular probation. The reincarceration rate for boot camp graduates (41%) was not significantly different from the diversion center residents (38%) and was significantly higher than the reincarceration rate for probationers (33%).

Similarly, Souryal and MacKenzie (1995) report that probationers were less likely than SAI graduates to undergo revocation for a new crime; no significant differences were observed for arrests or revocations for technical violations. The evaluation also indicated that there were no significant differences between boot camp graduates and prison releasees for arrests, revocations for new crimes, and revocations for technical violations.

Florida

Two evaluations also are available for Florida's shock incarceration program (Florida Department of Corrections, 1990; Souryal & MacKenzie, 1995; see also U.S. GAO, 1993). Youthful male offenders who are sentenced to boot camp spend 90 to 120 days in military drills, work, physical exercise, and counseling. After program completion, these offenders are released to regular probation supervision.

An evaluation conducted by the Florida Department of Corrections (1990) found that 6.4% of boot camp graduates, as compared to 10.6% of parolees, were reincarcerated for technical violations. Boot camp graduates were reincarcerated for new misdemeanors at a higher rate than the parolees (2.1% vs. 0.5%), and 16.7% of both groups were reincarcerated for new felonies. Tests for statistical significance were not conducted for these differences in outcomes, and the comparability of these groups is questionable.

In a more sophisticated analysis, Souryal and MacKenzie's (1995) evaluation introduces statistical controls for group differences. The authors report that compared to parolees, boot camp graduates and dropouts had significantly lower rates of reincarceration for new crimes. No significant differences in arrests or revocations for technical violations were revealed between these groups. Souryal and MacKenzie (1995) conclude that the similar postrelease performance of program graduates and dropouts sheds doubt on the effectiveness of the boot camp experience.

New York

New York's shock incarceration program has been evaluated extensively (Aziz, Korotkin, & MacDonald, 1990, 1991; NYDCS & NYDP, 1990, 1991, 1992, 1993; see also U.S. GAO, 1993). This program has the typical military-like components but also emphasizes treatment for participants. After completion of the 6-month incarceration phase, offenders may be released to intensive supervision parole.

The earliest evaluation indicated that for a 12-month follow-up period, shock incarceration graduates were reincarcerated for technical violations at a higher rate than parolees who had been eligible for shock but received regular incarceration (NYDCS & NYDP, 1990). Six months later, Aziz et al. (1990) evaluated a larger group of early program participants. They found that shock incarceration graduates (a) did not differ significantly from those sentenced before the program existed but (b) were significantly less likely to be reincarcerated than a comparison group of parolees who had been eligible for boot camp but received traditional incarceration. Although differences between the program graduates and parolees were significant at 12 months, they were insignificant when the samples were followed for 18 months.

A similar pattern is seen in subsequent annual evaluations of the New York shock incarceration program. Each of these studies compared boot camp graduates to three other groups: offenders sentenced before shock incarceration was available ("preshock" group); offenders who were eligible for shock incarceration but received traditional sentences instead; and offenders who were sentenced to boot camp but were removed before program completion ("dropouts"). In each study, the results indicated a lower rate of reincarceration among boot camp graduates than any of the comparison groups (Aziz et al., 1991; NYDCS & NYDP, 1992, 1993).

Even so, although percentage differences in recidivism occur across all follow-up periods, longer follow-ups indicate that reincarceration rates for boot camp graduates do not differ significantly from those of the comparison groups. The most recent evaluation, for example, reveals statistically significant, lower reincarceration rates for boot camp participants for 12- and 24-month follow-ups. When recidivism rates are compared after offenders are in the community for 36 months, however, the differences are not significant: The reincarceration rate for the boot camp offenders is 49.2%, whereas the rate for the other comparison groups ranges from 50.9% to 54.5% (NYDCS & NYDP, 1993).

New York's most recent report provides separate analyses for female graduates who have been under community supervision for 12 months. Female boot camp graduates are less likely to be reincarcerated than the comparison groups, but this difference is not statistically significant (NYDCS & NYDP, 1993).

Because of several methodological problems, the results reported above (and in many other evaluations reviewed here) must be viewed with caution. These studies did not use an experimental design and no statistical techniques were employed to control for group differences. Indeed, the potential for selection bias makes evaluating group differences risky. It is possible that some factor may have played a role in determining which offenders eligible for assignment to the boot camp program received regular incarceration instead of placement in the boot camp. If this factor is related to recidivism, then the reincarceration rate for the prison sample would be artificially inflated. Furthermore, the sample of inmates incarcerated before the program existed (the preshock comparison group) would have included some of these "eligible" inmates, thus inflating this group's reincarceration rate as well.

Finally, and perhaps most questionable, in making comparisons to the control groups, the evaluations focus on boot camp *graduates* as opposed to all those who *entered* the program. The overall value of a correctional placement, it can be argued, is its effectiveness with *all* offenders in the program, not just those who are its successes. This is particularly relevant when comparisons are made with other groups (e.g., prison populations) that do not have the option of removing "failures"—poorer candidates for reform—from the "program." As a result, any successes achieved by the boot camp program versus other interventions may have less to do with the program per se than with the fact that the program is composed of offenders—"graduates"—who are less prone to recidivate (e.g., more motivated to change, less criminogenic initially).

Louisiana

In the Louisiana Shock Incarceration (LSI) program, inmates begin by spending 90 to 180 days in military training, exercise, treatment, and education activities. Graduates of LSI are returned to the community under intensive supervision parole, which becomes gradually less restrictive over the first year following release.

MacKenzie and her colleagues have conducted several evaluations of the LSI program (MacKenzie, 1991; MacKenzie & Shaw, 1993; MacKenzie et al., 1993; Shaw & MacKenzie, 1991, 1992; Souryal & MacKenzie, 1995). Overall, the results are not promising.

MacKenzie (1991) reports, for example, that boot camp graduates are more likely to be rearrested than dropouts, parolees, or probationers, although these differences become nonsignificant when control variables are introduced. In a subsequent analysis, MacKenzie et al. (1993) observe that LSI graduates are slightly more likely to fail (i.e., abscond, be revoked, or jailed) on community supervision than parolees and probationers but less likely to fail than those who did not complete boot camp. Similar results are reported by MacKenzie and Shaw (1993). Finally, Souryal and MacKenzie's (1995) study indicates that although LSI graduates are less likely than parolees or boot camp dropouts to undergo revocation for committing a new crime, the program's graduates are more likely than parolees and probationers to receive revocation for technical violations.

Changing Antisocial Attitudes

Attitude change has been suggested as another means of assessing the potential effectiveness of boot camps to reduce offender criminality. Studies have examined the impact of boot camps on several types of attitudes, including perceptions of the program and staff, self-confidence, and motivation. Changing antisocial attitudes appears especially critical, because these have been associated most closely with criminal involvement (Andrews &

Bonta, 1994). If a boot camp placement can alter antisocial attitudes, then the potential to reduce recidivism is commensurately enhanced.

Research assessing the effects of boot camps on antisocial attitudes typically uses quasi-experimental designs to make comparisons among the attitudes of program graduates, program dropouts, and regular prison inmates at the beginning and end of shock incarceration (Burton, Marquart, Cuvelier, Alarid, & Hunter, 1993; MacKenzie & Shaw, 1990; MacKenzie et al., 1993; MacKenzie & Souryal, 1993; Shaw & MacKenzie, 1991; Virginia Department of Corrections, 1992). The findings are largely consistent across the studies and can be summarized in four points.

First, prior to the program, those who eventually graduate from the boot camp program are more prosocial than those who later drop out. Second, some programs report that boot camp participants are more prosocial than regular prison inmates at intake. Third, from intake to the end of shock incarceration (or a comparable period for regular inmates), both boot camp graduates and regular prison inmates become more prosocial, although the boot camp groups may show slightly greater reductions in antisocial attitudes. Finally, a similar pattern is revealed when boot camp graduates are compared with dropouts. In these comparisons, it is clearer that the increase in prosocial attitudes is greater among the program's graduates.

At this stage, then, it is unclear that boot camps are substantially more effective than alternative correctional placements in attacking attitudes linked directly to criminal behavior. MacKenzie and Souryal's (1993) study of boot camp programs in six states may contain important clues as to which programs may be more effective in fostering prosocial attitudes. They found that although offender demographic and offense factors exerted no significant influence on attitudes, program characteristics were related to the development of prosocial attitudes (e.g., allowed offender to drop out, had higher rates of dropouts). Most instructive, they discovered that positive social attitudes were higher in boot camp programs that devoted more time to offender rehabilitation.

Conclusions

Although programs differ in their characteristics and the quality of evaluation studies is uneven, some tentative conclusions are possible regarding the effectiveness of boot camps. First, compared to other correctional interventions, it is not clear that boot camps achieve greater reductions in recidivism (see also Dickey, 1994; U.S. GAO, 1993). Admittedly, boot camp graduates appear to do as well as or better than offenders sentenced to regular incarceration, which suggests that public safety would not be jeopardized by using shock incarceration as an alternative to regular imprisonment. Even these results, however, must be viewed cautiously due to the methodological problems besetting the existing research. Particularly problematic are the selection bias produced by the exclusion of some offenders from shock incarceration programs and the focus on the success of graduates rather than all those who participate in boot camps.

Second, it appears that positive changes in offenders that may have resulted from shock incarceration do not last indefinitely after offenders return to the community. The eventual return to crime by many boot camp graduates suggests that something may be lacking in the way offenders are supervised in the community. As Burton et al. (1993) suggest, the apparent ineffectiveness of boot camps to reduce recidivism may reflect, at least in part, the "quality and nature of 'aftercare' services" (p. 51). If boot camps are to be a catalyst that effects short-term change among offenders (see Burton et al., 1993; MacKenzie & Shaw, 1990; MacKenzie et al., 1993; MacKenzie & Souryal, 1993; Virginia Department of Corrections, 1992), appropriate aftercare supervision and services that encourage prosocial attitudes and behaviors may prolong the success of offenders in the community.

Third, particularly in Louisiana but also in Georgia and New York, a substantial proportion of reincarcerations among boot camp graduates result from technical violations. This observation has led MacKenzie and Shaw (1993) to recommend that such violations be sanctioned not with reincarceration but with an intermediate sanction imposed in the community. This approach has a clear advantage: The prison time saved initially by a boot camp placement, which potentially reduces institutional crowding and related costs, would not simply be eroded through high rates of reincarceration.

Fourth, programs with more emphasis on treatment seem to produce lower recidivism rates. Compare, for example, Oklahoma and Texas, where treatment is de-emphasized, with New York. Although the data for Texas and Oklahoma are preliminary, they seem to indicate higher recidivism among boot camp graduates than the more treatment-oriented New York shock incarceration program. This finding, we should add, is consistent with the mounting evidence showing the effectiveness of correctional rehabilitation (Andrews & Bonta, 1994; Andrews, Zinger, et al., 1990; Gendreau & Ross, 1979, 1987; Palmer, 1992, 1994; Van Voorhis, 1987).

Finally, let us end with a further note of caution. Correctional boot camps receive much of their legitimacy from the widespread cultural belief that military service—especially the experience of being "broken down and built up" in basic training—fosters character and in past times transformed delinquents into upstanding citizens. This commonsense belief awaits empirical support, and whatever generic benefits military service has to the average soldier, its effects on criminal conduct appear weak and complex (see, e.g., Rand, 1987, pp. 150-153).

Sampson and Laub's (1993) reanalysis of the Gluecks' longitudinal data set (Glueck & Glueck, 1950) is particularly instructive. Given the period in which the Gluecks' study was initiated—in 1939 with boys 10 to 17—about two thirds of the sample entered the military. Sampson and Laub's (1993, pp. 163-164) multivariate analysis revealed that service in the armed forces had no significant effect on future criminal involvement. They also found that despite the rigors of boot camp, "officially delinquent boys" (placement in a juvenile correctional school) continued to evidence deviant conduct after induction into the military. Compared to a sample of nondelinquents, the delinquents were three times more likely to commit crimes in the military (64% vs. 20%) and over seven times more likely to be a serious offender and to receive a dishonorable discharge. The same pattern was manifested when measures of unofficial or reported delinquency were used (Sampson & Laub, 1993, pp. 129-131; see also Gottfredson & Hirschi, 1990, pp. 164-165).

In short, military service and thus the boot camp experience showed few of the transforming effects commonly attributed to them. Importing the technology of boot camps to corrections seems based more on cultural myths—perhaps buoyed by selective memories and Hollywood war movies—than on generalizable empirical evidence (see also Feeley & Simon, 1992, pp. 463-464).

Conclusions:
Beyond the Panacea Phenomenon

The history of U.S. corrections, suggests Finckenauer (1982), is strewn with one failed "panacea" after another. Correctional crises inevitably give rise to proposed "cure-alls" that raise "unrealistic or unsound expectations." The panaceas are attractive precisely because they promise so much, usually at so little cost. Such reforms seem destined to fall short of their promises, however, and in the end are relegated to the scrap heap of interventions that do not work.

Advocates of intermediate sanctions might have learned from Finckenauer's (1982) warning about the power and disappointment inherent in the panacea phenomenon (see also Rothman, 1980; Walker, 1989). Facing a seemingly intractable crisis of rising prison populations and shrinking fiscal resources, they might have been cautious in suggesting that intermediate sanctions could meaningfully resolve this crisis without jeopardizing public safety. The history of corrections should have taught that all reforms have limits. As our review of research suggests, the community control movement is no exception to this rule (see also Byrne & Pattavina, 1992; Clear & Byrne, 1992).

What lessons have we learned by examining the community control movement? We offer six conclusions, which we note as provisional and open to revision as more evaluations inform us further as to the limits and potential benefits of intermediate sanctions.

1. Control in the community will not resolve the correctional crisis in the United States.

Although small victories against the correctional crisis may be possible—indeed, victories that are meaningful within a given jurisdiction—intermediate punishment programs have not shown the general ability to defeat the powerful forces fueling the crisis. The endless flow of offenders into the system is created by forces beyond the control of criminal justice officials—forces such as the political decision to launch a war on drugs (Currie, 1993) and the deteriorating fabric and social misery of the nation's cities that are, predictably, fostering high rates of predatory violence (Currie, 1985, 1989; Hagan, 1993; Short, 1991). Similarly, governmental fiscal woes are deeply embedded in the nation's strained economy and incompatible public desires to consume government benefits and to pay lower taxes. In the end, without a substantially new vision, the current roster of criminal justice reforms will be hard pressed to effect more than cosmetic changes (Cullen & Wright, in press; Feeley & Simon, 1992).

2. More correctional control in the community will mean that more offenders will be detected committing crimes and, especially, violating conditions of their supervision.

Intermediate sanctions generally have shown that if more resources are devoted to watching offenders in the community, more offender misbehaviors are discovered. In particular, the daily life habits of offenders that violate the stiffer supervision conditions imposed by intermediate sanctions will come under scrutiny. Petersilia and Turner (1993c) note that "frequent drug testing, alone, is likely to generate high rates of technical violations. . . . Putting drug-dependent offenders in a program that forbids drug use, provides frequent drug testing, and provides no assured access to drug treatment virtually guarantees high violation rates" (pp. 319-320).

3. The success in detecting technical violations is inconsistent with the need to reduce prison crowding and the concomitant fiscal crisis.

The research indicates that the potential savings in prison space and thus in finances are eroded by the high rates at which offenders are reincarcerated for technical violations. Again, as Petersilia and Turner (1993c) observe, such violations are inevitable when offenders are subjected to "more stringent conditions and closer supervision" (p. 319) than regular probationers or parolees. As a result, commentators suggest using community-based intermediate sanctions, not prison, to punish technical violations. This approach would seem to merit further examination.

4. Intermediate punishments are unlikely to deter criminal behavior more effectively than regular probation or prison placements.

Intermediate sanctions have not demonstrated the consistent ability to deter markedly offenders' recidivism. Notably, this finding is consistent with the general criminological research, which suggests that criminal justice punishments have marginal influences on future criminality (Braithwaite, 1989; Finckenauer, 1982; Paternoster, 1987; but see Wright, 1994). Deterrence theory, in short, may be incorrect or, at least, circumscribed in the conditions under which it is applicable. Relatedly, the detection and selective incapacitation of offenders for technical violations, which are achieved at an enhanced rate by community control programs, also are unlikely to accrue substantial reductions in crime: The research indicates that technical violations are a weak predictor of criminal recidivism (Petersilia & Turner, 1993c).

5. Intermediate punishments appear to be more effective if coupled with treatment interventions.

Although obtained as a secondary by-product of most evaluations, there is evidence that community control programs that add on treatment services achieve reductions in recidivism. This finding is consistent with the growing criminological literature indicating the potential effectiveness of rehabilitation interventions, especially in community settings (Andrews & Bonta, 1994; Andrews, Zinger, et al., 1990; Gendreau & Ross, 1979, 1987). Importantly, to the extent that community control programs have greater resources and more officer-offender contacts, they may provide the opportunity to channel offenders into treatments that address criminogenic needs—sources of criminality that are not targeted or affected by surveillance and punishment. Furthermore, community corrections agencies may be in a unique position to develop treatment services that can be grafted to intermediate sanction programs (see Gendreau et al., 1994).

6. Without more evaluation research using randomized experimental designs (or quasi-experimental designs), it will be difficult to reach more definitive conclusions about the effectiveness of intermediate sanctions.

To be sure, existing evaluations are informative and allow us to develop useful ideas about the effectiveness of community control interventions. In the absence of a body of methodologically sound research, however, it becomes difficult to conclude with confidence that anything works. When an evaluation is plagued by fundamental defects in its design, any positive findings on a program—for example, that home incarceration reduces recidivism—are open to two interpretations: The program really works, or the results are an artifact of biased methodology. In this situation, the positive findings are at best suggestive of what works and at worst could form the basis for an intervention that is ineffective or harmful.

In the end, a pressing need exists to increase the number of rigorous studies on the effectiveness of community control programs. Evaluation research is not unlimited in what it can tell about how the world operates, but with a more adequate knowledge base, perhaps we will have a stronger reason to move beyond grasping at panaceas that ultimately prove disheartening failures. The challenge is to embrace a more informed approach, which recognizes the limits of reform but is committed to laying a sounder, more scientific basis for understanding how the benefits of correctional interventions, small and not so small, might be achieved.

The Principles of Effective Intervention With Offenders

Paul Gendreau

Criminal justice practitioners and policymakers have been repeatedly informed that offender rehabilitation has been a failure; in the words of Martinson (1974), "Nothing works." Even though Martinson (1979) eventually recanted his views, the antirehabilitation rhetoric took firm hold, particularly in the United States, for a variety of sociopolitical reasons (Cullen & Gendreau, 1989). Many state jurisdictions subsequently embraced the new epoch of deterrence (Martinson, 1976), which was presumed to have considerable promise in reducing offender recidivism.

But the data have continued to accumulate testifying to the potency of offender rehabilitation programs. This evidence is readily accessible in a variety of published offender treatment outcome literature reviews since the nothing works credo became fashionable in the later 1970s (Andrews & Bonta, 1994; Andrews, Zinger, et al., 1990; Basta & Davidson, 1988; Borduin, in press; Cullen & Gendreau, 1989; Garrett, 1985; Gendreau, 1981, 1989; Gendreau & Andrews, 1990; Gendreau, Cullen, & Bonta, 1994; Gendreau & Ross, 1979, 1981a, 1981b, 1983-1984, 1987; Gottschalk, Davidson, Gensheimer, & Mayer, 1987; Greenwood & Zimring, 1985; Hollin, 1993; Izzo & Ross, 1990; Lipsey, 1992; Marshall & Pithers, 1994; Palmer, 1978, 1983, 1992; Ross & Fabiano, 1985; Ross & Gendreau, 1980; Ross & McKay, 1978).

What are the broad results emanating from this literature? If one surveys all studies that include control group comparisons, as Lipsey (1992) did in his impressive overview of 443 programs, 64% of the studies reported reductions in favor of the treatment group. The average reduction in recidivism was 10%. When the results were categorized by the general type of the program, for example, employment, reductions in recidivism were as high as 18%.

The thrust of my work and that of my colleagues such as Don Andrews and Jim Bonta has been to look into the "black box" of treatment programs. Unlike Martinson and his followers, we believe it is not sufficient just to sum across studies or file them into general categories. The salient question is what are the principles that distinguish between effective and ineffective programs? What does it means that an employment program was offered?—what exactly was accomplished under the name of "employment"? As a result of endorsing the perspective of opening the black box, we have been able to generate a number of principles of effective and ineffective intervention. Our analyses in this regard have revealed that programs that adhered to many of the characteristics described in the next section reduced recidivism in the range of 25% to 80% with an average of about 50% (Andrews, Zinger, et al., 1990).

Identifying Principles of Effective Intervention

Before specifying the principles, I briefly describe the information sources used to generate the principles and list exemplary studies, noting those that best illustrate the principles.

Information Sources

The principles are based on three types of information: (a) narrative reviews of the offender treatment literature, (b) meta-analytic reviews of this literature, and (c) individual studies and insights garnered from my clinical experience in the field, and that of colleagues, who have designed and run successful programs.

Narrative reviews have been until very recently the standard format for summarizing the offender treatment literature. The narrative review, unfortunately, is vulnerable to a number of problems that arise as a result of the subjectivity involved in assessing research studies in a qualitative manner (Glass, McGraw, & Smith, 1981). Meta-analytic reviewers attempt to address the problems of the narrative review by standardizing and interpreting the findings of diverse studies in as objective and quantifiable a manner as possible. Quantitative procedures and techniques are employed to ascertain the numerical strength of the relationship between treatment factors and outcome (cf. Bangert-Drowns, 1992). Meta-analytic procedures, however, are not a panacea. There are occasions when only a narrative review is possible (e.g., Marshall & Pithers, 1994), and sometimes conclusions from the two types of review processes correspond (Gendreau & Andrews, 1990). The growing consensus seems to be that the quality of meta-analytic reviews is superior (Beamon, 1991), as my colleagues and I (Andrews, Zinger, et al., 1990) discovered when meta-analysis revealed some important relationships between treatment factors that were overlooked in earlier narrative reviews (e.g., Gendreau & Ross, 1987). Indeed, meta-analyses have recently led to important advances in our knowledge about the effectiveness of psychological treatment in general (Lipsey & Wilson, 1993).

Exemplary Programs

Space does not permit a detailed review of all the individual programs that, in my view, are particularly meritorious. For those readers who wish to go beyond the principles discussed here to inspect at first hand some of the primary source material, several of the best programs can be located in Ross and Gendreau (1980), an edited volume with commentary on the studies by the editors and updates of some of the original studies by the program designers themselves. More recently, Andrews, Zinger, et al. (1990, Table 1, pp. 403-404) have supplied the references to 35 program evaluations designated "appropriate correctional service." All but 2 of the 35 studies found reduced recidivism; 20 of these programs lowered offender recidivism rates by at least 25% compared to their control groups (some studies involved more than one treatment-control comparison).

There are at least a dozen programs that I believe satisfy most of the effective principles described later and that can be recommended as good models for future program development. Family therapy programs for juveniles of either the family systems or multisystemic type have been noteworthy for their therapeutic integrity (Barton, Alexander, Waldron, Turner, & Warburton, 1985; Borduin, in press; Gordon, Arbuthnot, Gustafson, & McGreen, 1988; Wade, Morton, Lind, & Ferris, 1977). Other praiseworthy juvenile programs were those of Barkwell (1980); Chandler (1973); Collingwood, Douds, and Williams (1980); Davidson, Redner, Blakely, Mitchell, and Emshoff (1987); Lee and Haynes (1980); Platt, Perry, and

Metzger (1980); Ross and McKay (1976); and Walter and Mills (1980). Several of the programs have been replicated in every type of facility or program possible (community residential, courts, mental health, probation, police, reformatory).

Some innovative probation-based adult programs that featured cognitive behavioral strategies and matching of client, treatment service, and treatment provider characteristics were those of Andrews and Kiessling (1980) and Ross, Fabiano, and Ewles (1988). There are, unfortunately, few good examples forthcoming from adult institution samples; two exceptions were Jesness (1975) and Wexler, Falkin, and Lipton (1990).

I now turn to the principles of effective and ineffective programs. They are set forth as succinctly as possible; in a few instances, however, clarification is required. It should be noted that meta-analysis is the principal source of information for "effective" Principles 1(b), 2, 3 and "ineffective" Principles 1 through 6. The rest are based on a combination of narrative reviews, selected experimental studies, and clinical knowledge.

Principles of Effective Intervention

1. Services

Services should be intensive and behavioral in nature.

   a. Intensive services occupy 40% to 70% of the offenders' time while in a program and are of 3 to 9 months' duration.
   b. Behavioral strategies are essential to effective service delivery.

Interested readers might wish to consult two highly recommended texts on the theories underlying behavioral programs (Liebert & Spiegler, 1990) and the what and how of various behavioral interventions (Spiegler & Guevremont, 1993). Because I often find confusion among practitioners as to what is meant by the term *behavioral,* here follows a thumbnail sketch of behavioral program principles.

Virtually all offender behavioral programs are based on the principles of operant conditioning. At the core of operant conditioning is the concept of *reinforcement,* which refers to the strengthening or increasing of a behavior so that it will continue to be performed in the future. The most efficient and ethically defensible way to achieve this goal is to use positive reinforcers (something prosocial the offender considers pleasant or desirable) and to ensure that reinforcers are contingent (contingency management) on the behavior being enacted. In contrast, punishment, which is used much less frequently by behavioral therapists, attempts to weaken or suppress behavior by providing unpleasant or harmful consequences.

Three types of positive reinforcers are used to strengthen behavior. They may be tangible (money, material goods) or activities (shopping, sports, music, television, socializing) or social (attention, praise, approval). Behavior modifiers usually employ the last two types of reinforcers because they are natural consequences of a person's life. Positive reinforcers fit nicely into a powerful concept called the Premack principle, which simply states that making a high-probability behavior contingent on a lower-probability behavior will increase the frequency of the latter. Social reinforcers are much to be preferred because they are cost-effective and require little effort to satisfy contingency management practices. Most programs include a general menu of reinforcers, with efforts made to individualize them where possible.

There are many types of behavioral programs. The three described next are prevalent in the offender behavioral treatment literature. A well-designed program will employ at least two of the following, as each overlaps to some degree with the others.

a. *Token economies*—A reinforcement system for motivating offenders to perform prosocial behaviors. Tokens can be tangible or symbolic, that is, points. They are most often used with groups.

b. *Modeling*—The offender observes another person demonstrating a behavior that he or she can benefit from imitating. Andrews and Bonta (1994, pp. 202-203) include an excellent summary of how modeling should be carried out with offenders.

c. *Cognitive behavioral*—There are several schools of cognitive behavioral therapy (see Spiegler & Guevremont, 1993). Fundamentally, they are intended to change the offender's cognitions, attitudes, values, and expectations that maintain antisocial behavior. Problem solving, reasoning, self-control, and self-instructional training are frequently used techniques. Cognitive therapists stress that a good therapeutic relationship, involving empathy, openness, and warmth, is necessary for effective cognitive therapy.

2. Behavioral Programs

Behavioral programs should target the criminogenic needs of high-risk offenders. Treatment is more effective when it is matched with the offender's risk level. Higher-risk offenders are much more likely to benefit from treatment than low-risk offenders (see Chapter 2).

There are two types of risk factors—static and dynamic. A static risk factor is any aspect of an offender's past criminal history that is fixed in time (e.g., number of previous convictions). Dynamic risk factors are those aspects of the offender's everyday functioning that are amenable to change. Gendreau, Little, and Goggin (1995) have listed those dynamic risk factors that are the best predictors of recidivism and therefore the most promising targets for intervention—Andrews and Bonta (1994) refer to them as criminogenic needs. If these factors undergo positive changes, the offender's criminal behavior will be reduced. Some of these criminogenic needs involve antisocial attitudes, styles of thinking and behavior, peer associations, chemical dependencies, and self-control issues. There are also dynamic factors (or noncriminogenic needs) that if targeted for treatment will not lead to reductions in antisocial behavior (e.g., lack of self-esteem and feelings of personal inadequacy, such as anxiety and depression; Andrews, Bonta, & Hoge, 1990).

It is critical that behavioral programs employ risk assessment measures that measure a wide range of criminogenic need factors. Of the measures in widespread use that have been identified as comprehensive, reliable, and valid (Gendreau et al., 1995), the measure with the best predicted validities is the Level of Supervision Inventory (Andrews & Bonta, 1994).

3. Characteristics of Offenders, Therapists, and Programs

Characteristics of offenders, therapists, and programs should be matched. The responsivity principle is rooted in the notion that there can be potent interactions between the characteristics of individuals and their settings or situations (Gendreau, 1981; Gendreau & Ross, 1979). These authors have decried the simple-minded rationale of the time that programs should be limited to one treatment modality, for example, using only a token economy and ignoring all other behavioral strategies, and treating all offenders as if they all had identical personality traits, attitudes, and beliefs. We are indebted to Andrews, Bonta, and Hoge (1990) for developing and refining the concept of responsivity to guide treatment interventions. Their review provides summaries of intervention studies demonstrating that substantial variations in recidivism result from paying attention to responsivity factors. Andrews has also generated some impressive data of his own in this regard (see Andrews & Kiessling, 1980; Andrews, Kiessling, Robinson, & Mickus, 1986).

The principle of responsivity simply states that treatment programs should be delivered in a manner that facilitates the learning of new prosocial skills by the offender. Failure to do so means that programs can easily fail, as Arbuthnot and Gordon (1986) demonstrated when they found some of their clients did not succeed because they did not have the cognitive skills to understand the program material. Essentially, the responsivity principle is one of matching treatment × offender type × therapist's style. The three components of responsivity are the following:

a. Matching the treatment approach with the learning style and personality of the offender. As a case in point, offenders who prefer high degrees of structure or who are impulsive are likely to function better in programs such as graduated token economics, which initially provide considerable external control with concrete rules for appropriate behavior. Psychiatrically troubled offenders, on the other hand, will often perform more adequately in low-pressure, sheltered-living environments.

b. Matching the characteristics of the offender with those of the therapist. For example, offenders who are more "anxious" respond best to therapists exhibiting higher levels of interpersonal sensitivity.

c. Matching the skills of the therapist with the type of program. Therapists who have a concrete conceptual-level problem-solving style function best in a program that is highly structured.

4. Program Contingencies and Behavioral Strategies

Program contingencies and behavioral strategies should be enforced in a firm but fair manner.

a. Reinforcement contingencies must be under the control of the therapists.

b. Staff, with meaningful input from offenders, design, maintain, and enforce contingencies.

c. Positive reinforcers exceed punishers by at least 4:1.

d. Internal controls, for example, drug testing for substance abuse, are judiciously used to detect possible antisocial activities of clients.

5. Relating to Offenders

Therapists should relate to offenders in interpersonally sensitive and constructive ways and should be trained and supervised appropriately. Interpersonal skills have all but been ignored in the nothing works debate. This principle was initially formulated in 1979 (Gendreau & Ross, 1979) in the following words:

> To what extent do treatment personnel actually adhere to the principles and employ the techniques of therapy they purport to provide? To what extent are the treatment staff competent? How hard do they work? How much is treatment diluted in the correctional environment so that it becomes treatment in name only? (p. 467)

It is an essential component of what is called therapeutic integrity (Gendreau & Ross, 1983-1984). Most of the exemplary studies noted previously make mention of some of the four criteria described next; few of the studies that report no reductions in recidivism comment in this regard.

    a. Therapists are selected on the basis of interpersonal skills associated with effective counseling. Some of these factors are clarity in communication, warmth, humor, openness, and the ability to relate affect to behavior and set appropriate limits. With these sorts of skills, therapists can be effective sources of reinforcement and can competently model prosocial skills.

    b. Therapists have at least an undergraduate degree or equivalent with training in theories of criminal behavior and the prediction and treatment of criminal behavior.

    c. Therapists receive 3 to 6 months' formal and on-the-job or internship training in the application of behavioral interventions both in general and specific to the program.

    d. Therapists are assessed periodically on the quality of their service delivery.

    e. Therapists monitor offender change on intermediate targets of treatment.

6. Designing Program Structure and Activities

Program structure and activities should be designed to disrupt the delinquency network by placing offenders in situations (people and places) where prosocial activities predominate.

7. Providing Relapse Prevention Strategies

Relapse prevention strategies should be provided in the community to the extent possible. Relapse prevention is a strategy that originated in the alcoholism field and has begun to be adapted to offender populations such as sex offenders (Maletzsky, 1991). It is essentially an outpatient model of service delivery applied after the offender has completed the formal phase of a treatment program in prison or a community residential center. Elements of the strategy include the following:

a. Plan and rehearse alternative prosocial responses.

b. Monitor and anticipate problem situations.

c. Practice new prosocial behaviors in increasingly difficult situations and reward improved competencies.

d. Train significant others, such as family and friends, to provide reinforcement for prosocial behavior.

e. Provide booster sessions to offenders after they have completed the formal phase of treatment.

8. Advocacy and Brokerage

A high level of advocacy and brokerage should be attempted as long as community agencies offer appropriate services. Where possible, it is desirable to refer offenders to community-based services that provide quality services applicable to offenders and their problems. Therefore, it is vital that community services be assessed in this light in as objective a manner as possible (see, e.g., Correctional Program Assessment Inventory [CPAI]; Gendreau & Andrews, 1994). The reality, regrettably, is that many programs are lacking in most of the effective components noted earlier. As a case in point, a recent survey of 112 offender substance abuse programs using the CPAI reported that only 10% of the programs had programmatic elements that would indicate an effective service was being provided (Gendreau, Goggin, & Annis, 1990). A similar result, again using the CPAI, was found for a similar number of juvenile offender programs (Hoge, Leschied, & Andrews, 1993).

Principles of Ineffective Intervention

The first three principles of ineffective intervention are grounded in therapeutic approaches that have little in common with or are antagonistic to behavioral methods.

1. Traditional "Freudian" Psychodynamic and "Rogerian" Nondirective or Client-Centered Therapies

Offender treatment programs that have been based on these two approaches have emphasized the following processes:

    a. "Talking" cures

    b. Good relationship with client as a primary goal

    c. Unraveling the unconscious and gaining insight

    d. Fostering positive self-regard

    e. Self-actualization through self-discovery

    f. Externalizing blame to parents, society

    g. Ventilating anger

2. "Medical Model" Approaches

    a. Change in diet

    b. Plastic surgery

    c. Pharmacological, for example, testosterone suppressants

3. Subcultural and Labeling Approaches

Subcultural and labeling approaches emanated from the sociological theoretical perspectives of the same name. For a detailed review of how these two "sociological" strategies attempted to "treat" offenders see Andrews and Bonta (1994, pp. 196-200).

Subcultural theory emphasizes respecting the offender's culture and "doing good for the disadvantaged" by providing access to legitimate opportunities. Labeling theory operates on the principle that the criminal justice system stigmatizes youth and therefore offenders should be diverted from the system.

Neither approach favors behavioral-style interventions for offenders. If a program must be offered, nondirective therapies are preferred, and in the case of labeling theory, sanctions such as restitution are considered to be worthwhile alternatives.

4. Programs, Including Behavioral, That Target Low-Risk Offenders

5. Programs, Including Behavioral, That Target Offender Need Factors That Are Weak Predictors of Criminal Behavior (e.g., anxiety and depression)

6. "Punishing Smarter" Strategies

The so-called punishing smarter strategies became popular in community corrections in the mid-1980s. In the classic paper of the time, it was stated, "we are in the business of increasing the heat on probationers . . . satisfying the public's demand for just punishment . . . criminals must be punished for their misdeeds" (Erwin, 1986, p. 17). The programs that resulted are commonly known as intensive supervision programs (ISPs). ISPs usually include some or all of the following components:

a. Greatly increasing contact between supervisors and offenders

b. Home confinement

c. Frequent drug testing

d. Restitution

e. Electronic monitoring

f. Shock incarceration

g. Boot camps

Because punishing smarter strategies have become so popular in the United States—that they are not in other comparable Western societies is an interesting question in itself—the following data will be of interest. Gendreau and Little (1993) completed a preliminary meta-analysis of the punishing smarter literature. The analysis consisted of 174 comparisons between a punishment group and a control group. The authors found that these programs produced, on average, a slight increase of recidivism of 2%. Also of note is that Cullen, Wright, and Applegate's review of the sanction literature (Chapter 4) and

Andrews, Zinger, et al.'s (1990) meta-analysis of a subset (14 studies) of the sanction literature reached an identical conclusion—that these sanctions do not reduce recidivism. At this writing, the author has added 50 more comparisons to their meta-analysis and will report on the revised database shortly.

Indeed, of the entire punishing smarter literature, only two studies have been found that reported reductions in recidivism of more than 20% (Gendreau, Paparozzi, Little, & Goddard, 1993; Pearson, 1987a). Both were programs in New Jersey; one was evaluated by Frank Pearson and the other was Mario Paparozzi's Bureau of Parole program. Their distinguishing feature is that each attempted to provide as much treatment services as possible. The Bureau of Parole evaluation is of particular interest, because it used a carefully chosen matched control group. In addition, this program deliberately targeted high-risk offenders, provided significantly more treatment services to the ISP than the regular probation control group, and examined the quality of implementation of the program and probation officer supervision style. Unfortunately, the quality of services provided in either New Jersey program could not be determined.

With colleagues, I have addressed the matter in detail elsewhere of why punishment and punishing smarter programs have been failures (Gendreau & Goddard, 1995; Gendreau & Ross, 1981a). The information can be located in three separate sets of literature that go back approximately 30 years and approximate 25,000 references. They are the animal and human experimental-learning literature (Walters & Grusec, 1977), the human behavior modification literature (Matson & DiLorenzo, 1984) and the social-psychological literature on resistance processes in attitude change and how to influence behavior (Cialdini, 1993; Eagly & Chaiken, 1993).

Briefly, the conclusions are as follows:

1. There is no experimental evidence that most of the sanctions currently in use are effective punishers that reliably suppress behavior. The exception to the list is fines, which are rarely used in ISPs. As well, ISPs almost invariably target behaviors that are *not* predictors of criminal behavior, such as fitness or obeisance. Only five reliable and potent punishing stimuli have been experimentally identified: electric shock, some forms of drug-induced aversion, overcorrection, time-out, and fines.

2. For any of the effective punishing stimuli to work, the following rules must apply without exception:

   a. Escape from the punishing stimuli is impossible.

   b. The punishing stimulus is applied immediately and at maximum intensity. Also, it is applied at the earliest point in the deviant response chain and after every occurrence of the deviant behavior.

   c. The punishers should not be spread out and should be varied.

Obviously, it is virtually impossible to meet these criteria in the real world in which offenders live, unless some sort of unbelievably efficient Orwellian environment is envisioned by adherents of punishing smarter programs.

3. Punishment only trains a person what not to do.

4. When punishment is inappropriately applied, several negative consequences can occur, such as producing unwanted emotional reactions, aggression, or withdrawal—or an increase in the frequency of the behavior that is punished!

5. People who appear to be resistant to punishment are psychopathic risk takers, not neurotic or under the influence of a substance, or have a previous history of being frequently punished. All of these characteristics are to be found, in varying degrees, among offenders more than other clinical groups.

6. The social psychology of attitudes and attitude change nicely documents how many people inoculate themselves from threats and coercion by the way they choose to interpret "evidence," employing self-relevant reasons that disregard negative consequences, and have affective schema, that is, free-will arguments or ego defenses, that are resistant to attitude change. The social-psychological literature on influence has established that the principles of reciprocity, liking, authority, and commitment, among others, are necessary to change behavior (see Cialdini, 1993). The means by which these principles operate make it a rather doubtful proposition that they could be employed effectively, given the way sanctions programs are structured (Gendreau & Goddard, 1995). The reader is also reminded that behavioral programs require therapists to establish an open, trusting, and empathic relationship.

When proponents of sanctions try to justify the use of sanctions as umbrellas under which effective treatment programs might reside, they minimize the fact that a surround of sanctions can create a miasma in which it is difficult to establish supportive relationships or sustain the predominant use of positive reinforcers vis-à-vis punishers. The offender behavior modification literature is replete with examples of the disastrous consequences that befall programs in which punishment and control are emphasized over all else (Ross & McKay, 1978).

Conclusion

In conclusion, the evidence is persuasive that specific styles of service delivery can reduce offenders' criminal behavior to a degree that has profound policy implications. We also have a clear idea as to what doesn't work. In fact, some of the programs that do not work, such as ISPs, have also been shown to be very costly and contribute to prison overcrowding (Gendreau et al., 1993). The next goal of the rehabilitative agenda, besides adding to the principles as more data accrue, is to address how we can overcome the sociopolitical and professional barriers to the implementation of high-quality offender services that have been found to be effective in reducing offenders' criminal behavior (Gendreau, in press; Gendreau & Ross, 1987).

Programmatic and Nonprogrammatic Aspects of Successful Intervention

Ted Palmer

Studies of Programmatic Factors

Since 1975, the effectiveness of correctional intervention has been examined in more than 20 literature reviews; from 1980 to the present, researchers in 9 meta-analyses have done the same. Most of these works covered an aggregate of 45 to 90 individual studies each; some focused on more than 100 studies and one even had several hundred.[1] Each reviewer or analyst drew conclusions about the effectiveness of correctional intervention as a whole, particular types of correctional intervention, or both. Several of these authors, for example, Romig (1978), Gendreau and Ross (1979, 1987), and Andrews, Zinger, et al. (1990), expressed largely positive views regarding effectiveness. Others, such as Martinson (1974), Greenberg (1977), and Whitehead and Lab (1989), expressed generally negative views. Perhaps the majority, including Rutter and Giller (1983), Gordon and Arbuthnot (1987), Gottschalk et al. (1987), and Lipsey (1992), emphasized mixed results.

To date, this large body of individual literature reviews and meta-analyses has never been examined in the aggregate, that is, as a single group or collection. In particular, such an examination has not been conducted relative to the question, Do correctional interventions reduce recidivism and, in that respect, protect the public? Such an overview of reviews and analyses could determine how the findings from these several large-scale works support and differ from each other as well as whether there is general agreement regarding particular interventions, thus providing more broadly based and reliable information about correctional effectiveness. Conclusions and generalizations that would result from such an overview would not, of course, constitute the final word on the subject, but they would require fewer caveats than those associated with any one, two, or even handful of literature reviews or meta-analyses alone.[2]

Caveats or qualifications regarding individual reviews and analyses that have been carried out to date either reflect or should have reflected various limitations associated with those works. For instance, they should have reflected the fact that approximately one of every two such works focused largely or entirely on one particular *setting,* such as an institution or community. This limitation, in turn, interacted with that of *offender-representation:* Because specific types of offenders were strongly represented in some reviews and analyses, other types, such as violent offenders in community-based programs, were necessarily underrepresented, at least with given types of intervention. Though the degree of representation received by various offenders may have been appropriate or unavoidable, this nevertheless placed or should have placed limits on the conclusions and generalizations that were drawn, as differing types of intervention may have been differentially effective with differing types of offenders. Despite this situation, a fairly wide range of offenders was included in most analyses and reviews, even though their degree of representation may have been unequal within and across those works and, especially, unequal in the individual studies included.[3]

Finally, another limitation related to *time,* and this applied to almost all meta-analyses and literature reviews. Although correctional interventions have been studied for 30 to 35 years at a moderately frequent and fairly steady rate, many analyses and reviews covered roughly 6 to 12 years. Many of these periods, for example, 1960 to 1972, 1974 to 1980, or 1978 to 1987 (and therefore the respective studies that were included in the analyses or reviews) did not necessarily or largely overlap. Though this truncated coverage was quite appropriate for specific purposes—and sometimes unavoidable (especially with earlier reviews and analyses)—it nevertheless constituted a limitation regarding conclusions about intervention's overall effectiveness. It was also a source of inconsistent findings or conclusions from one analysis or review to the next.

Even if the limitations associated with most individual literature reviews and meta-analyses were small to moderate, an overview of those and the remaining works *collectively* could provide not only added and more reliable information about the effectiveness of correctional approaches *as a whole,* but in addition, a broadly based and perhaps more objective or balanced composite profile of several often-used *approaches.* An overview could especially provide such a profile if the studies that are examined are collectively not just numerous but unselected and, if they are, again collectively, widely representative and inclusive as to settings, types of offenders, and time periods. The resulting overview or integration of the many individual meta-analyses and literature reviews that are now available could thus provide a perspective that might help policymakers, practitioners, researchers, and others better sort out and assess various conclusions that have been drawn regarding effectiveness.

Methods

To obtain a broad overview of correctional research findings, we examined some 32 meta-analyses and literature reviews—the two basic forms of study conducted to date. We reviewed the results from all delinquency-centered U.S. and Canadian meta-analyses that have been published thus far—namely, Andrews, Zinger, et al. (1990); Davidson, Gottschalk, Gensheimer, and Mayer (1984); Garrett (1985); Gensheimer, Mayer, Gottschalk, and Davidson (1986); Gottschalk et al. (1987); Izzo and Ross (1990); Lipsey (1992); Mayer, Gensheimer, Davidson, and Gottschalk (1986); and Whitehead and Lab (1989).[4] In addition, we examined the findings from approximately 15 general, or multitopic, literature reviews, in which several types of intervention were covered. These were Gendreau and Ross (1979, 1987); Genevie, Margolies, and Muhlin (1986); Gordon and Arbuthnot (1987); Greenberg (1977); Johns and Wallach (1981); Lab and Whitehead (1988); Lipton, Martinson, and Wilks (1975); Lundman (1984); Panizzon, Olson-Raymer, and Guerra (1991); Romig (1978); Rutter and Giller (1983); Van Voorhis (1987); Whitehead and Lab (1989); and Wright and Dixon (1977). Martinson (1974) and Palmer (1975, 1978, 1983) were also included, although their observations often related to the Lipton et al. (1975) study sample.[5]

The sample of general literature reviews may not have included all multitopic, large-scale works, but it did, in the aggregate, encompass a very wide range of views and outcomes published from 1955 to the present—quite possibly the full range. Though the sample emphasized reviews that have been perhaps the most widely and most often quoted, the general literature reviews were otherwise unselected and every effort was made to represent their full range of findings and conclusions, whether positive, neutral or mixed, or negative. The sample of multitopic literature reviews, when aggregated, was very inclusive as to settings, types of offenders, and time periods.

Finally, we examined the results from eight special-topic reviews, literature surveys focused mainly or exclusively on a single approach or intervention (such as family intervention). These were Altschuler and Armstrong (1990); Armstrong (1988); Brody (1976); Geismar and Wood (1986); Graziano and Mooney (1984); Krisberg, Rodriguez, Baake, Neuenfeldt, and Steele (1989); Parent (1989); and Schneider (1986) and Ervin and Schneider (1990). Many of the above-mentioned *general* literature reviews had included the single approach or intervention that was focused on in these respective, special-topic reviews. The general reviews, of course, had each included several other approaches as well.

Individually, the above-mentioned meta-analyses and literature reviews focused entirely or primarily on adjudicated youths in institutional or community settings or both. Each analyst or reviewer purposely selected and emphasized individual studies in which a treatment, or experimental ("E"), program was compared with a traditional, or control ("C"), program. Each program's performance measure, that is, its outcome or effectiveness criterion, typically involved a behavioral indicator, such as arrests, convictions, detentions or incarcerations, or suspensions; however, revocation, unfavorable termination, or similar status criteria that *reflected* behavior were not uncommon.

The authors of these meta-analyses and literature reviews generally organized them according to type of intervention, method, general (or generic) approach, and so forth. In this context, *type* refers to the program feature, for example, vocational training, that was used by an author (analyst or reviewer) to characterize the collection of experimental programs—the treatments or interventions—that he or she had grouped together for purposes of analysis and discussion. For instance, a reviewer may have grouped 15 separate studies that each emphasized vocational training and that differed from their control or comparison program in that respect. He or she may then have given those studies the generic label *vocational training* and may then have proceeded to determine whether—or in the case of meta-analysts, to what degree—the various E-programs within that group outperformed their respective Cs or vice versa.

The types of intervention that are included in the present overview of meta-analyses and literature reviews are confrontation; areawide strategies of delinquency prevention; social casework, social agency, or societal institution approaches to delinquency prevention; diversion; physical challenge; restitution; group counseling or therapy; individual counseling or therapy; family intervention; vocational training; employment; educational training; behavioral approach; cognitive behavioral or cognitive approach; life skills (skill oriented, skill development); multimodal approach; probation or parole enhancement; intensive probation supervision; intensive aftercare (parole) supervision; and community-based approaches versus institutional intervention.

Not all individual meta-analyses and literature reviews touched on every subject area; in fact, many addressed fewer than half. Nevertheless, if the findings, conclusions, or even the basic data displays from any analysis or review bear on any given subject area (e.g., confrontation), they are mentioned in the results presented below. (See Appendix A regarding the strength of these results.) More precisely, they are referred to in connection with the given approach *unless* the overall research quality of the individual studies in that approach was very questionable, for example, if the percentage of random-assignment studies or quasi-experimental studies was either known to be, or seemed likely to have been, other than high. This situation, however, was uncommon.

Results

When the overall collection of 9 meta-analyses and 23 literature reviews is examined, the following emerges:

Confrontation

Confrontation, that is, direct deterrence efforts, such as "Scared Straight" and shock probation, has rather consistently been considered unsuccessful.[6] No reviewer or analyst reported positive results for confrontation as a whole or even for several individual studies. Gendreau and Ross (1987); Lab and Whitehead (1988); Parent (1989); Whitehead and Lab (1989); Andrews, Zinger, et al. (1990); and Panizzon et al. (1991) found this approach made no difference in recidivism; Lundman (1984) concluded its results were mixed at best; and Lipsey (1992), based on the largest sample size of all, found it had the weakest—in fact, the most negative —results of the approximately 20 types of intervention he studied (ES = –.24). (ES means "effect size." This is the statistic used in meta-analysis to estimate the degree of difference—for example, difference in recidivism rates—between a treatment or experimental group and its control. This statistic indicates the number of standard deviation units by which one group outperforms another. An ES of .10 corresponds to a difference of about 10% in the recidivism rates of the experimental as compared to the control or traditional programs, and ESs of .20 and .30 correspond to differences of approximately 20% and 30% respectively.[7] A minus sign in front of an ES means that the treatment or experimental group or program performed worse than its control [Glass, McGraw, & Smith, 1981; Hedges & Olkin, 1985].)

Areawide Strategies of Delinquency Prevention

Such strategies as community organization efforts encompassing entire neighborhoods or other sizable portions of large urban settings and efforts by street corner gang workers have uniformly been judged unsuccessful in reducing crime and delinquency (Lundman, 1984; Romig, 1978; Rutter & Giller, 1983; Wright & Dixon, 1977).

Social Casework, Social Agency, and Societal or Institutional Approaches to Delinquency Prevention

Such approaches as child guidance clinic and public agency referrals or services have generally been considered unsuccessful with little qualification (Gordon & Arbuthnot, 1987; Panizzon et al., 1991; Romig, 1978; Rutter & Giller, 1983; Wright & Dixon, 1977) or *usually* unsuccessful (Gottschalk et al., 1987). Gendreau and Ross (1987), however, although in general accord with those conclusions, also described positive outcomes for early intervention efforts that involved (a) the Perry preschool component of Head Start, (b) specified family techniques, and (c) cognitive problem solving. In addition, Lipsey (1992) found that casework services that occurred outside the justice system had substantial impact on delinquency (ES = .16).

Diversion

Although diversion has often been viewed as having little effect on recidivism (Gensheimer et al., 1986; Greenberg, 1977; Romig, 1978; Whitehead & Lab, 1989, relative to nonjustice system diversion), some reviewers have added that a modest percentage of such programs are clear exceptions to the rule (Gendreau & Ross, 1987; Panizzon et al., 1991). Other reviewers have listed a number of positive-outcome programs or differentially positive programs (Andrews, Zinger, et al., 1990; Gendreau & Ross, 1979; Johns & Wallach, 1981, with "service-oriented" efforts). Still others have listed as many positive as nonpositive programs (Lab & Whitehead, 1988) or concluded that diversion is probably *as* effective (Rutter & Giller, 1983) or *at least* as effective (Lundman, 1984) as further penetration into the justice system. Finally, Whitehead and Lab (1989) have indicated that, collectively, diversion programs within the justice system have a higher percentage of positive outcomes than programs categorized as "nonsystem diversion," "probation/parole/community corrections," or "institutional/residential." Diversion, of course, encompasses a wide range of program components and general interventions, from recreation, advocacy, and resource brokerage to vocational or educational training and group or individual counseling; moreover, the frequency as well as duration of client contacts varies considerably (Gensheimer et al., 1986), and differing meta-analyses and literature reviews have emphasized somewhat different components and general interventions.

Physical Challenge

Evaluations of physical challenge, such as Outward Bound and Vision Quest, have been mixed and wide ranging. In some analyses and reviews, the studies collectively showed little if any impact on recidivism (Gendreau & Ross, 1987; Panizzon et al., 1991; Romig, 1978); in others, conflicting outcomes appeared (Greenberg, 1977). In still other analyses, either positive outcomes were reported (Garrett, 1985) or such programs were presented as part of a broader category that was itself positive (Lipsey, 1992). Across all analyses and reviews, however, individually and collectively these programs were small in number and often the same.

Restitution

Restitution has been systematically studied and discussed by relatively few analysts or reviewers. Though Lipsey (1992) found that 13 such programs collectively had an average effect size of only .08 and a mean recidivism reduction of about 8%, other researchers described a number of successful

($p < .05$) individual programs in well-controlled E/C studies conducted during the mid-1980s (Ervin & Schneider, 1990; Galaway, 1988; Schneider, 1986; Schneider & Ervin, 1990). A few successful restitution programs were observed in the 1970s as well (Heinz, Galaway, & Hudson, 1976; Wax, 1977).

Group Counseling or Therapy

The group counseling or therapy approach presents an especially mixed but, on the whole, somewhat negative picture. Although only one analyst or reviewer found it almost entirely unsuccessful (Romig, 1978), most concluded it was (a) usually unsuccessful, (b) successful only under certain presumably somewhat limited conditions, or (c) unclear as to its promise (Garrett, 1985; Gordon & Arbuthnot, 1987; Lipton et al., 1975; Van Voorhis, 1987; Wright & Dixon, 1977). When judged unclear, this was partly because few good evaluations were thought to exist (Panizzon et al., 1991). Other analysts and reviewers focused on individual instances of success or else concluded—or presented data that either implied or directly indicated—that group counseling or therapy might be as often successful as unsuccessful (Gendreau & Ross, 1979; Genevie et al., 1986; Gottschalk et al., 1987; Greenberg, 1977). Finally, Andrews, Zinger, et al.'s (1990) data display suggested that group approaches can be successful if they are carefully focused and, in general, other than "nonbehavioral"; and Lipsey (1992) found that whereas group approaches that operated within the justice system showed fairly modest recidivism reductions on average (ES = .07), those outside the system had substantial reductions (ES = .18).[8]

Individual Counseling or Therapy

Individual counseling or therapy had similarly mixed results, though studies of it were less often considered qualitatively questionable. For instance, Romig (1978), Genevie et al. (1986), Gordon and Arbuthnot (1987), and Gottschalk et al. (1987) concluded that few—perhaps 20%—of these programs reduced recidivism. In fact, Gottschalk et al. (1987) found this generic approach (though not "client-centered therapy" in particular) the least successful of the several they studied. At the same time, the data display in Andrews, Zinger, et al. (1990) indicated—possibly in contrast to Gottschalk et al.'s (1987) finding—"nondirective client-centered/psychodynamic counseling" did not reduce recidivism. Others concluded that individual counseling or therapy sometimes did work in institutional (Lipton et al., 1975) or community (Panizzon et al., 1991) settings, though perhaps only under particular conditions or for certain types of offenders (Rutter & Giller, 1983). Still others pointed to specific instances of success (Gendreau & Ross, 1979, 1987). Though Lipsey (1992) found no overall impact in nonjustice system settings (ES = −.01), this approach seemed, again on average, to reduce recidivism to a modest degree when implemented in justice system settings (ES = .08).

Family Intervention

Family intervention presented a more promising but still somewhat mixed picture. For instance, positive or very promising overall assessments were made by Van Voorhis (1987) and Garrett (1985). Gendreau and Ross (1979), Johns and Wallach (1981), and Gordon and Arbuthnot (1987) either highlighted or noted specific studies that showed promise. Similarly, Graziano and Mooney (1984) concluded that despite research shortcomings and the few experimental studies involving recidivism, family intervention was "the most promising approach" of all, at least when behavioral programming was used. Other analysts and reviewers stressed that although success sometimes occurred, it seemed even more conditional. For instance, Geismar and Wood (1986), Andrews, Zinger, et al. (1990), and Romig (1978) each concluded—or suggested via their data displays—that although nonfocused family interventions do not ordinarily reduce recidivism, those carefully structured or focused with regard to family problems or client needs often do succeed. Still, Rutter and Giller (1983) and Panizzon et al. (1991) highlighted frequent research shortcomings and other deficiencies. Although they collectively mentioned instances of short- and longer-term success, they believed definite conclusions about family intervention's effectiveness were premature. Finally, Lipsey (1992) found that on average such interventions within the justice system produced or were associated with essentially no recidivism reductions (ES = .02), whereas those outside the system had moderate impact (ES = .10).

Vocational Training

Analysts and reviewers of vocational training routinely found this approach associated with lower recidivism in about one of every three studies (Lipton et al., 1975; Romig, 1978; Wright & Dixon, 1977; in Gottschalk et al., 1987,

50% of all outcomes were positive when vocational and educational training were reported as a single unit). The influence of vocational training alone was difficult to assess, as the studies in which it appeared generally included one or more employment components as well (e.g., job referral, placement, or experience), and they sometimes contained an educational training feature, too. Genevie et al. (1986) found "inconsistent" results for vocational training, with some positive and some negative outcomes. Lipsey (1992), on the other hand, found a sizable negative impact on recidivism (ES = –.18) when such programs were operated within the justice system. For nonjustice system programs, however, he analyzed vocational and employment studies together and observed no net impact (ES = –.02).

Employment

Work experience programs were associated with positive outcomes in about one of every three such operations that were found in the data displays of Lab and Whitehead (1988) and Andrews, Zinger, et al. (1990). Genevie et al. (1986) considered work-study among the few promising or successful approaches, and Lipsey (1992) found employment the single most powerful justice system intervention (ES = .37), though his sample of studies was quite small in this instance. At the same time, employment (analyzed together with vocational studies, as mentioned above) had no apparent effect on recidivism in the case of justice system programs (ES = – .02)—and the sample was much larger in this instance.

Educational Training

Educational training, which usually consists of standard or special academic programming, remedial education, and/or individual tutoring, was associated with positive outcome in some two of every three studies discussed by or listed in Lipton et al. (1975), Romig (1978), and Andrews, Zinger, et al. (1990). Gottschalk et al. (1987) reported a positive outcome for one third of all programs in which educational training was a component though not necessarily the "primary intervention." Nevertheless, Lipsey (1992) found no net impact of this approach on recidivism (ES = .00) for all studies combined (only nonjustice system programs were reported), and Genevie et al. (1986) described their results as "inconsistent."

Behavioral Approach

The behavioral approach, for example, contingency contracting and token economies, was most widely recognized as having many positive results and being among the strongest of all. Lipsey (1992), who analyzed this approach separately from the "skill oriented" (see "Life Skills," p. 142), found its average effect sizes (ESs) to be .25 and .20 for justice and nonjustice system programs, respectively; Garrett (1985) obtained an ES of .18 for institutional and community residential settings combined; Mayer et al. (1986) found ESs of .50 and .33 (unweighted and weighted, respectively, for sample size) for settings that also included community nonresidential programs; Gottschalk et al. (1987) obtained positive outcomes for 64% of all studies in which the behavioral approach was the primary intervention; Andrews, Zinger, et al. (1990) found this approach to have a significantly higher ES (.29) than the nonbehavioral (.04); Geismar and Wood (1986) concluded that the behavioral approach outperformed the nonbehavioral on family intervention (the focus of their review); and Gendreau and Ross (1979, 1987) as well as Rutter and Giller (1983) noted several instances of success. (The 1983 reviewers nevertheless found few high-quality designs and believed long-term effects on recidivism were unclear.) Johns and Wallach's (1981) relatively few studies involved more successful than unsuccessful outcomes. Graziano and Mooney (1984) found a small but increasing number of long-term reductions for behavioral interventions and described this approach as promising.

The above findings centered on recidivism reduction. Collectively, the studies included predelinquents as well as adjudicated offenders. Only Romig (1978) and Panizzon et al. (1991, focusing on community settings alone) concluded that the behavioral approach had shown relatively few positive effects on recidivism. Whitehead and Lab's (1989) meta-analysis suggested that the overall results for this approach were only mildly positive, though 31% of all behavioral programs had a phi coefficient of +.20 or more.

Despite these differences, the positive and often strong findings for the behavioral approach seem clear. It might be noted that this method (e.g., contingency management, behavior contracting, and token economies) has commonly been used to help implement *other* categories, such as family intervention and vocational or educational training, not just to encourage and reinforce socially acceptable behaviors per se or to discourage specific unwanted behaviors. As a result, the behavioral approach has perhaps been as much a generic technique as a general approach per se. This applies to the cognitive behavioral approach as well, though to a much lesser degree.

Cognitive Behavioral or Cognitive Approach

The cognitive behavioral or cognitive approach has sometimes been analyzed as a subset of the behavioral and sometimes as separate from it; in both cases it has been considered positive and promising (Garrett, 1985; Gordon & Arbuthnot, 1987; Izzo & Ross, 1990, based on some 46 programs, with recidivism as an outcome). Panizzon et al. (1991), however, indicated it has had relatively few reported instances of success with regard to recidivism (these authors called this approach "social-cognitive interventions"). Gottschalk et al. (1987) and Andrews, Zinger, et al. (1990) singled out too few "cognitive therapy" and "cognitive behavioral" approaches for meaningful quantitative analysis, but Gottschalk et al. (1987) separately reported a successful outcome for 45% of the 20 studies in which "modeling/role playing" was included. This particular feature appeared to constitute a sizable part of Panizzon et al.'s (1991) as well as Izzo and Ross's (1990) earlier-mentioned, broader categories of "social-cognitive interventions" and "cognitive programs," respectively. (The latter categories, in turn, sometimes appeared under other labels, e.g., "social skill training," "social perspective taking," "negotiation skill training," "interpersonal skills training," and "role-playing and modeling.") More broadly, several of these categories might be considered interpersonal skills training, whether or not the latter is placed in the cognitive behavioral or cognitive category, or for that matter, under "skill oriented" per se (see "Life Skills," below). Obviously, some category boundaries remain fluid in this relatively new research area.

Life Skills

The approach called "life skills" (Garrett, 1985), "skill oriented" (Lipsey, 1992), or "skill development" (Lipton et al., 1975) is a mixture or group of categories that individually consist of approaches already discussed. Collectively, that is, from one analysis or review to the next, the groups in question partly overlap. In Garrett (1985), "life skills" consisted of academic training, vocational training, outdoor experience (Outward Bound), and drug programs; in Lipsey (1992) "skill oriented" contained not only "academic educational/tutoring" (other than "school based") and outdoor experience ("wilderness/Outward Bound; survival training") but interpersonal "social skills" training (e.g., via role-playing); and in Lipton et al. (1975), "skill development" referred exclusively to educational and vocational training, with some work exposure and job placement. This substantively diverse yet conceptually coherent (albeit broad) category was among the more successful approaches—or perhaps, dimensions—observed by Lipsey (1992) in the case of justice system programs (ES = .20). Within the nonjustice area, it was the most successful one by far (ES = .32). (See Note 8. Lipsey, 1992, separated the skill-oriented approach from one he analyzed as "behavioral.") Garrett (1985) found "life skills" not just successful (ES = .28 on recidivism) but even more so than the behavioral approach (ES = .18). Finally, Lipton et al. (1975) reported positive outcomes for skill development approaches that were "specialized" rather than "standard" in nature, especially regarding educational programs.

Multimodal Approach

The multimodal approach (e.g., such combinations as—hypothetically—work-study + counseling + restitution) was found, in general, to be the second strongest category analyzed by Lipsey (1992): ESs were .25 and .21 for justice and nonjustice system programs, respectively. Panizzon et al. (1991) also presented some positive findings regarding this approach (called "combined therapeutic" intervention), specifically for community settings. Palmer, in earlier reviews, suggested the apparent or at least probable importance of multimodal programming (first called the "combined-modalities approach," 1978, pp. 48-49; and later called "broad-based" or "extensive"—but not necessarily intensive—intervention, 1983). Relatively few analysts or reviewers have focused specifically, let alone systematically, on this aspect of programming—programming that reflects the idea that certain combinations of elements may have considerably more relevance to clients and, in that sense more power, than any of those elements alone. This general absence of focus reflects most analysts' and reviewers' emphasis to date on what might be called single-feature or salient-feature analysis.

Probation and Parole Enhancement

Probation and parole enhancement have generally been described as additions to standard supervision in the form of more contacts (often made possible by reduced caseloads); service or control elements, such as family and collateral contacts; or, in recent years, electronic monitoring. Before the early 1980s, these enhancements received somewhat mixed reviews. Greenberg (1977), Wright and Dixon (1977), and Romig (1978) suggested that enhancements, including reduced caseloads, made little difference; however, Martinson (1974) considered special probation programs possibly the only promising intervention. Lipton et al. (1975) furnished several examples of positive or promising outcome, and Palmer (1978), after examining all recidivism studies reviewed by Lipton et al. (1975), observed that 50% of those in probation and 71% of those in parole had outcomes in which Es outperformed Cs by 15% or more. In the 1980s, Gendreau and Ross (1987) suggested that although increased supervision produced fairly small recidivism reductions by itself, improvement could be substantial if well-selected, *new* program elements were added. The three meta-analysts who reviewed this area collectively obtained a range of results: Lipsey (1992) found that reduced caseloads and other enhancements made only modest differences (ES = .08 and .07, respectively);[9] Whitehead and Lab (1989) found that 35% of their "probation/parole/community corrections" programs had satisfied their standard of success (phi = .20 or more); yet Gottschalk et al. (1987) found that 60% of the programs in which probation played a role had positive (E > C) though not necessarily statistically reliable ($p < .05$) outcomes. Thus, as before, reviews were mixed and sometimes mutually inconsistent.

Intensive Supervision

Intensive Probation Supervision (IPS). Programs using intensive probation supervision during the 1980s were reviewed by Armstrong (1988) and Krisberg et al. (1989). In many such programs the control-and-surveillance component and the service provision component were emphasized or augmented considerably more than in the enhancements of the 1970s. These reviewers found that no clear conclusions could be drawn about effectiveness because too few well-designed or even adequate studies had been conducted. More recently, looking at programs for adult offenders, Byrne and Pattavina (1992) concluded that questions about the diversionary impact and cost-effectiveness of IPS programs still cannot be answered. They also believed that "the majority of IPS program evaluations do not support the notion that 'intensive' supervision significantly reduces the risk of offender recidivism" (p. 296). Drawing on results from the evaluation of a Massachusetts IPS program (Byrne & Kelly, 1989) and from randomized field experiments in three California sites (Petersilia & Turner, 1990), however, they suggest that better recidivism outcomes are likely in programs giving more attention to higher quality and quantity of treatment, as opposed to emphasizing surveillance and control.

Intensive Aftercare (Parole) Supervision. A detailed review of intensive aftercare supervision was conducted by Altschuler and Armstrong (1990), who found that too few acceptable studies existed to allow for reliable conclusions. Nevertheless, well-designed experiments by Barton and Butts (1990), Gruenewald, Laurence, and West (1985), and Fagan, Forst, and Vivona (1988), collectively suggested that multicomponent probation and aftercare interventions that are carefully conceptualized and relatively intensive can be at least as effective as standard approaches. The 1985 and 1988 experiments involved high-risk, violence-prone or violent youths who would otherwise have been institutionalized.

Community-Based Approaches
Versus Institutional Intervention

Since the mid-1970s, literature reviewers and, later, meta-analysts have considered community-based approaches (a) *no less* effective than institutions (Greenberg, 1977; Lundman, 1984), (b) possibly (Wright & Dixon, 1977) or probably (Rutter & Giller, 1983; Van Voorhis, 1987) more effective or slightly more effective, and (c) *more* effective or more often effective with respect to reducing recidivism. Regarding (c), Lipsey (1992) found that community-based programs had larger ESs than programs implemented in institutions; Andrews, Zinger, et al. (1990) found that "appropriate treatment" programs in the community had a substantially higher ES (.35) than similarly categorized programs conducted in institutions (.20); Whitehead and Lab (1989) obtained a 2.5:1 ratio of successful community programs to successful institutional ones; and Izzo and Ross (1990) found that proportionately more effective programs had occurred in community settings. No reviewers or analysts considered the institutional approach better than the community-based in terms of recidivism, at least not for unselected, heterogeneous populations of offenders. This was independent of Brody's (1976) view that institutional programs are largely unsuccessful in themselves (Sechrest, White, & Brown, 1979)—a conclusion that not all reviewers shared. These findings from meta-analyses and literature reviews do not ipso facto mean that institutional programs or settings have had little or no positive effects.

Trends Regarding Effectiveness

This overview of meta-analyses and literature reviews suggests three inter-related points regarding programmatic factors.

1. Less Effective Approaches

For individual programs grouped together and analyzed according to their salient program feature—a component they shared—several such groups or "generic approaches" were substantially less likely than others to have been associated with reduced recidivism (see Appendix B). (When analyzed this way, each of these groups was in effect treated as an entity, that is, as a homogeneous or undifferentiated conceptual unit. The distinguishing program feature was, if only by implication, often the quantitatively most "salient" feature as well.) In five groups or generic approaches, individual studies had (when aggregated within each approach) the lowest percentage of successful outcomes (recidivism reduction) or an average effect size that was relatively low: confrontation, areawide strategies of delinquency prevention, diversion (at least "nonsystem"), group counseling or therapy, and individual counseling or therapy. The results for most of these approaches, especially the last three, were far from entirely negative. In fact, these particular results were basically mixed—with modest-to-moderate overall recidivism reductions being the rule and partially counterbalancing the various negative findings. At any rate, these three approaches could not, in toto, be described as "successful," whether in comparison to other approaches or on their own.

2. Effectiveness of Individual Programs

Although the E-programs that constituted each generic approach that was listed in the "Studies of Programmatic Factors" section above did not collectively (when aggregated) outperform their C-programs fairly often (e.g., in two E-programs out of every three), a substantial percentage of E-programs that made up those or other approaches did individually outperform their Cs. They did so in terms of perhaps the most commonly used criterion for describing the success or failure of individual programs. More broadly, using the $p < .05$ criterion of statistical significance, individual E-programs outperformed their Cs in about 25% to 35% of all programs across all generic approaches combined; Cs led Es in under 10%. (This finding was based on a separate substudy; the figures were 33% and 7%, respectively. They applied to all 20 generic approaches combined, not just to the 5 "less effective" ones.)[10] In addition, using *any* degree of recidivism reduction ($p < .05$ or not), Es led Cs in about 65% of all programs, whereas Cs were ahead in some 30%—again, for all groups (all 20 generic categories) combined. (This criterion is designated E > C.) These percentages differed considerably from one generic approach to the next.

It should be kept in mind that because the E > C differences did not necessarily reach $p < .05$, many of them almost certainly arose from chance variations alone and were therefore of limited reliability. Nevertheless, findings that did reach $p < .05$ indicate that even if a researcher *had* grouped various programs within a single, broad category but had also reviewed those programs individually, he or she would have found statistically successful individual programs within that category. This would have applied to almost any category, including diversion, group counseling or therapy, and individual counseling or therapy. This is the case even though some of those categories (generic approaches) may have been considered unsuccessful as *categories,* for example, because of frequent inconsistencies across individual-program outcomes or because of a low average effect size. Such findings might lead one to ask, Why did some diversion programs work but not others? Why did some group counseling programs, and some individual counseling programs, succeed, whereas many others did not? Even among categories that had some of the best overall results *as* categories (see below), why were some behavioral programs, life skills programs, and family intervention programs successful, whereas others were not? A hypothesis regarding such questions is presented in Item 3 of "Unimodal and Combination Approaches," below.

3. More Effective Approaches

Returning to the level of generic approach rather than individual program, the following interventions were (a) those most often or proportionately most often considered successful or promising from an E-better-than-C perspective (whether or not one used $p < .05$); or (b) those that seemed, on balance, to have the strongest positive results (e.g., the largest average effect sizes or recidivism reduction): behavioral, cognitive behavioral or cognitive, life skills or skill oriented, multimodal, and family intervention.[11] To be sure, a number of meta-analysts and literature reviewers did not find some of these approaches, for example, "behavioral" and "family intervention," to be successful, let alone among the most successful. Differing assessments regarding success occurred for several other generic approaches as well, including physical challenge, group counseling or therapy, individual counseling or therapy, and probation or parole enhancements.

Unimodal and Combination Approaches

As mentioned earlier, these differing assessments (and even various inconsistencies as to whether or not given approaches were successful—or just how successful or promising they were) resulted from several factors, including differences in the various analyses and reviews with respect to time period covered and the settings that were involved (e.g., diversion vs. probation vs. institution). Moreover, these differences were often associated with substantial differences in the composition of the offender samples that appeared in the various analyses and reviews. In addition, some approaches may have been more relevant than others with regard to the typical offender samples with which they were used in any one setting.

Even if few differences had existed regarding time period, setting, and sample, no approach would likely have emerged as a guaranteed or even highly reliable success. This, we believe, would probably have reflected the following situation (the three items that make up this situation are interrelated and culminate in Item 3).

1. Each approach (also called a *category*) actually contained more than one *program component*. For instance, many of the individual programs that made up the group counseling category also contained substantial amounts of another component: *vocational training*.[12] Still other programs in that category included some *educational training* or individual counseling. Thus "group counseling" was in fact a multimodal rather than unimodal approach in that its programs collectively involved more than one component, that is, more than group counseling alone.

2. It follows from Item 1 that several mutually different combinations of program components existed or could have existed in each category, for example, within the group counseling (GC) category (at least they could have easily existed if a category contained numerous individual programs). For

instance, in some individual programs in the GC category, the combination of components was GC plus vocational training. In other such programs, the combination of components was GC plus educational training (etc.).

3. We hypothesize that within any category only some combinations of program components reduced recidivism. More precisely, only some combinations were effective with a large portion of offenders who were involved in individual programs in the category.[13] This hypothesis implies that it was these particular combinations that collectively accounted for most or all of the approximately 33% of individual E-programs that significantly outperformed their C-programs.[14] The remaining combinations—in effect, the remaining individual programs (with *their* particular sets of components)—were insufficiently relevant, inadequately or inappropriately applied, or both.[15] This hypothesized mixture of (a) sufficiently and insufficiently relevant plus (b) properly and improperly applied combinations would help account for the fact that no generic program approach examined thus far, such as group counseling or behavioral, would probably have emerged as being highly reliable in terms of effectiveness, even if time period, setting, and offender samples were quite similar across the meta-analyses and literature reviews. Items 1 through 3 are further discussed in Appendix C.

Which particular combinations of E-program components have yielded positive results with large portions of their populations, and which ones have not, has seldom been *systematically* explored and, in that sense, remains largely unknown.[16] It is clear that several experimental programs that combined a number of elements have significantly reduced recidivism when compared to their control programs. In one fairly recent example, restitution, counseling, and recreation were combined in the E-program, and restitution and standard probation characterized the C (Panizzon et al., 1991; Schneider & Schneider, 1985). Combinations found in other successful E-programs for juveniles include the following (these studies also involved random assignment to E and C conditions, and the programs may be characterized as multimodal):

a. Job placement and job counseling, individual counseling, and remedial education if needed (Shore & Massimo, 1979). This was the Boston Program (Vocationally Oriented Psychotherapy).

b. Individual counseling, pragmatically oriented discussions, routine supervision, family counseling if needed, and academic training as well as individual tutoring if needed (Lee & Haynes, 1980). This was the CREST Program (Clinical Regional Support Teams).

c. Counseling, pragmatically oriented discussions, limit-setting and control-centered discussions, recreation and socializing experiences, and academic training as well as individual tutoring if needed (Barkwell, 1980; Palmer, 1974). This was the California Community Treatment Project and the similar Winnipeg Program.[17]

Other instances include the Los Angeles Camps Programs (Palmer & Wedge, 1989), CaVIC ("Canadian Volunteers in Corrections"; Andrews & Kiessling, 1980), and the Danish Program (Bernsten & Christiansen, 1965).[18] These programs, and those mentioned above, each targeted two or more of the following factors: (a) Skill/Capacity Deficits, (b) External Pressures/Disadvantages, and (c) Internal Difficulties.[19] The various programs' *range of components*—for example, from remedial educational and/or job placement to family or individual counseling—allowed them to address that *range of targets* simultaneously or successively. This breadth of intervention seems relevant to moderately serious and very serious offenders—individuals whose deficits and difficulties are themselves often broad and intertwined. (Regarding the existence of multiple needs and problems among offenders—including their "internal [psychological] difficulties"—see Andrews & Wormith, 1989; Elliott, Huizinga, & Menard, 1989; Palmer, 1992.)

Though examples of successfully combined components thus exist, what is unknown is whether any given combinations—combinations that were effective in individual E-programs—were fairly *reliably* effective. It is not known if those or even rather similar combinations were associated with recidivism reduction in a large majority of the studies in which they appeared (not just in the above examples). Moreover, it is not even known if those particular combinations really *did* appear in several studies, even though it is clear that some combinations or portions of large combinations occurred in more than one. The absence of such information generally reflects the fact that clearly delineated combinations have hardly been focused on in the first place and have rarely even been hypothesized as such for purposes of systematic research. (Of course, to help corrections officials clearly and reliably delineate *any* combinations in the first place and then to generate sets of studies in which various combinations are systematically compared with each other to determine which ones are more effective, researchers and others should first develop relatively standardized descriptions of or definitions for the several features or components that may make up any given combination.)

Research on Combinations

General Considerations and Scope

To identify combinations that may be reliably effective, one would need a long-term, multistudy research effort in which the outcomes of similar or identical combinations from individual E-programs would be compared across studies. These studies need not have occurred only within the same generic category, such as group counseling or vocational training. In this research effort, the first or broadest task would center not on the question, Which E-program combination (EPC) is the *most* effective? Or even, Which EPCs are *more* effective than others? Instead, it would focus on, Which EPCs are effective at all, particularly across most (or at least a sizable portion) of their studies?—that is, What constitutes those combinations?

Given this task, initial efforts would not center on comparing the outcomes of two or more E-program combinations with *one another*—combinations that would each have been effective relative to their respective Cs (in individual studies) and differentially effective relative to each other (across studies). Instead, such efforts would focus on comparing the outcomes of various Es, on the one hand, with those of their respective *Cs,* on the other, to determine if those E-program combinations, when aggregated across the individual studies, commonly outperformed the aggregated Cs. The Es whose outcomes would be compared with those of Cs would be a preestablished set of similar or identical EPCs, for example, counseling, routine limit-setting supervision, pragmatically oriented discussions, restitution if and as feasible, and certain other components if needed (academic training and individual tutoring; job placement plus job-centered discussions).

Combinations of Program Components

To date, research on combinations has hardly existed; rarely has it been discussed in detail. Instead, as indicated, researchers have centered their analyses of intervention effectiveness around single-program features or components, that is, around a distinguishing or salient feature of given programs. These features have often been "programmatic," as in the case of counseling or educational training. Often, however, they have involved "approaches," as for instance, with the "behavioral," "cognitive behavioral," and "confrontation"—not that these lacked specific content or subject matter focus.

In analyzing the given program component or approach, researchers have used that feature as the equivalent of an independent variable, and they have, we believe, produced much knowledge and many important leads as a result. While occupied with that already large task, however, they have not tried also to take on the following challenge (moreover, the basic information needed to address this challenge seriously was generally unreported in individual studies—and, by itself, this gap would have made the third and fourth steps of the challenge impossible to implement adequately):

1. Based on prior research and theory, delineate one or two combinations of features, such as combinations of program components, that one hypothesizes to be effective across various E-programs.[20]

2. Analytically use each of those combinations, that is, each one in turn, as the equivalent of a single, independent variable.

3. Determine, via systematic comparisons across various E/C studies in which a given, hypothesized E-combination appears, whether that combination is in fact successful in many or most of those studies. (As an alternative, at least take Step 4.)

4. Determine, via the same type of systematic, cross-study comparisons, not only (a) which particular program components (i.e., which subset of features or factors within the total combination) appear most often in the programs that are successful (see Note 17) but also, if possible, (b) their degree of success as well, for example, their effect size. (Also determine the relative emphasis given to the features that make up the total combination.)

Researchers have not yet hypothesized and used any specific combinations of program components for the purpose of systematically studying them *as* combinations. Certainly, no such combinations have been widely discussed, let alone generally accepted as prime candidates for such research. Nevertheless, discovering various combinations that commonly yield positive results with large portions of their offender samples should be, we believe, one of corrections' most important tasks for the next 10 or more years.[21] As indicated, some successful combinations have been observed, but their degree of reliability or generalizability is unclear.

Studies of Nonprogrammatic Factors

Complicating the already challenging task of accurately identifying effective combinations is experimental and direct experiential evidence that attests to the role of other than programmatic factors. Moreover, some such factors may have to operate simultaneously if one wishes to address the skill or capacity deficits seriously, the external pressures or disadvantages, or the internal difficulties mentioned above.[22] Two summary examples will illustrate the type and range of nonprogrammatic factors and conditions in question—most or all of which eventually operated or existed simultaneously, yet some of which were a precondition for others (see also Gendreau & Andrews, 1990; Gendreau & Ross, 1983-1984).

Type and Range of Factors

From 12 years of research and observations involving California's Community Treatment Project (CTP), the following were identified as significant contributors to reduced recidivism and other indices of success:[23] "small caseloads; intensive [frequent] and/or extensive [broad-based] contacts; individualization and flexible programming; . . . personal characteristics and professional orientation of [parole] agent; specific abilities and overall perceptiveness of agent; explicit, detailed guidelines [intervention strategies]" (Palmer, 1994, p. 92; in press).[24] These probably played the key role in producing the project's 50% reduction in violent offending, as compared to the well-matched controls. This effect covered not just the period of parole supervision (agency jurisdiction) but several years of postdischarge follow-up as well.

Based on several years' experience with the Canadian Volunteers in Corrections (CaVIC) program and related efforts, the following were considered key ingredients of successful intervention:[25] "(a) use of authority by correctional worker; . . . (b) anticriminal modeling and reinforcement, by worker; . . . (c) a problem-solving strategy; . . . (d) use of [appropriate] community resources; . . . and, (e) a particular quality in the worker/offender relationship" (Andrews & Kiessling, 1980, pp. 445-446; Andrews, Zinger, et al., 1990, pp. 375-376; Cullen & Gendreau, 1989, p. 33).

In general, the types of factors or conditions listed in those examples support or, we believe, even make possible the appropriate implementation of generic program components such as educational training, vocational training, and counseling. They may even facilitate the adequate implementation and maintenance of such components or general strategies or methods as the behavioral and cognitive behavioral. At any rate, these factors are other than programmatic in content and they may often be important in their own right, regardless of the particular program components or types of approach they facilitate. The impact of such factors and conditions can be illustrated by briefly focusing on staff characteristics and staff-client (offender) inter-actions.

Staff Characteristics

Findings such as the following have been repeatedly obtained regarding staff characteristics, such as personality features (including modeling quali-ties) and professional orientations.

1. In the CaVIC program,

Probation officers, [whether] volunteers or professionals, who were interperson-ally sensitive to conventional rules of conduct (above average on the Socialization Scale) were the most effective one-to-one supervisors according to [various reports, to] the officers' actual behavior during audio-taped sessions with proba-tioners, the attitudinal gains exhibited by probationers, and recidivism rates.
    Among low risk probationers, . . . the professional status of officers was unrelated to recidivism. [However, a]mong the higher risk probationers, . . . volunteer supervision was significantly more effective than professional super-vision, particularly so among [certain] young unsocialized probationers. . . . Nevertheless, such matching effects seemed to exist for even "the indigenous [volunteer] workers . . . only [when they] possess[ed] the preferred personality dispositions, [e.g.,] high empathy/socialization." (Andrews & Kiessling, 1980, pp. 453-455)

2. In the Youth Center Research Project,

The non-specific factor of client positive regard for staff potentiated whatever specific treatment effects were present and contributed about as much to outcome as did type of treatment. . . . Where specific overt behaviors are targeted in a behavioral [i.e., behavior modification] program, greater changes can be made when the client feels positively toward staff; similarly in a transactional analysis program, greater changes on attitudinal and self-report measures can be obtained where good relationships exist. (Jesness, 1975, pp. 759, 777)

*3. Related though somewhat different results were obtained in the
   Cooperative Behavior Demonstration Project:*

> Where there was high mutual regard or high mutual dislike between client and
> caseworker, the differences in recidivism were great. Only 10% of those showing
> high mutual regard failed; 40% of those showing high mutual dislike failed. . . .
> The association between positive regard and recidivism was more likely a conse-
> quence of differences in the caseworker's behavior toward the client than of
> common client characteristics. (Jesness, Allison, McCormick, Wedge, & Young,
> 1975, pp. 153-154)

Staff-Client Interactions

In addition, the following type of findings have been obtained regarding
aspects of staff-client interaction, such as matching, and particular qualities
in the relationship:

1. In the Santa Monica probation study,

> *"Relationship/Self-expression"* officers [change agents] achieved their best
> results with youths who were Communicative-alert, Impulsive-anxious, or Ver-
> bally hostile-defensive; they did less well with those who were Dependent-
> anxious.
> *"Surveillance/Self-control"* officers had their greatest difficulties with indi-
> viduals who were Verbally hostile-defensive or Defiant-indifferent; they did
> considerably better with those who were Dependent-anxious.
> *"Surveillance/Self-expression"* officers seemed uniquely matched with proba-
> tioners who Wanted to Be Helped and Liked. (Palmer, 1965, pp. 19-20)

2. In the Camp Elliott study,

> The interaction between the maturity level of the subjects and the supervisor
> characteristics significantly affected later success rate of subjects. Not only were
> the treatment methods of some internally-oriented supervisory teams effective
> in increasing the success rates of high maturity offenders, but also, the treat-
> ment methods [of those same teams] were markedly detrimental to the success
> chances of low maturity offenders. Furthermore, the externally-oriented super-
> visory team had the reverse effect on high and low maturity subjects. (Warren,
> 1971, p. 245)

3. Finally, in California's CTP, for the overall sample,

> Boys who were closely matched with their CTP worker had a failure rate . . . of
> 23 percent over a fifteen-month parole follow-up. Those not closely matched had
> a failure rate of 49 percent ($p < .01$). . . . After twenty-four months, the failure
> rates were 34 and 57 percent, respectively ($p < .05$). (Palmer, 1973, p. 101)[26]

Besides the staff and staff-client factors, two other nonprogrammatic com-
plications enter the picture—offender differences and setting.

Offender Differences

Several studies have indicated that intervention can have different impacts
on offenders with differing personalities, interpersonal styles, or developmental levels.[27] For instance,

1. "Conflicted" youths in the Community Treatment Project, that is, a particular,
   large subgroup of youths within the experimental group (Es), averaged 34 arrests
   per 1,000 months on parole; however, "Power Oriented" youths in that same
   intensive program averaged 55 arrests.[28] In addition, during a 4-year postparole,
   that is, postdischarge, follow-up, the arrest rates were 32 and 68 for those same
   E- subgroups, respectively (Palmer, 1978).
2. In the Fricot Ranch study, "neurotic or emotionally disturbed delinquents" (Es)
   who were assigned to an interpersonally supportive, small-living-unit program,
   had a 24-month postprogram recidivism rate of 48%; for "nonneurotics," that is,
   the remaining Es from that program, the rate was 75% (Jesness, 1971-1972).
3. In the CaVIC program, "relationship oriented counseling (the worker's use of
   nondirective, empathic messages) correlated with decreased crime rates among
   the clients who had above average empathy scores but [it] increased criminal
   behavior of those with less empathic skills, especially when the clients were also
   low on the Gough Socialization Scale" (Andrews & Kiessling, 1980, p. 420).
4. A study of Project Outward Bound (a wilderness program) "showed that program
   to be [more] effective with those delinquents who were 'reacting to an adolescent
   . . . crisis' [e.g., to situational stress or to an identity crisis], than with the more
   immature, emotionally disturbed, or characterologically deficient boys" (Kelly
   & Baer, 1971; Warren, 1972, p. 7).

During the past 15 years, such offender differences have been minimized
or largely ignored in connection with program planning. Especially in the past

10 years, offenders have been mainly distinguished from each other in terms of risk level, although very different personalities may have the *same* level and might respond quite differently to the same program. Thus, for example, almost all individuals in the CTP and Fricot programs were high risk; yet their responses differed widely. Moreover, program differences can sometimes outweigh the risk factor. For instance, in the Los Angeles probation camps, some types of programs were more effective with higher-risk youths than with middle risk. This, too, reflects an offender-program interaction (Wedge & Palmer, 1989).

Setting

A program's impact may also differ by type of youth, depending on the *setting* in which intervention occurs. For instance, Mueller's (1960) study found differential impact as a function of assignment to institutional, non-institutional or open institutional, and direct parole settings in the case of "conforming and overinhibited" youths, "aggressive or insecure" youths, and "emotionally disturbed" youths, respectively. Similarly, Reiss's (1951) study found differential impact of assignment to home and community placement versus closed institutions on youths with "relatively strong personal controls," those with "relatively weak personal controls," and those with "marked social deterioration or very immature personalities." Sealy and Banks (1971) observed that "the difference in success rate between open and closed institutions is greatest for boys of the lowest levels of maturity and is negligible for boys of higher maturity" (p. 257), and the Borstal (Manheim & Wilkins, 1955) as well as Highfields (Weeks, 1958) studies found differential impact of open versus closed institutions with more as well as less amenable youths (or higher- and lower-risk youths). In addition, Palmer (1974) found differential impact of initial institutionalization versus initial community programming to be a function of youths' subgroup or personality type combined with their degree of problems or vulnerability (Mueller, 1960; Palmer, 1974; Reiss, 1951; Sealy & Banks, 1971; Weeks, 1958). Several of these examples were summarized and discussed by Warren (1971); related findings are seen in Kobrin and Klein (1982) with respect to juvenile diversion settings. Finally, Brill (1978) observed that postinstitutional adjustment reflected an interaction between high versus low institutional program structure, on the one hand, and youths' level of preprogram conceptual development, on the other. These and related findings were further reviewed by Reitsma-Street (1984).

Further Challenges in Knowledge Building

Scope of Study

Our review of nonprogrammatic factors, such as staff characteristics and staff-client interactions, indicates it is not enough to study programmatic factors and program components alone. This is true even if we broaden the concept of program components to that of "operations" overall and if we include among the operations various "formal aspects" of programming or programs shown in Appendix D. These aspects include such specific features or items as basis of case assignment (e.g., geographic, available case opening or living unit space, person match, program match) and offender-staff ratio or caseload size.[29] At any rate, even "operations" is not enough; nonprogrammatic factors should be studied as well.

And nonprogrammatic factors (e.g., staff characteristics) should involve more content areas than those suggested earlier. For instance,

1. "Staff characteristics" should encompass more than personality features and professional orientations—that is, treatment and intervention orientations—and should include various background characteristics (e.g., age, gender, ethnicity, type and amount of training and job-related experience).

2. "Staff-client interactions" should include not just matching and particular qualities in the relationship. In fact, some interactions would involve program features themselves. These interactions could be considered specific features within "operations,"—that is, program operations—and in that context they would include two significant subcategories: (a) *"goals and areas of focus"* (e.g., enhancing or promoting a nondelinquent or noncriminal self-image, modifying attitudes toward adults or establishment, reducing apathy and indifference, improving or altering family and parental relationships) and (b) *"processes and lines of approach"* (e.g., gaining client's confidence in worker, expressing personal concern for and acceptance of client, programming or rehearsing client for specific life situations).[30] Item (b) is often just called "process," and it encompasses much of what has frequently been labeled the black box.

3. "Offenders" should encompass more than just "personal characteristics," such as developmental level, personality type, and generic psychological variables (e.g., cognitive complexity, locus of control, affect awareness, impulse control). Rather, it should include background characteristics and sociodemographic features as well.

4. "Setting," that is, program setting, should involve more than various formal or structural aspects (e.g., justice system or nonjustice system jurisdiction and sponsorship, public or private, size, physical condition), in addition to its "type" (e.g., institution or community); it should also include management and decision-making styles, social climate dimensions, and so on.

The preceding features are listed in Appendix D, as are several others. This list constitutes a general guideline and provides examples of the type and range of programmatic and nonprogrammatic features that might ideally be recorded in connection with any given operation (intervention, program, service). The list consists of what might be called data items or elements. Data items supply the content basis of systematic knowledge—the *what* of "what do we know, in objective terms" (Palmer, 1978, p. 114). Other things being equal, the more items one can work with, the greater the chance of developing a comprehensive picture of any given phenomenon—in this case, a particular intervention program. By the same token, if only a few data items have been singled out, for example, a few variables that describe the offender population or particular strategies that are used, basic limitations will soon appear. The program will be difficult or impossible to describe in a detailed, systematic way and, therefore, hard to replicate. In addition, numerous similarities and differences that exist between that program and others may be impossible to pin down or validate scientifically.

The Global Approach

Underlying Issues

Clearly, the combinations research described earlier should include examination of programmatic and nonprogrammatic dimensions alike—operations, staff, offender, and setting factors. The examination should be done simultaneously, because each such factor exists not in a vacuum but together with the others, and they can jointly, that is, interactionally, bear on outcome. (These four types of factors will also be called "areas." Each area consists of numerous *features*—sometimes called "characteristics," "items," or "variables." In this context, "examining" or "studying" means determining whether, or to what degree, a factor or feature contributes to an outcome, for example, to reduced recidivism.)

We will now discuss a research strategy designed for studying all four factors or areas simultaneously. This strategy—the "global approach"—emphasizes the premise that programs are functional entities. Given this perspective, researchers' approach would not proceed by examining only one or two of the above-mentioned areas (e.g., *operations*) or only one or two features (e.g., group counseling, restitution) that fall within any such area. Instead, they would begin by examining programs as a whole, as totalities or integrations of (a) *operations,* goals, strategies, and specific techniques, on the one hand, and (b) the *staff* who implement those operations with particular *offenders* in specified *settings,* on the other.[31]

Following are key theoretical reasons for not just (a) studying features individually and (b) assembling and using those features that were found to be associated with successful programs, as a basis for creating a new, multi-feature program. (This approach—the "aggregate *individually successful features* strategy"—would be called the "building block" method. It contrasts with the "global" approach, in which *combinations of features* that are found to exist across particularly successful programs provide the key basis, or at least one fundamental basis, for establishing new programs.)

1. Although research might identify (a) *an individual feature* (such as family counseling) that is associated with a successful program or group of programs (say, programs that mainly target 15- to 18-year-old males in community settings) and although it may also identify (b) a *different* individual feature (say, confrontation) from a different successful program or set of programs that may focus on largely the same target and setting as the above, the following could occur and might even be common: If and when those two identified features are subsequently joined with each other (i.e., aggregated) to establish a new, multifeature program, those particular features—which had not originally been part of the same, real-life program—might in fact not function well together. They might not be operationally compatible or otherwise mutually feasible in the new program, or they may be only minimally so. (This can include but may go beyond simply being inefficient, and it could apply to *any* number of individual features assembled this way, not just two.)[32]

2. Even if those individual features proved operationally compatible when joined together to create a new program, they might not be jointly strong enough to reduce recidivism significantly or often. Were this the case, it might mean that those respective features had not, by themselves, been critical elements of success in their respective individual programs or groups of

programs—they may indeed have contributed substantially but might still not have made the significant difference by themselves. Instead, they may have made their important contribution to successful outcome (at the $p < .05$ level) only when combined with certain other features that had not been studied and therefore were not identified as being related to success. (In short, although the first feature's role in that *combination* might indeed have been essential, it may have been no less essential than that of the combination's remaining features—which were not studied.) With respect to a newly established program, the individual features that had been identified as successful from their respective studies and then aggregated to create that program might not have been a sufficiently strong combination, even if they turned out to be mutually compatible and otherwise feasible in that context.

Via the focus on whole programs, the global approach is intended to directly identify combinations that *are* likely to function together in a newly created program and that have a reasonable to very good chance of being strong enough to make a major or even crucial difference in outcome. In any case, they would probably be a stronger, not just a more compatible, combination than one assembled from *individually* identified and subsequently aggregated features (as in the building block method). Thus we hypothesize that the global approach, although no surefire guarantee of success, would have a good chance of identifying sets of features that can form the nucleus of successful new programs; at least, it might well provide a very promising, empirically derived mix of ingredients. As its product would more fully and directly reflect real-life programs, it would not essentially be a statistical aggregate of individually identified features.

Basic Steps

In implementing the global approach, the basic steps and related considerations are as follows.

1. *Select a main target of study,* such as a category of offenders (such as 16- to 19-year-old urban males) who have been focused on in many programs that were, perhaps, each conducted in a similar type of setting (e.g., an institution). The programs collectively will have almost certainly included a mixture of generic program approaches, for example, vocational training in some programs, group counseling in others, and the behavioral in still others.

This group of programs, and the specific subgroup of programs on which the global approach will focus (see Step 2, below), can include any given mix. Those respective approaches—that is, each such "program component" (say, group counseling)—would be examined (via Steps 3 and 4) as simply another one of the program's *several* features, programmatic or nonprogrammatic.

2. *From among the many programs that involve the main target, select only those in which the E-program performed well above average,* for example, outperformed its C by at least 40% on recidivism or some other important measure[33] (see Andrews, Zinger, et al., 1990, regarding unusually successful programs that were found for various offenders or offender subgroups). An alternative selection standard—one that is somewhat easier but still high—would involve at least a 25% difference between the E-program and its C. This alternative would allow one to select and, via Steps 3 and 4 below, examine more studies than if one used the 40% standard.

E-programs that outperformed their Cs by 40% or more could be called "guides," as they could provide important clues and could thereby "lead." Es that outperformed Cs by 25% or more (or that constituted the upper 25% of all programs in which Es outperformed Cs by any amount) could be considered "prominent."[34] Because the E/C performance difference would be quite substantial in each case, it would seldom have resulted from chance or "noise" alone (given reasonable sample sizes). In addition, the E-program could be presumed to have definitely worked with respect to increasing public protection and to have important planning implications for the target at hand and perhaps for similar ones as well.[35]

3. *For each guide or prominent program identified in Step 2, record descriptive information on as many of its specific operations, staff, offender, and setting features as possible,* using, for example, items such as those in Appendix D. In accordance with the premise ("Premise A") that each program is an integration of its several features, record and systematize data on as wide a range of subject areas and as large a number of features within those areas as is feasible. In that respect, allow the "overall"—that is, the substantively intact—guide or prominent program (not just one feature that is extracted from it or perhaps even a few such features) to be part of the subsequent analysis, described in Step 4.

Before reviewing Step 4, please note the following. Given the above-average and the well-above-average performance of prominent and guide programs, respectively, it is reasonable to assume that the several recorded features that make up those programs were mutually compatible—or that a number of those features were sufficiently compatible. In addition, and again in light of the programs' considerable success, it would be prudent to address the possibility that any given feature or combination of features that helped make up those programs may have made a *major* contribution to the programs' outcome. (This possibility exists even though the feature or combination's absolute and relative contribution is, of course, unknown. What *is* known is that the overall collection of features or, perhaps, certain subgroupings of features, very likely produced much, most, or nearly all of the respective programs' success, for exmaple, the sizable recidivism reduction in the E-program.) At any rate, (a) given the respective features' possibly *important* role, rather than a possibly minor one and (b) in accordance with Premise A, it would be best to allow *each* known feature to enter into, and in that respect contribute to, the analysis (as in Step 3). Because this broadly inclusive approach might well result in the recording of numerous features, this brings us to the next step: culling out. This step helps identify *which* of the possibly (or probably) numerous features will be particularly useful and which ones would most likely be useful, with regard to the target at hand (e.g., the offenders and setting).

4. *Compare the features recorded in Step 3 with each other.* Directly compare—across all the respective, successful programs—all the information that was recorded about those programs (organized in the form of data items that systematically described the programs). This step allows one to identify which features or combinations of features reappear in, or may be common among, the various guide or prominent programs. Here, the special goal is to identify any features or combinations that are shared by most such programs, say, by four of the six guide or prominent programs whose several recorded features have been compared with each other.[36]

The assumptions, here, are that such shared features or combinations of features can be considered especially strong and would be particularly useful or likely to be useful in creating successful new programs. Implicit is the view that, on average, features that are often observed in strong programs will probably be quite reliable or at least especially useful for major planning purposes. (This applies even though such features are not necessarily the *most* reliable and useful ones.) At the same time, however, features or combinations that appear in, say, even one third of these above-average programs can themselves have important implications; moreover, their presence across these programs may not, in effect, be largely attributable to measurement error and other statistically based noise.

5. *Use those shared features or combinations as a key basis for creating new programs,* that is, as major or even central elements of those programs.[37]

In sum, the global approach ensures examination of intact programs, not just one feature alone or even a small number of features. Researchers directly compare all features that are known to have existed in all the individual programs that have met certain high standards of success for specified targets. Given that known success on the part of these guide or prominent programs (collectively, the global approach program sample), the following seems reasonable: (a) If any programs should be carefully examined, it is they; and (b) features that not only helped make up those respective programs but that are also repeated across a sizable portion of them (and in that sense are shared by them) may be particularly useful in creating additional successful programs.

Thus, the global approach allows a wide range of relevant features and combinations to be compared across E-programs that each have strong credentials in terms of the degree to which they outperformed their Cs. The central idea is to identify those features or combinations that are usually shared across or are at least common among those strong programs for use as a key basis for creating new programs or improving present ones.

Review and Implications

Combinations Research

To describe and understand successful programs better and thereby help create new ones, researchers and others should systematically examine combinations of features. The conceptual and analytic framework for the meta-analyses and most literature reviews completed to date includes (a) grouping various individual programs by distinguishing or salient features and (b) examining and interpreting those grouped programs collectively within that unimodal context. This unimodal framework has excluded or greatly de-emphasized serious consideration of the programs' combined features and thus their wider context and actual complexities. A future strategy should seek a broader and more realistic description and understanding of correctional intervention. One key to achieving that goal lies in the systematic study of combinations of features. To date, however, the particular combinations that have commonly yielded positive results with large portions of offender samples are largely unknown, though some definite leads exist. Systematically identifying such combinations is a major challenge, and addressing this challenge should become one of the main research priorities in corrections.

The information that is needed to reflect intervention's complexities and understand its successes will seldom be obtained by organizing analyses around unimodal or single-element questions such as, Does vocational training work? Is family (or individual or group) counseling effective? How successful are behavioral approaches? Such questions can remain relevant throughout the 1990s and beyond, especially if they are more focused or differentiated—for example, Which *kinds* of counseling or behavioral approaches work? And for whom? Nevertheless, researchers should now directly and systematically address questions such as, What combinations of components substantially contribute to success? The combinations that are studied should include not just the programmatic, such as particular types of family counseling and cognitive behavioral input, but also specified staff and staff-client interactions; settings and client differences should be examined as well. It is important to recognize clearly and address concretely the fact that, for example, a vocational training program is not *just* vocational training and a counseling program involves more than counseling, irrespective of the particular varieties (e.g., parent management training, guided group interaction) that might be described and regardless of where and to whom the program is applied.

Even partial answers regarding the nature of effective combinations can substantially reduce blanket responses to questions such as the above ("Is . . . counseling effective?")—responses that are far from precise and possibly, if inadvertently, misleading. This especially applies to sweeping assertions, such as "Counseling does not work"; "Probation enhancements do not work"; and "Behavioral approaches do work (or do not work)," with the typical implication that the stated outcome ("It works," "It does not work") is preponderantly or almost always the case or that the named approach is solely or very largely responsible for it. Answers or partial answers regarding the nature of effective combinations can thus reduce the chances of drawing premature, overstated, or overly generalized conclusions about various approaches and summarily dismissing, generally overlooking, or even inappropriately extolling them.

Caveats Regarding More and Less
Successful Programmatic Approaches

Given the considerations discussed above, it follows that the assessments presented earlier regarding numerous literature reviews and meta-analyses of respective programmatic approaches should themselves be considered valid in a restricted sense only. Those reviews of intervention effectiveness accurately delineated single *portions* of programs, that is, individual components that were a common denominator across given programs and were often associated with recidivism reduction or with a relative lack thereof. (The programs in question, for example, group counseling programs, had been grouped together *based* on that common denominator.) However, although those portions (also called distinguishing or salient features) may have been important and possibly even crucial with regard to recidivism, they might not have been decisive by themselves, and in some cases they may have added relatively little.[38] In any event, they may not have been the only factors that made a sizable contribution to success (or lack thereof).

Through the use of "combinations research," we may learn, for example, that the behavioral, the cognitive behavioral, or the family intervention approaches have shown considerable promise not only because—or not *mainly* because—their programs featured that particular component, and not even because they may often have included certain other less salient programmatic components, services, or activities. Instead, their relative success may have partly reflected the following, hypothesized fact (besides programs' overall relevance to client needs): Those approaches were implemented (or were more often implemented than were other approaches) under what might be broadly called "appropriate conditions"; in that respect, they were relatively *well* implemented. Key ingredients or constituents of those conditions may have been (a) certain staff characteristics and staff-client interactions, (b) differential intervention by type of offender, or (c) the use of particular settings. Combinations (i.e., "multiple-features") research may even show that diversion, group counseling, and other presently *less* promising approaches can be improved, if they too are implemented or more often implemented under such conditions. Still other conditions, for example, those involving caseload size and frequency of contact, may play a role as well.

Obviously, then, the conclusions we drew earlier regarding the more and the less successful or promising approaches could be misleading, unless they are carefully qualified and placed in a broader context, one that emphasizes the role of several programmatic and nonprogrammatic features and conditions combined. This is true even though the findings as well as conclusions in question (a) contain important kernels of truth, (b) are an integration of considerable information and a widening of perspective, and (c) provide leads for future research and programming. They provide information about correctional effectiveness that is more broadly based or reliable than before. Nevertheless, corrections researchers need to develop better information, information that is more complete and more likely to produce successful new programs.

Matching the Tool With the Task

To develop the needed information, one should use a tool, that is, an approach, that can be focused on, integrate, and reflect features (a) whose content can encompass the programmatic and nonprogrammatic, (b) whose analytic structure can range from the simple to the complex and from the individual to the combination, (c) that may be numerous,[39] and (d) some of which may exist during certain program phases only and may occur in a particular sequence only.[40] Researchers should be able to examine and interrelate many of the features as well as combinations of features that may play an important role in programs' often complex operations. Moreover, they should be able to do so without overly simplifying or greatly curtailing the content, structure, and so forth of the programs or depicting the programs in a highly abstract or very incomplete way. To be sure, some abstraction and representation is both unavoidable and desirable.

The global approach is a good choice for identifying, integrating, and representing features characterized by points (a) through (d), above. This especially applies to features that involve relatively lengthy combinations that may simultaneously cut across various content areas or that include a number of features within given areas. Though the global approach can produce detailed information about program inputs (features) commonly associated with unusually positive outputs (outcomes), it neither can nor must reflect almost every nuance and interaction.[41] As to meta-analysis, this approach can itself be focused on several features at once—features that collectively may encompass various content areas. Despite recent advances (Cook et al., 1992), however, this approach seems less useful than the global in identifying and integrating the complexities, patterns, and sequences that often characterize intervention (Palmer, 1994). It should therefore not be substituted for the latter. This is independent of the global approach's specific focus on guide and prominent programs—programs that meta-analysis neither emphasizes nor is limited to.

Closing Remarks

Knowledge about the frequency with which intervention works and does not work has rapidly advanced in recent years, mainly due to careful meta-analyses and detailed literature reviews. Together, these studies have helped change the atmosphere surrounding correctional intervention from one of widespread gloom and frequent indifference to one of considerable hope and interest. Nevertheless, progress in identifying *key ingredients* of successful programs has been relatively slow. This is partly because most analyses and reviews have been centered on whether intervention worked (more precisely, on how often it worked) and partly due to the particular analytic framework and tools that were used. (*Ingredients* is synonymous with features and combinations thereof.)

Because of the approach that has been used, even if the focus of effectiveness research was shifted from "whether" to "why," progress in identifying key ingredients would probably remain slow—certainly slower than necessary—if one continued to rely solely or even primarily on meta-analyses and literature reviews, and especially if one used an essentially unimodal framework. Moreover, important qualitative limitations would exist regarding the nature and scope of any progress, whatever its speed. To make faster and better progress in identifying key ingredients one needs a broader and more integrated analytic framework and tool than those used to date to determine whether intervention works and, if so, which "types" (broad program categories) are successful.

The framework and approach that are needed would give particular emphasis to programs as composites and often-complex wholes; at the same time, they would require program descriptions that are considerably more detailed and systematic than before. Whether brisk or moderate in pace, the needed progress would therefore call for altered directions and emphases and for new or added efforts. But then, what science that has continued to grow rather than plateau and that has avoided or overcome long periods of diminishing returns has not required change and effort—not to mention flexibility or creativity regarding concepts and methods?

To initiate the needed progress, a strong, first-time emphasis on multiple-features analysis is now needed, within and across the operations, staff, offender, and setting areas. Administrative and organizational factors and conditions should be examined as well. Given this emphasis and given a continuity of effort, in 10 to 15 years, corrections research can be in a far stronger position than it is today with regard to understanding scientifically how and why intervention works and how to create successful programs.

Appendix A

Regarding those results, the question arises, Are they based on the *same* individual studies or on *different* ones? More specifically, Did the group of meta-analysts and literature reviewers who assessed a given approach (e.g., vocational training) collectively examine mainly the same or different studies in connection with that approach? (On average, seven analysts or reviewers assessed any given approach.) This question is thus the extent to which identical studies were used by, and therefore copresent across, the different authors in their reviews and analyses. The answer is important for the following reason: Conclusions that one might draw about an approach's effectiveness or ineffectiveness that are based mainly on *identical* studies, that is, on repetitive evidence from one author to the next, would carry less scientific and practical weight (though not ipso facto *little* weight) than conclusions based mainly on *different* nonrepetitive studies and thus on converging evidence. (*Evidence* refers to the individual studies that make up a given approach—more specifically, to their identity or difference and thus to their "overlap" or "nonoverlap," from one author to the next, within a given approach. *Author* is synonymous with analyst or reviewer, or a/r.)

We addressed this question of study overlap by determining if the conclusions, inferences, or data displays provided by each a/r regarding any given approach involved largely the same individual studies or mainly different ones than those examined by each remaining a/r. For the large majority of approaches, we found that a/rs had not based their conclusions or inferences on evidence that when examined across those a/rs, turned out to involve mostly the same studies. Instead, they had mainly used what turned out to be converging evidence—that is, nonidentical (nonrepetitious) individual studies. Except for a few generic approaches (confrontation, physical challenge, vocational training, and educational training), differing rather than identical studies clearly dominated across the a/rs collectively. This partly reflected the different time periods, settings, and so on, that were studied.

This dominance of nonrepetitious studies was observed regarding virtually the entire spectrum of generic approaches—that is, whatever the degree of a/r-judged *effectiveness/*

ineffectiveness had been regarding the respective approaches. Also observed within that spectrum were all or nearly all approaches that consisted of the following (i.e., they composed it when *we* compared, collated, or integrated all the a/r judgments of effectiveness or ineffectiveness, plus the available recidivism rates or reductions, and available effect sizes, for all the approaches collectively): (a) only the five approaches that were the *most,* or the proportionately most often, successful or promising; (b) only the five approaches that were the *least,* or the proportionately least often, successful or promising (see the section, "Trends Regarding Effectiveness"). Moreover, by addressing the original question (Are the results based on the same or different studies?) from a different angle, a separate analysis indicated that most individual authors had reviewed no more than a moderate percentage of the studies examined by all the authors *collectively* in connection with any given approach. In short, an analysis based on an alternative framework but focused on the original question produced results that were very similar to those mentioned above.

Individually and collectively, the preceding set of results means that the generalizations that appear in the text regarding the effectiveness or ineffectiveness of various generic approaches can be considered stronger—better anchored or more broadly based—than they would have been if the various a/r assessments of those approaches had reflected mainly repetitive evidence (for details and specific quantitative findings, see Palmer, 1994).

Appendix B

Each of the former groups, when compared to each of the latter, had a considerably lower percentage of programs that showed (a) statistically superior performance ($p < .05$) for Es versus Cs, or (b) Es outperforming Cs by any amount, even short of $p < .05$. Moreover, such groups, respectively, have often been called ineffective or unsuccessful because (c) their E-programs collectively did not outperform their respective Cs fairly consistently (e.g., in at least two thirds of the individual programs that made up the respective groups)—they did not outperform them that often in terms of Success Criterion (a) or (b), above. Because several programs within a given group had a positive outcome in terms of (a) or (b) whereas several others had a "no difference" outcome ($E = C$) or even a negative outcome using those same criteria, the overall results for that group, collectively, were sometimes characterized as inconsistent. Implicitly or explicitly, some reviewers and analysts equated frequent inconsistency with lack of success for the overall group. (To be sure, even modest inconsistency reflected lack of absolutely guaranteed or even highly reliable success.) Obviously, even if two thirds of the studies of a given approach had been successful, one third would not have been successful, and considerable inconsistency or difference could then be said to have existed. If one then highlighted the fact of inconsistency and especially if success were required to occur almost all the time, the given approach might have been called unsuccessful, even though most programs had reduced recidivism (though not necessarily at the $p < .05$ level) and few if any had increased it.

Appendix C

The Role of Labels

Together, Items 1 through 3 reflect a fact or circumstance that needs to be increasingly recognized: Few if any *categories*—e.g., vocational training (VT) are programmatically unimodal—that is, consist of only one component, such as VT—even though their label (in this case VT) may suggest they are. That fact in turn reflects the virtual certainty that within most categories, only a minority or small minority of the *individual programs* that make up those respective categories are themselves unimodal. (*Unimodal, one dimensional,* and *single component* are synonymous. Again, *category* and *approach* are synonymous, and they are also identical to *generic approach* and *generic category.*)

In short, the following occurred regarding meta-analyses and most literature reviews to date: Rather than the respective *categories* being unimodal, a unimodal *label* was used to describe them. More specifically, a label (such as vocational training) had been used (a) as an abstraction for conceptualizing and more easily describing any given category (and ipso facto its constituent programs) and (b) as an analytic unit for statistically organizing, examining, and summarizing the given categories (and again their respective programs) more manageably and reliably. Thus, for any given category, the label that was used to distinguish a number of experimental programs from their controls had intentionally reflected one program component alone (e.g., vocational training); and that "number of . . . programs," when grouped and labeled, thus became a category or approach, in this case vocational training.

The Reality of Combinations

Often, to create a given experimental program physically, a specific component or element (e.g., vocational training) had simply been substituted for, or else added to, one in the traditional (i.e., the control) program.[42] That substitute or added component (vocational training) is the one that was then (i.e., later) likely to be used as a label, as it constituted a distinguishing component or feature (and in that sense was a "salient" feature or element). In short, the label conceptually and analytically distinguished the experimental (E) programs from their controls (Cs).[43] Yet the fact that one component *distinguished* an E-program from its C did not mean that the E—or, for that matter, the

C—literally and necessarily *contained* only one component[44] (*component, feature,* and *element* are synonymous). Instead, as indicated, experimental programs were usually combinations of approaches (i.e., each E-program involved more than one component or feature, not just, say, VT); and in reality, any given combination included components that may have been later (and elsewhere) used as labels for at least two generic categories (for instance, the combination may have consisted of any one of the following sets of components: VT and group counseling, VT and individual counseling, or VT plus one or more other components).

Some E-programs had been labeled vocational training not necessarily because they contained (a) much of it or (b) more of it than anything else,[45] but mainly because VT was a basis for (c) distinguishing those programs from the more traditional ones. Yet as indicated, many of those VT programs included other components as well—for example, a moderate amount of recreation, a small amount of group counseling, or perhaps one other element, whether or not in moderation.[46] (Vocational training, of course, has simply been used as an example; other components, or approaches, could have been used instead. For instance, components other than the distinguishing or salient one existed in programs and thus, in approaches, are labeled counseling or educational training, whether in connection with institutional or community settings. This also applied in programs labeled behavioral or cognitive behavioral,[47] and in those called probation enhancements and intensive probation. The latter two, for example, may have included not just increased contact and reporting but substance abuse counseling or life skills training.)

Unimodal labels notwithstanding, then, many E-programs that collectively made up a given generic category were themselves made up individually of combinations of components; and as mentioned earlier, these combinations often differed from one program to the next within the given category. In addition, meta-analyses and literature reviews already indicated that many individual programs within a given category were successful or promising, whereas many others were not. Moreover, successful and unsuccessful programs were found in every or almost every generic category (e.g., group counseling, vocational training, and the behavioral); and, as indicated, these individual programs typically contained more than one component.

It was with this backdrop that we hypothesized the following: For any generic category (e.g., vocational training or individual counseling) *only some combinations of components were effective* with a large portion of offenders who were involved in the category's respective programs. (Together, these components constituted individual programs.) This hypothesis implies that if a large proportion of the combinations of components that existed within a generic category were *not* especially effective, that overall category might well have been considered only moderately effective, because the overall category substantively was basically a direct reflection of the individual programs (i.e., of the programs' combinations of components). By the same token, the hypothesis implies that generic categories that were described as the most successful or promising were those that contained the highest proportion of effective combinations or at least the lowest proportion of ineffective ones. Yet even here, a category's *distinguishing* feature (e.g., vocational training) would not, by itself, have necessarily or entirely accounted for that category's relative promise, even though the feature may have often exerted more influence than others that were present.

In connection with promising *individual programs* grouped within a given category, we hypothesize that the programs' salient feature had operated in concert with other features, though not necessarily all others. Together, this group of features (i.e., the combination) had adequately or fairly adequately addressed delinquency-related needs of the respective offender samples; at least, it did so to a greater extent than did (a) the control programs' combinations and (b) the combinations that existed in less successful or promising (S/P) experimental programs. Insofar as that is true, it follows that each category's (not just each program's) salient feature (e.g., vocational training) operated not alone but in a context that involved various components. For S/P categories (and thus for their more-S/P *programs*), this combination of components was more relevant or more often relevant to offenders than was the combination that operated for non-S/P programs—programs that, to be sure, may have had the same salient feature. This is apart from the fact that nonprogrammatic features, such as staff characteristics and various types of staff-offender interactions, probably contributed to program outcome themselves.

Appendix D

Researchers should increasingly attend to a core of standard or benchmark items, each of which may bear on various aspects of client adjustment and development. These items would involve information in at least four areas—operations, staff, offender, and setting—and organizational or administrative features might constitute a fifth. Whenever opportunity allows, items such as the following would be collected, examined, and described.[48]

I. Operations

A. Formal Aspects

Basis of case assignment (geographic, available case opening or living unit space, person match, program match, other); offender-staff ratio or caseload size; living unit size; extent of initial diagnostic workup; direct intervention-centered contacts (frequency, number, total hours, total duration); collateral contacts (frequency, number, total hours, etc.); number of intervention approaches or modalities; quantitatively salient or dominant intervention(s) or combination (e.g., individual counseling and educational training); programmatically, operationally, or dynamically central or dominant intervention(s) or combination; supervision of staff (type, amount); postprogram or postdischarge contacts.

B. General Features

1. Approaches, Modalities, and Intervention Patterns

Confrontation, areawide strategy of delinquency prevention, social casework, social agency, or societal institution approach to delinquency prevention, diversion, physical challenge, restitution, group counseling or therapy, individual counseling or therapy, family intervention, vocational training, employment, educational training, behavioral, cognitive behavioral or cognitive, life skills (skill oriented, skill development), multimodal, probation and parole enhancement, intensive probation supervision, intensive aftercare (parole) supervision, standard probation supervision, standard aftercare (parole) supervision, milieu intervention, work release, recreation and cultural enrichment, involvement in community activities, advocacy and legal assistance, crisis intervention, medical approaches (specified), imprisonment or institutionalization, coeducational or noncoeducational, other components or activities (family assistance, referral to other agencies, work assignments, day passes, furloughs, other).

2. Orientations and Schools

Eclectic, rational-emotive, reality therapy, existential, transactional analysis, Gestalt, behavior modification, analytic (neo-Freudian), I-level, conceptual level, differential association, general theory, habilitation or developmental, integrated theory, social bonding, social learning, subcultural deviance, subcultural strain (blocked opportunity), other (specified).

C. Specific Features

1. Goals and Areas of Focus

Enhancing or promoting a nondelinquent or noncriminal self-image, modifying attitudes toward adults or establishment, teaching values and controls, increasing self-awareness and self-acceptance, reducing illegal behavior, reducing apathy and indifference, improving or altering family and parental relationships, altering peer influence and pressure, everyday practical adjustment, client-worker relationship, other.

2. Processes and Lines of Approach

Gaining client's confidence in worker as understanding or capable, expressing personal concern for and acceptance of client, exposure to masculine (feminine) adult models, "programming/rehearsing client for specific life situations," ego bolstering via success experiences, using positive peer influence, using authority (legitimate power or force), using internal stress as stimulus or motivator, doing the unexpected, client's participation in case planning and decision making, concreteness versus abstractness of verbalizations and interpretations, other.

II. Staff

A. Background Characteristics

Age, gender, ethnicity, amount of training, type of training, amount of experience, type of experience, work status (professional, paraprofessional, volunteer, other).

B. Personal Characteristics

Strength of feelings, expressions, and opinions; sharpness or alertness; criticalness; past personal difficulties, felt as such; satisfaction with own work and accomplishments; socially desired qualities; socially undesirable qualities; aggression or hostility; other.

C. Treatment Orientations

A type versus B type, instrumental versus expressive, relationship/self-expression or surveillance/self-expression or surveillance/self-control (Palmer, 1965), I_2 or Cfm or Mp-Cfc, or Na or Nx worker (I-level system; Warren, 1971), other classifications, general factors (orientation toward change and activity, use of own past experiences as primary basis for working with others, other).

III. Offenders

A. Background Characteristics

Age, gender, offense history, base expectancy (or standardized risk score or level), IQ, grade level attained, school status at intake, work history, work status at intake, marital status, parental status (client's parents, client as parent), residence (urban, semiurban, rural), neighborhood (high, medium, low delinquency), socioeconomic status, ethnicity.

B. Personal Characteristics

Developmental level (interpersonal, psychosocial, moral, ego, conceptual, and/or other), classification or personality type (Warren, Quay, Schrag, Megargee, other); trait clusters: communicative or alert, passive or uncertain, defiant, indifferent, alienated, dependent, independent, other (Palmer); specific factors or generic variables (cognitive complexity, locus of control, internalized standards, affect awareness, impulse control, planfulness or foresight, persistence, rigidity or inflexibility, social consciousness, other) (Gibbons, 1965; Hunt, 1971; Kohlberg, 1976; Megargee & Bohn, 1979; Palmer, 1965; Quay, 1984; Schrag, 1971; Warren, 1971).

IV. Setting

A. Formal Aspects

Jurisdiction and sponsorship (justice system; nonjustice system, public; nonjustice system, private; other), size (offender population), physical condition (age, upkeep, space), adequacy of services (food, clothes, medical, other), level of physical security, accessibility to community.

B. Type

Adult prison or youth institution; jail; camp, ranch, farm; halfway house; day care center; other community center (specified); group home; free community (natural setting, e.g., family, relatives, independent placement); management and decision-making styles; social climate dimensions (Moos, 1975); homogeneous offender grouping (e.g., by Quay types) versus nonhomogeneous grouping; coeducational versus noncoeducational (Moos, 1975; Quay, 1964).

Notes

1. The median number of studies was 75. Lipsey's (1992) analysis, which included more than 400 individual studies, is the broadest and most systematic to date.

2. Such an overview would also contain less by way of average "measurement error" regarding program effectiveness. In any given literature review, this measurement problem would reflect, for example, an accumulation of (a) errors whose size is often small to moderate, and/or (b) random fluctuations. These inevitably occur when researchers try to measure or estimate the

"true" recidivism rate associated with any individual program. To some degree, this problem also exists in large-scale meta-analyses that focus on many such programs.

3. In any one analysis or review, the limitations (regarding conclusions or generalizations) that reflected or should have reflected various emphases or even exclusions were sometimes large. This applied not just to (a) individual studies that made up the analyses and reviews but also to (b) certain characteristics of the offenders covered in those studies. The latter emphases or exclusions generally resulted from responses by decision makers—for example, agency administrators, program planners, or managers—as to the nature and seriousness of given individuals' offenses or to the apparent extent of their social or psychological difficulties. Nevertheless, in most reviews and analyses, the approximately 45 to 90 studies that were examined collectively contained a wide range of offenders. As a result, most types of offenders seemed to be reasonably well represented in most reviews and analyses, even though the less common individuals may still have been quite infrequent or virtually absent, particularly in connection with certain interventions (approaches). The limitations in question existed whether the given review or analysis focused on a range of interventions—for example, counseling, vocational training, and cognitive behavioral—together or on one intervention alone.

4. One correctional meta-analysis we knowingly excluded was conducted in Western Europe on adults and involved only 16 studies (Losel & Koferl, 1989). The only other meta-analysis not included in our review of results involved 20 studies of preadjudicated, at-risk youths only (Kaufman, 1985).

5. In the results presented below, Gottschalk et al.'s (1987) analysis will be used instead of Davidson et al.'s (1984) work not only because the two were very similar as to the studies they examined and the methods they used, but also because Gottschalk et al.'s (1987) investigation was more detailed in some respects. Johns and Wallach (1981) expanded on Wright and Dixon (1977), which covered 1969 through 1974.

6. Though shock probation is often called *split sentence,* these subcategories sometimes differ from each other. In addition, both such categories can be distinguished from *shock incarceration*—a somewhat newer intervention, to which the above findings do not refer (Parent, 1989; Parisi, 1980; Vito, 1984).

7. This relatively straight-line relationship also exists whether one uses, as a *baseline,* a control or traditional program recidivism rate that is 40%, 50%, or even 60%. The straight-line relationship disappears, however, when, for example, one's control or traditional baseline drops well *below* 40%, especially when one's ES is .40 or more (Cohen, 1988, p. 181).

8. An earlier account (Palmer, 1991) stated that "probation and parole enhancements had no positive impact, *nor did broadly labeled approaches such as counseling and skill-oriented programs*" (p. 335, emphasis added). The italicized statement is incorrect, however. It was based on preliminary information only (Lipsey, 1989) and did not reflect findings in Lipsey's final report (Lipsey, 1992). That report indicates (a) skill-oriented programs were, on average, successful; and (b) particular forms of counseling produced—again, on average—slight to moderate recidivism reductions. Both (a) and (b) applied to justice and nonjustice system programs combined.

9. Lipsey (1992) analyzed "reduced caseload" programs and "intensive supervision" programs together and referred to them generically as "probation/parole reduced caseloads."

10. These figures were the unweighted averages of all 270 separate juvenile delinquency studies that were reported collectively in 14 of the 32 meta-analyses and literature reviews. These 14 constituted all analyses and reviews—from among the 32—in which statistical significance was either routinely reported or was derivable from the numbers presented, for example, from sample sizes and recidivism rates. This substudy was conducted by the author as part of the present overview.

11. Although an earlier analysis (Palmer, 1991) had included vocational training (VT) among the "most successful approaches," it would have been more accurate to use the "life skills or skill oriented" category instead. Though VT had usually been included *within* the skills category—this being a considerably broader and, indeed, a relatively successful or promising category—VT was not, by itself, among the generally successful, let alone the most successful, approaches.

12. This is apart from the fact that many individual programs in the vocational training category themselves included group-counseling activities.

13. This does not preclude effectiveness for unimodal—that is, single- rather than multicomponent—programs that may in fact have existed relative to the given category.

14. The 33%, of course, may have been partly accounted for by unimodals. In any event, it applied to all generic categories combined, not necessarily to any one in particular. For purposes of illustration, we are applying it to any given category—for example, the group counseling approach.

15. Some combinations may have been relevant and adequate but not to a significantly greater or lesser degree than their control program. In any event, they may not have been relevant to as large a proportion of the client sample as were the more successful combinations.

16. A paucity of knowledge also exists not only regarding the particular emphasis that has been given to any one feature—say, any one component, compared to others—but also regarding the sequencing of various features in relation to each other. Such a paucity also exists with respect to the relative contributions those features have made to success.

17. To be sure, it is not known for certain if the effectiveness of any given program (e.g., CREST; Lee & Haynes, 1980) was largely accounted for by (a) a particular *subset* of the various features mentioned above or (b) either that same subset or a different one in combination with other *types* of factors (staff characteristics, staff-client interactions, or intervention strategies and techniques). We believe (b) applies. In addition, the content of the given combination varied somewhat for different types of clients, as did the relative weight of its components.

18. Of the last two programs, one focused mainly on adults and the other exclusively on them.

19. *Skill/Capacity Deficits:* Various—often major—developmental challenges, frequently including deficits in life and social skills, such as educational and vocational deficiencies. *External Pressures or Disadvantages:* Major environmental pressures or stresses, or major social disadvantages, also including comparatively limited or reduced family, community, and other supports or social assistance. *Internal Difficulties:* Long-standing or situational feelings, attitudes, and defenses; ambivalence regarding change; particular motivations, desires, and personal and interpersonal commitments (Palmer, 1992).

20. We assume that more than one effective combination exists in connection with the many E-programs studied to date.

21. Such studies of combinations would be complicated by the following (which is a hypothesis): What sometimes contributed to the absence of an E/C recidivism difference was the fact that certain features that should have been present in an E-program were either absent or, when indeed present, were insufficiently or inadequately used in addressing critical though not always obvious needs. This could have occurred even in otherwise sophisticated and well-implemented programs.

22. As implied earlier, more than one such target area may have to be appropriately and sufficiently addressed to help many individuals substantially improve their coping skills and adjustment techniques, change their attitudes toward others and their interactions with them, or modify their self-image and increase their self-understanding. This personal growth and internal change could often provide considerable public protection in the long run. Because such advances would increase the individuals' internal controls, they would be particularly relevant to commu-

nity-based programs (in which the incapacitation factor is absent), whether or not strong *external* (supervisory) controls exist.

23. CTP was a large, multiphase, multiyear, well-implemented and well-matched, random assignment study of serious repeat offenders in an intensive, rehabilitation-centered, in-lieu-of-institutionalization program that operated in one large and two medium-sized California cities. It was operated by the California Youth Authority and researched via National Institute of Mental Health funds (Palmer, 1974; Warren, 1971).

24. Several of these and other factors were originally singled out after the first 7 years of this 12-year project. Among them were, "a. Matching of specific types of clients [offenders] with certain types of workers [agents]. b. Level of ability and perceptiveness of workers. c. Intensive and/or extensive intervention by workers with regard to several areas of the client's life—made possible by low caseload assignments. d. Emphasis on the working through of the worker/ward relationship as a major vehicle of treatment" (Palmer, Neto, Johns, Turner, & Pearson, 1968, p. viii).

Personality characteristics and professional orientations were specified by Palmer (1967), and guidelines plus intervention techniques were later provided by Palmer and Grenny (1971). These guidelines and techniques were major extensions—in some cases, modifications—of carefully field-tested approaches that had already been described by Warren et al. (1966). After the early 1970s, the CTP offender classifications and intervention guidelines were incorporated, albeit in simplified and somewhat modified form, in the Wisconsin and (soon thereafter) the National Institute of Corrections's client management classification (CMC) system and treatment prescriptions (Arling & Lerner, 1981).

25. This Ottawa, Ontario, study involved random assignment of adolescent and adult probationers to either regular probation officers or citizen volunteers. Of the probationers, about 80% were males, 56% were 16 to 19 years old, and 33% were 20 to 29 (Andrews & Kiessling, 1980).

26. Regarding particular "types" of youth within CTP's overall sample,

> Among "conflicted" youths, those described as "neurotic, acting-out" (with little felt-anxiety) performed better when assigned to matched parole agents [those specifically matched with the "acting-out" youths, not just matched, skilled, and/or sensitive in general] than to all remaining agents, combined [the latter being skilled, sensitive, etc., but only matched to one or more *other* subgroups and not specifically matched to "neurotic, acting-out" youths]. . . . Similarly, among "power oriented" youths, those described as "manipulators" performed better with matched agents [i.e., agents specifically matched to power oriented youths] while those called "subcultural conformists" [e.g., gang-involved youths who want to consider themselves delinquent] did not. (Palmer, 1975, p. 148)

27. Although the various combinations can have greater or lesser positive impact on differing offenders, this does not mean the particular combinations that have *lesser* impact ipso facto have *little* impact per se and therefore little relevance to the given offenders. They sometimes do, however, have little positive impact.

28. Naturally, no individuals literally had 1,000 months on parole. 1,000 is simply a time-standardized amount that involves a multiplier, and it is used strictly for ease of presentation. The actual numbers (still standardized regarding follow-up period) are 0.34 arrests per 10 months for Es and 0.55 for Cs.

29. To distinguish structurally those formal aspects from the program components reviewed on pages 135-146, those components (e.g., vocational training) could be thought of as general

features. The distinction in question would be viable despite the fact that "general features" would also include *additional* approaches and modalities (e.g., work release; recreation and cultural enrichment; involvement in community activities; advocacy and legal assistance; crisis intervention).

30. "Goals and areas of focus" is sometimes called "strategies or techniques"; "processes and lines of approach" is also called "specific processes and methods."

31. The view that a program is a "functional entity" and the fact that its several features *coexist* (simultaneously or successively) does not automatically mean that all those features actively (let alone positively) *interact* with each other, closely, efficiently, or at all. Because some degree of interaction (e.g., in the sense of jointly contributing to an outcome) is probably quite common and may even be the rule, however, interaction is emphasized in the global approach.

32. A hypothetical example of, say, three such features might be the following: First, a certain behavioral (or perhaps cognitive behavioral or individual counseling) approach; second, a particular restitution approach; and third, a particular type of staff member (or perhaps staff-client relationship). Though *each* of these three features (independently of the others) might be associated with a successful program or sets of programs, those individual features might not be particularly compatible. In any case, they might not, by themselves, be the key to the respective program's or programs' success (see Item 2 in the text). This would apply whether or not those programs targeted the same offenders and settings.

33. When E-programs outperformed their Cs by any amount, however small, the average recidivism reduction was 17% to 22%. When *all* E- and C-programs were examined, not just those in which Es outperformed Cs, the average reduction was 10% to 12% (Palmer, 1991).

34. Guide programs would, of course, include all prominent ones. Presently, guides probably make up a small portion, perhaps 15%, of all experimental studies whose Es outperformed their Cs by any amount (including, as in Note 33, "amounts"—E/C differences—that did not reach $p < .05$). Because this estimated portion is an overall average, differing portions—some higher, some lower—undoubtedly exist across the several "types" of programs (e.g., the cognitive behavioral and the confrontational).

35. To increase the initial benefit from global approach research, the various guide or prominent programs that are selected should mainly focus, collectively, on similar offenders and, if possible, similar settings, such as first- or second-time juvenile offenders, on probation (see Step 1). In later research efforts, the targets might be more varied.

36. The "most-such programs" standard implies the following: The global approach does not require that an individual feature (or group of features) "pass" a standard statistical test—for example, $p < .05$—before it can be viewed, say, as "reliably shared" (or otherwise "sufficiently shared") and appropriate for certain purposes. Instead, this approach depends on convergence of evidence or accumulation of instances. The fact that the global approach involves only *guide or prominent* programs—operations in which the E/C performance difference is already large—helps compensate for the further fact that at present this approach would generally have to focus on a fairly small number of programs. In effect, Step 2 produces higher built-in reliability than would otherwise exist—that is, "noise" is substantially reduced at the start (though not, of course, eliminated). Because sharp E/C differences are required by virtue of Step 2, information regarding each program can carry more weight than it would if a more typical range of differences were involved. Partly for this reason, the global approach can produce good to excellent findings, even though it cannot, or can only seldom, provide essentially ironclad results. Strong findings can ordinarily suffice with respect to program planning or improvement, even though indisputable evidence would be preferred.

37. It is reasonable to assume that features that are repeated across a number of successful programs and are in that sense "shared" by them are probably much more likely to be positive than negative or even just superfluous. When features from several such programs are compared with each other (as in Step 4), this may largely filter out the negative and perhaps most of the superfluous features that might have existed in any one or two programs—features that could therefore have been recorded in Step 3. (Given their strong *positive* features, many programs can function reasonably well—sometimes very well—despite the presence of certain negative and superfluous features. Even those programs would undoubtedly perform better without the negatives, however; and they would likely be more efficient, not to mention more cost-effective, absent the superfluous features.)

38. Being a crucial or even an essential ingredient (e.g., a sine qua non) is one thing, and in fact there may be several such features. Being "largely responsible" for a given outcome, however—that is, being the dominant or predominant factor—may be a different matter and one difficult to prove.

39. That is, a large number of *differing* features may exist, and because they are potentially important contributors to outcome, they should each be considered in the analysis.

40. All items apply collectively: Items (a) and (b) apply across features and within and across programs. Item (c) applies especially, but not exclusively, across programs; and item (d) applies within programs.

41. As described in this chapter, the global approach depends on guide or prominent programs, and these programs will almost certainly have been well implemented. Nevertheless, any program can be examined globally, whatever its level of success and implementation.

42. Not uncommonly, the experimental and control (or comparison) programs differed not just in one but in several respects. To simplify this presentation, however, we will emphasize the former situation.

43. It was used to reflect the E-programs' overtly salient feature, whether or not that feature was also quantitatively dominant. Such usage directly accounted for the unimodal—that is, the single-component—descriptions that have characterized meta-analyses and most literature reviews to date.

44. In some cases, traditional programs may have lacked the distinguishing component entirely. In other instances, their difference from Es regarding that component may have only been one of degree—albeit a substantial degree, for example, as in many probation enhancement programs. Yet whether the difference involved type or degree, many Es and Cs each contained still other elements.

45. To be sure, they *may* have contained a lot of it or more of it than anything else.

46. Some or all of the latter, nonsalient components may often have been considered too routine—and perhaps also part of the C-program—to have been focused on or otherwise singled out in various program descriptions. Through the years, most program descriptions have in fact been sketchy in this regard.

47. Moreover, it applied regardless of what the primary focus or vehicles of those behavioral or cognitive behavioral programs may have been—for example educational achievement or discussion group.

48. Each area contains two or more subdivisions—for example Area 1 (operations), Subdivisions A, B, and C. Across the four areas, there are 10 subdivisions in all. In areas I-A, II-A, III-A, and IV-A, all items are mutually exclusive. Within these areas, separate information would therefore be needed on all items or on as many as possible. In other areas, say, I-B and the first section of IV-B, all items make up a single set of alternative choices. Within these areas,

information would be collected on only the particular item(s) describing the program or setting in question. (For further details, see Palmer, 1978, 1994.) In most studies, individual researchers would be unable to gather information on most items from all 10 subdivisions collectively. They might be able, however, to do so with many subdivisions individually. This applies even though the list is not exhaustive, particularly in areas I-C, II-B, and II-C.

Developing Community Corrections

An Implementation Perspective

Philip Harris
Stephen Smith

We have all heard the messages of failure in corrections: Treatment does not work; reform efforts only make matters worse; and community corrections has widened significantly the net of social control, resulting in more punishment at greater cost. Unfortunately, these claims are sometimes true. Fortunately, they are not *always* true. We take the position that the primary cause of failure and success rests with the ways in which policies and programs have been implemented. We agree with Walter Williams (1976), who nearly two decades ago argued that "lack of concern for implementation is currently *the* crucial impediment to improving complex operating programs, policy analysis and experimentation" (p. 267).

To develop a useful perspective on implementation we need to begin by exploring the meaning of the term *implementation*. Implementation is not simply the event during which a policy is put into effect or a program design is put into action; rather, *implementation includes a process of mutual adaptation between the vision and goals of those who initiate development or adoption of an innovation and the organizational or system environments in which the innovation is applied.* This component of our definition builds on the notion of implementation as "mutual adaptation," introduced by Berman and McLaughlin (1975), in which they emphasize the mutual reshaping of an innovation and its organizational setting over the life of the innovation. We have added the element of persons to the definition, recognizing that implementation involves commitment, negotiation, and sometimes faith. Putting together the concepts of enacting a program design and allowing the design to take shape through mutual adaptation, we can define *implementation* as a *process of interaction between program innovators, organizational administrators, external stakeholders, and line staff through which a program design and its organizational and political environments adapt to each other to meet the needs that stimulated development or adoption of the program design.*

The need to focus on implementation has two components: (a) the need to know whether or not a program or policy works and (b) the need to find ways to maximize the potential of an innovation. The first of these needs emerges from an observer or evaluator perspective. The second is a need of the innovator or proponent of an innovation—the individuals or groups that have a stake in the innovation's effectiveness.

On the basis of judgments made about the effectiveness or usefulness of a program, replication or abandonment decisions are made. Every innovation design lays out relationships between a set of changes in the way business is done, on one hand, and a set of objectives, on the other. To determine whether or not the design has merit, we must know whether or not the enacted design is the same as the conceptualized design. Failure of a program to achieve its objectives may have little or nothing to do with the program's design but may instead be due to inadequate implementation. Unless we can appraise the program's implementation, we may never know the difference (see Kelling, Edwards, & Moore, 1986; MacKenzie, Shaw, & Gowdy, 1990). Furthermore, conclusions regarding the potential effectiveness of an innovation cannot be regarded as valid unless adequate testing of its underlying assumptions has occurred.

What evaluators frequently argue is that the extent and manner of implementation affects the innovation's impact, perhaps to a greater extent than the innovation itself (see, e.g., Palumbo, Musheno, & Maynard-Moody, 1984). The evaluations reviewed by Byrne, Lurigio, and Baird (1989) of intensive supervision probation and parole programs in Georgia, New Jersey, and Massachusetts underscore the value of assessing extent of implementation. Of particular interest is the evaluation of an Intensive Supervision Program (ISP) program operated in 13 sites throughout the state of Massachusetts. This multisite effort provided a forum for comparing the degree of implementation on a site-by-site basis. The evaluators (Byrne & Kelly, 1989) created a "degree of implementation" scale and with it examined program variation in outcome. They found an inverse relationship between program implementation and offender recidivism; in other words, the more fully the intensive probation supervision (IPS) program was implemented, the more likely recidivism "decreased significantly across a range of alternative outcome measures" (Byrne et al., 1989, p. 35).

Unfortunately, evaluators in the area of community corrections rarely supply details regarding the implementation process. Although it is important to asses the extent to which a program design is implemented and although information on correlates of successful implementation provides important guides for assessing a system's readiness for innovation, what is often needed by people in the field is the sharing of knowledge about how these things came about.

The second need to focus on implementation—to find ways to maximize the potential of an innovation—can be attached to the perspective of persons or groups who have a stake in the success of the innovation. Their concerns are twofold: (a) that the environmental conditions that interact with the program design are as close to the ideal as possible and (b) that the program design is logical, feasible, and relevant to the needs of the system. Much like the gardener who tills a plot of land; removes the weeds; tests the soil and adds lime or fertilizer to correct the pH balance; and continues to weed, fertilize, and water after planting, innovators recognize the need to attend to environmental conditions that can affect program outcomes, beginning well before the program is put into action and continuing as long as program development is desired.

In this chapter, we focus on this second set of needs by identifying process principles and best practices associated with implementing community correctional policies and programs. We do not differentiate the implementation problems associated with policy implementation from those associated with program implementation. We have found that in the community corrections literature, programs—in particular program technologies—have been the focus of evaluation. It would be more accurate to conclude, however, that community corrections programs can emerge within the context of policy development or, conversely, independent of any change in policy. Although we rarely make direct reference to the interaction between policy and program, our references to the need for clarity at the level of mission and vision, derived from an organizational perspective, imply that program implementation is most likely to be successful if it occurs in concert with implementation of policy.

The Implementation Context of Community Corrections

Viewing community corrections from an implementation perspective results in a much different assessment of the field than using a policy or philosophical perspective. An implementation perspective focuses attention on the content of policies and programs only insofar as they affect the process of acceptance, adoption, and use. From this perspective, we are more interested in concepts such as negotiation, marketing strategies, information systems, and commitment than we are in specific technologies of community corrections, such as restitution, home confinement, or intensive supervision probation. For example, the shifts in terminology from "alternatives to incarceration" to "intermediate sanctions" to "intermediate punishments" may have meaning from the perspective of correctional philosophy, but from an implementation perspective, the newer labels imply both a response to marketing information and a desire to be clearer about the purposes of suggested innovations.

An account of the recent history of community corrections is useful to understanding the dilemmas of implementation. Most previous accounts have not taken an implementation perspective (see, e.g., Corbett & Marx, 1992) but, instead, have focused on philosophical shifts. A reconstruction of this history underscores the fact that the development of community corrections has been largely reactive: a reaction against imprisonment.

The 1970s have been identified as a period in which rehabilitation was dealt a near-fatal blow: A conclusion that rehabilitation failed to affect criminal behavior was widely disseminated, producing a shift in sentencing and correctional objectives toward retributive aims. The liberal agenda, a reaction against the abuses of intrusive treatment programs combined with indeterminate sentences, centered on procedural fairness and rights of the accused. Conservatives took advantage of the message that treatment does not work to build support for the more punitive aims of the system. Like many, more recent reformers, they argued that their reforms would result in less imprisonment. Instead, we saw a growth in prison use and consequently in available prison space.

The greatest irony of this period for corrections is that the perceived failure of rehabilitation appears to have been a failure of implementation. For Ted

Palmer (1975, 1992), the problem was one of simplistic evaluation methods: A more careful analysis showed that different categories of youths benefited from different treatment approaches. Others have argued that implementation was often faulty and that fidelity to the program design rarely occurred (Quay, 1977). This last argument, the failure to exploit our knowledge of rehabilitative approaches, is echoed by Jerome Miller (1986):

> One might conclude we went through a great renaissance in corrections in the 1960's in the United States—characterized by massive infusions of funds into rehabilitative programs, psychoanalysis, psychotherapy, intensive treatment programs, etc. This of course is a great myth. The language of rehabilitation was popular—the reality was virtually nil. (p. 231)

As prison populations grew, liberals began to emphasize the problems of prison crowding and the high cost of incarceration. Sentencing reform in the form of sentencing guidelines and mandatory sentences proliferated, as did arguments in favor of alternatives to incarceration for nonviolent offenders. The conservative agenda, well entrenched during the entire decade of the 1980s, was saved by the war on drugs and the wave of violence ushered in by the growth of illegal drug markets. The number of prisons and prison populations continued to grow. Ironically, alternative community-based approaches often backfired, resulting in stronger and larger nets of social control.

Given the failure of the alternatives approach to stem the tide of prison construction, liberals revised the semantics of their arguments and began using a term believed to be more compatible with existing correctional policies—*intermediate sanctions*—to describe community approaches. The strategy and goal accompanying this new term was to build a range of sanctions between probation and prison, based on a belief that the presence of options linked proportionally to offenses would reduce the number of offenders sentenced to prison. This message was given a significant boost by the more recent development of the term and accompanying equivalency arguments of *intermediate punishments* (Morris & Tonry, 1990). Although prison construction continues, even in the face of horrendous budget cuts in education, health, and social services, there is growing interest in intermediate punishments as a strategy to control the cost of corrections.

From an implementation perspective, however, the problem over the past two decades for those seeking to reduce U.S. dependency on imprisonment has been reliance on strategies that are based on a reaction against something,

namely prisons. Consider the following quote from the National Advisory
Commission on Criminal Justice Standards and Goals (1973):

> A basic principle underlying the philosophy of community-based corrections is
> that all efforts consistent with the safety of others should be made to reduce
> involvement of the individual offender with the institutional aspects of correc-
> tions. The alienation and dehumanization engendered in jails, workhouses, pris-
> ons, and even probation services, is to be avoided wherever possible. (p. 232)

It was suspected that some of the more vocal spokespersons for the alternatives movement did not approve of the use of prisons at all. No doubt that
suspicion was widely shared (Smith, 1982), and so the notion of alternatives
became the equivalent of being soft on criminals, of not caring about public
safety, and of being opposed to punishment.

Reactive strategies are inherently weak but are especially counterproductive when opposing forces are well entrenched. Given the fact that goals such
as public safety and retribution are more clearly attached to imprisonment
than to "alternatives" to incarceration, the "alternatives" strategy could not
have overcome the trend toward greater use of prison. Proponents of community corrections, however, built their strategies on negative reactions to
imprisonment, the form of punishment around which all other forms revolve,
at least in this country. Unfortunately this reactive view cannot be translated
into a comprehensive picture of corrections around which key system actors
can rally. Consequently, community corrections was always vulnerable to
whatever philosophy dominated the existing system. Co-optation has been the
rule, not the exception.

As an example, home confinement was first introduced as an alternative to
incarceration as a way of "avoiding the psychological destructiveness of
incarceration, allowing the use of community treatment resources, avoiding
the severing of family and community ties, and maintaining adequate control
of offenders without the expense of incarceration" (Renzema, 1992b, p. 46.)
Acceptability of this innovation necessitated a shift in goals from a benevolent
alternative to incarceration to an alternative form of punishment. According
to Renzema (1992b), its use has been linked most frequently to the goal of
reducing jail crowding. Even when attached to electronic monitoring, however, home confinement as implemented has not been shown to have increased
the imposition of prison caps, prevented prison construction, or increased
community safety.

Although adopted to reduce the flow of offenders to prison, the use of home confinement has more often been to increase the level of punishment for less serious offenders. Renzema (1992b) even goes so far as to argue that home confinement plus electronic monitoring, as with other forms of community correction, could be used to serve a rehabilitative aim, but typically the duration has been insufficient and pattern of use unrelated to behavior of the offender (Gendreau & Ross, 1979, 1987; Renzema, 1992b, p. 50).

We conclude that these technologies of community corrections have been implemented in a vision vacuum and that a more comprehensive view of the potential effects of home confinement and its relationship to the larger mission of corrections might have produced a more complex and worthwhile application. Certainly, the goal of incapacitation could be well served alongside a program designed to reinforce specific desired behaviors. Whether this combination of goals is desirable is quite another matter.

Community Corrections, Reactive Planning, and the Need for Vision

From one perspective, community corrections can be regarded as a conglomeration of fads—of technologies that have proliferated without any reason other than a need to relieve our crowded prison systems (Byrne & Pattavina, 1992; Cochran, 1992). One significant consequence of this growth in community corrections technologies has been a greater acceptance of the concept of community corrections. As a means of reducing prison populations we have witnessed little success, but the range of options is growing, as is familiarity with the different forms they can take. Unfortunately, we know little about the effectiveness of newer forms of community corrections approaches or intermediate sanctions. Their proliferation appears to be driven by considerations other than those for which they were originally intended.

Growth of interest in community corrections programs has had nothing to do with knowledge of program effectiveness. Byrne and Pattavina (1992) express surprise at the growth in the use of boot camps, absent evidence of their effectiveness. At the same time, they advocate continued proliferation, arguing that the crises of prison overcrowding and the cost of incarceration require communities to "do something." This need to do something is clearly reactive; even if evaluations find modest successes, we will have lost the battle unless we can express and become energized by knowing what it is we want.

Ellickson and Petersilia (1983) observe the superiority of planning strategies that are proactive or adaptive over those that are reactive. Reactive, or crisis-oriented, strategies are typically narrow in focus and endanger other programs that may be useful to the system. Even broadly focused efforts to develop a range of community corrections programs within a community corrections policy can fail to bring about significant change in the sanctioning of offenders if a comprehensive revision of the system's mission and vision are not undertaken first. In several sections of this chapter, we use the developments of Georgia's community corrections programs as examples of good implementation practices. Yet during the time these developments took place, Georgia's prison population continued to rise. The inability of the Georgia Department of Corrections to capitalize on its successes and argue for keeping a more risky portion of the offender population in its community corrections programs speaks to the absence of a systemwide vision.

Delaware officials, on the other hand, have implemented a comprehensive sanctioning system with levels of sanctions and a means for addressing offender behavior and offender needs simultaneously. Its sentencing accountability guidelines incorporate discretion regarding stepping up or down the original sanctions, depending on offender behavior. As Governor Michael Castle (1991) reports, Delaware began the process of responding to a prison crisis by developing consensus among key groups and stakeholders that the current system was a failure. Once this was agreed to, it was easier to begin planning a new model of corrections. The process was not one of placing blame; rather, it was one of developing an idealized design. The result of this process was development of a new correctional philosophy expressed in terms of prioritized goals.

In Delaware, the second phase of implementation was the creation, by means of legislation, of the Sentencing Accountability Commission (SENTAC). This commission conducted debates and discussions among a wide range of constituent groups, identified goals of these constituents, developed plans that incorporated these goals, and then brought the process back to a centralized planning group for refinement. The resulting system of sanctions has widespread support, flows from clear statements of vision and mission, and provides a wide array of services to offenders within a range of levels of supervision.

The need to begin with a vision and plan backward cannot be overemphasized. *Without a clear sense of what we want, we have no way of assessing what we have.* Theorists express this notion of an ideal in different ways,

Ackoff (1984) speaks of idealized designs, Lippitt (1983) speaks of preferred futuring, Elmore (1982) and Redlinger and Shanahan (1986) advocate backward mapping, and Weisbord (1992) speaks of ideal futures, but the idea is the same. *What would your correctional system look like if you could design it from scratch?* Once we have consensus on this question, planning has direction.

The rush to adopt new innovations, however, often occurs without adequate planning, thus leading to a lack of commitment, particularly at the direct service level, and to system instability. Donald Cochran (1992), for example, observes that "given the lack of research and reliable information behind the new intermediate sanctions, policies and practices are generally based on political considerations accompanied by the buzz-words *punishment and innovation*" (p. 309).

Simply adding new technologies to a system merely adds to its complexity. Without a thematic structure to tie the pieces together, this increased complexity weakens the system's capacity to maintain order and damages its capacity to implement anything successfully.

Conditions Conducive
to Effective Implementation

The literature on program and policy implementation provides a wealth of suggestions regarding ways to explain the level of failure observed in criminal justice innovations. Many of the authors attempt to develop generalizations about the implementation process based on theoretical arguments. Several writers, however, have specified very clearly correlates of success and failure derived from analyses of large numbers of implementation efforts (Ellickson & Petersilia, 1983; Faust, 1993; Harris, 1983-1984; Larson, 1980; McGarry, 1990; Petersilia, 1990a). Larson (1980) lists five factors common to failure of federal programs: (a) vague or unrealistic goals, (b) lack of support from key persons in the implementation process, (c) inadequate implementation procedures, (d) complexities of intergovernmental accommodations and actions, and (e) forces in the economic environment that affect resources and priorities. In a similar vein, Harris (1983-1984) observes with respect to attempts to establish alternatives to incarceration that past failures are best explained by (a) mixed, fuzzy, or counterproductive goals; (b) lack of a genuine attempt to achieve stated goals; (c) a climate increasingly hostile in its treatment of criminals; and (d) insufficient attention to political and professional interests.

These lists of correlates of successful implementation are useful to funding agencies for evaluating potential grant recipients and to evaluators seeking to explain the relative success or failure of implementation of a program or policy, and we look to them for the knowledge they provide.

Perhaps the most thorough and well-documented study of program implementation in criminal justice was conducted by Ellickson and Petersilia (1983). Based on an analysis of 37 case studies covering several different types of programs (criminal career programs, computerized information systems, victim and witness programs, and programs designed as alternatives to incarceration), six correlates of successful implementation were identified that can serve as the basis for both understanding implementation failure and improving the chances of implementation success.

1. *Sincere Motivation at Initiation.* It is often the case that program designs are constructed or adoption of an innovation is considered for reasons that have little to do with the goals of the program design. Past experience demonstrates that agency administrators have used innovations as a means to obtain funds that are then used for other purposes, to gain local political support, and to co-opt internal leaders. Ellickson and Petersilia (1983) distinguish opportunistic adoption of an innovation from situations in which innovation occurred in response to a need felt by local practitioners.

2. *Support From Top Leadership and Each Group Whose Cooperation Is Required for Implementation and Use.* Four categories of stakeholders are identified as being critical sources of support during the implementation process: (a) the top leadership of the organization within which the innovation is to take place, (b) the program director, (c) practitioners within the organization, and (d) practitioners from external agencies whose cooperation is needed.

3. *Staff Competence.* If implementation of an innovation requires new behaviors or skills, the capacity and willingness of those staff members who will implement the innovation to learn these behaviors are critical to achieving success. In addition, resources must be made available to provide relevant training.

4. *A Benefit-Cost Surplus.* For all stakeholders in the system, the benefits of implementing the innovation must outweigh its costs relative to the option of returning to status quo. This condition, as with the next two, emerges *after* adoption of the innovation. Development of incentives prior to enacting an innovation, however, provides some degree of predictability with respect to benefits.

5. *Clarity of Goals and Procedures.* Although goals continue to take shape as a program or policy is implemented, continual articulation of goals and procedures helps to ensure fidelity with respect to the innovation's design. The danger in allowing goals to remain unclear is that individual implementors are free to attach their own interpretations of goals to the decisions they make, thus introducing the likelihood that contradictory outcomes are defined as indicators of success by different people in the same system. Procedural fuzziness further complicates matters in that the integrity of the program design is jeopardized.

6. *Clear Lines of Authority.* During the implementation process, questions of interpretation continually arise. In some cases, policy decisions are required to be made without time for extended debate. To maintain consistency in the evolution of the innovation, mechanisms for resolving differences of opinion or solving problems are needed (Ellickson & Petersilia, 1983, pp. 22-23).

An analysis of observations made by Harland, Warren, and Brown (1979) of 10 restitution programs funded by Law Enforcement Assistance Administration (LEAA) reveals four additional conditions associated with implementation success.

1. *Extent of Innovation.* In some cases, an innovation is merely an expansion of an existing program. For example, the addition of an intensive drug and alcohol program to an intensive probation unit should present relatively little problem for implementation. In other cases, the innovation is new, but those working in the system have experience with the technology on which the innovation is based. In still other situations, attempts are made to implement an innovation in systems that lack previous experience. It was found that the greater the gap between current practices and those practices required by the innovation, the more difficult the implementation. Often, the issue is a

matter of how big a leap of faith initiators of change are asking key actors in the system to make. In the latter, more difficult case, credibility and trust based on prior innovation efforts appears necessary.

2. *Administration-Practitioner Gap.* The presence of a working relationship with practitioners as users of an innovation, at the point where adoption occurs, facilitates successful implementation. If practitioners view those who administer a program as outsiders, cooperation will be more difficult to obtain as credibility and trust have not been established.

3. *Procedural Complexity.* Particularly with respect to multiagency programs in which case-level decisions are required, the more decision makers involved in screening cases, the more difficult it is to control the implementation process. This finding is supported by the arguments raised by Pressman and Wildavsky (1973) and Nakamura and Smallwood (1980) regarding the effect of the number of consents that must be obtained and the likely success of implementation. The more consents that are needed, the shakier are the chances for successful implementation.

4. *Structural Stability.* Resignations or transfers of key players in an organization, particularly of those persons who administer new programs, can be costly to implementation efforts. In some cases, these instabilities are the death knell of an innovation. Although such changes cannot always be predicted, their importance to the implementation process suggests that steps be taken to ensure structural stability for an appropriate period of time.

Petersilia's (1990a, p. 130) more recent analysis of an 11-site IPS demonstration project elaborates nine conditions of successful implementation, listed in Table 7.1. We note three important additions in this list to the earlier Ellickson and Petersilia (1983) list. First, it is clear that proponents must be prepared with a theory that connects the proposed innovation to specific desired outcomes. To be able to articulate this theory no doubt contributes to the attractiveness of the innovation. Second, small changes are more likely to gain acceptance than broad ones, especially if normative changes are required. Finally, a stable organizational environment, much as was noted by Harland et al. (1979) is consistent with successful implementation.

What can we make of these lists of ideal conditions? First, it appears that *the closer the fit between a program or policy and the environment in which*

TABLE 7.1 Petersilia's Correlates of Success

1. The project addresses a pressing local problem.

2. The project has clearly articulated goals that reflect the needs and desires of the "customer."

3. The project has a receptive environment in both the "parent" organization and the larger system.

4. The organization has a leader who is vitally committed to the objectives, values, and implications of the project and who can devise practical strategies to motivate and effect change.

5. The project has a director who shares the leader's ideas and values and uses them to guide the implementation process and ongoing operation of the project.

6. Practitioners make the project their own, rather than being coerced into it—that is, they "buy into" it, participate in its development, and have incentives to maintain its integrity during the change process.

7. The project has clear lines of authority: There is no ambiguity about "who is in charge."

8. The change and its implementation are not complete and sweeping.

9. The organization has secure administrators, low staff turnover, and plentiful resources.

it is to be enacted, the better its chances of successful implementation. This notion of "fit" applies to the structure of a program: the alignment of its authority structure with the authority structure of the larger system; the program's goals and the extent to which they meet significant and widely recognized needs of the larger system; and the procedures or ways in which different parts of the system interact around cases. Second, *commitment to the innovation at all levels of the system appears necessary*—among the leadership of the agency involved, among program management, among line staff, and among key players in the program's political environment. Third, *resources must be made available to support the program at a level consistent with its structure and purpose.* Our restatement of these conclusions in Table 7.2 as main conditions associated with successful implementation is intended to highlight the themes that will guide our discussion, but our emphasis will be not on conditions but on the processes by which these conditions are established.

Missing from the lists of attributes of successful implementation is information about *how* they are generated under conditions in which they are not already in place and how innovators manage when one or more of these conditions cannot be met. In the following sections, we address the processes

TABLE 7.2   The Three Main Conditions Associated With Successful
                Implementation

---

1. There is a close fit between the program and the environment in which it is enacted.

2. Commitment is made to the program at all levels of the system, from external stakeholders to line staff.

3. Resources are made available to support the program at a level consistent with its structure and purpose.

---

by which each of these three conditions has been met in previous efforts in community corrections. In doing so, we draw on several examples in the literature and those about which we have more direct information, supplementing these case studies with conclusions drawn by other scholars who have studied community corrections as well as others who have commented more generally on implementation in the public sector.

Ellickson and Petersilia (1983), like other writers on implementation, found that attributes of programs, although often correlated with success, are less predictive of success than are attributes of the implementation *process* and of the organizational setting. This finding is best explained by several observations that pertain to the adaptation of innovations.

Process and Management:
Two Components of Implementation

Before discussing what we know about the adaptation of innovations, however, let us return to our definition of the term *implementation* to clarify an apparent discrepancy in its use. David Wilson (1992) has argued that *implementation* has to do with the management of individuals, whereas *process* is the component of change that pertains to the political and historical context of an innovation. According to this definition, implementation begins with a fixed, preconceived design and is focused on bringing about compliance with all its facets. In fact, when we use the term *implement,* this idea of carrying out something already defined is what we have in mind. We do not entirely disagree with this formulation, as our definition of implementation implies. In fact, what Wilson (1992) contributes to this discussion is that implementation necessarily involves the shaping of individual behavior so that a program design has a reasonable chance of being tested and developed. On the other hand, he misses the observation that even at the line level, implementation involves process elements: Negotiation and adaptation are components of the interactions that occur between managers and staff, between staff members, and between staff and clients, when line staff play out the activities specified in a program design. Their own goals, biases, knowledge, and skills in many ways affect the extent to which the program as enacted looks like the program as it was envisioned by its designers.

This variation in behavior is of concern to innovators, managers, and evaluators alike. Strategies for improving the match between design and practice include involving line staff in the design process, providing incentives for careful and thorough compliance with the design, imposing negative sanctions for failure to carry out activities as they were specified in the design, as well as monitoring and feedback systems and intensive staff training programs. The task of the manager is to see that program inputs and outputs are true to the program design.

Divergence from the program design can lead to improved implementation of the concepts and purposes of the program. Grau (1981) describes how probation department staff restructured the department in response to an experience in which a program design was forced on line staff. The director of the Tacoma, Washington, probation department adopted in its entirety a model of probation services that would have eliminated individual caseloads and replaced them with staff specialization and probation teams to work with pooled caseloads. Conflict between the director and his staff resulted in resignation of the director, but more important, the new director enabled his staff to reshape their work. The goals of the original program model remained the same—improved knowledge and use of specialized services—but the officers retained their own caseloads.

Adaptation need not be this extreme, but some modification of a program design is inevitable if it is to be effectively used. Although there is much talk about replicating program models, each new program site is different from all others, thus producing a need for differences in the program itself. In fact, some evaluators argue that if we look closely enough we find that replication is a myth (Alkin, 1990); in our attempts to generalize from experiences with a program technology, we may be comparing programs that share little more than the same label.

From an "action science" perspective (Argyris, Putnam, & Smith, 1985), the reaction of an organization to intervention is a source of understanding the organization. Informal structures in the organization, its values and norms, and the absence of effective planning are often exposed in the early stages of a program's implementation. Assuming that someone is paying attention to these data, modifications can be made to the program and to its relationship to the larger system that facilitate continued program development. Failure to do so can be disastrous.

At each stage of the implementation process, then, management, or the manipulation of behavior to carry out plans, is necessary to give structure to the program. Compliance alone, however, can undermine achievement of the goal for which the program was intended. We have seen examples of programs designed to reduce the number of offenders heading to prison that failed to do so. It may be that although the program design was carried out faithfully, adaptation of the program's environment to the program was incomplete.

The process we are describing presents us with a dilemma: How can change and stability be maintained simultaneously? Change in any organization can be chaotic and frustrating. Continuous change, in fact, may work against successful implementation. It is likely that implementation is best facilitated by alternating periods of adaptation with periods of conformity to an agreed-on program design.

This episodic pattern of adaptation has recently been advocated by Tyre and Orlikowski (1993) in their discussion of strategies for adapting new technologies to organizations. Typically, a large window of opportunity to manipulate staff behavior and the behavior of external stakeholders appears at the beginning of a program. This window of opportunity does not stay open, however, and if forced open may produce opposition to the program. Innovators and program proponents must find ways to create new opportunities for adaptation and take advantage of them. Program evaluations, minor crises, and retreats that focus on planning are among the types of disruptions to day-to-day operations that provide opportunities to rethink and refine a program design or to develop stronger environmental supports for the program.

This mix of management of a program design and the mutual adaptation that takes place as the program interacts with its environment is the core of implementation. Figure 7.1 illustrates this management-adaptation mix in four domains of program implementation we have identified in the literature on correlates of successful implementation. These four domains are program political environment, parent organization, program staff, and resources.

In this visual presentation of our conceptualization of implementation, we differentiate between the management component of implementation and

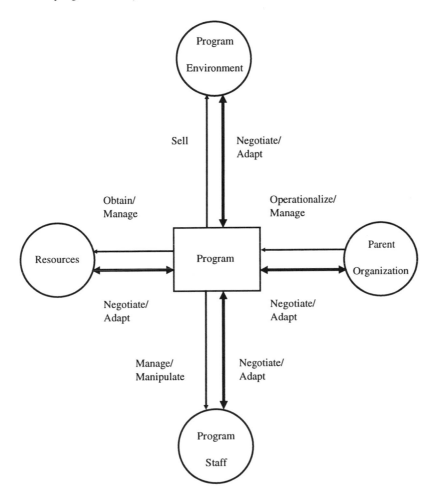

Figure 7.1. Program Implementation Process

mutual adaptation by depicting management as being unidirectional, using an arrow with a point at only one end. Mutual adaptation, on the other hand, is illustrated with a bold arrow with points on each end. Both the program and the domain undergo change in response to the other.

We have already discussed the importance of this combined management-adaptation perspective for understanding the interaction between programs and program staff. Programs are also typically located within a parent organization, thus requiring a complex of interactions with this larger structure. A home confinement program, for example, may reside within a probation department. The program director is likely a member of the probation department management team, and program staff consists of probation officers. The management of the program, then, is shared with the program director's superior, and both officials typically monitor the extent to which staff behavior complies with program design.

In the case of a new program, the appointment of a new director may mean the addition of a new member of the management team. It may also mean that resources will be distributed differently and the new program may steal staff from existing units. These changes in the organization are often matched by changes in the program that result from observations and judgments made by other managers in the department and the organization's CEO.

A new program also exists within a political environment that can include other criminal justice agencies, non-criminal-justice government agencies, interest groups, powerful individuals, and the media. To the extent that the program interacts with other agencies around the same clients, interorganizational adaptations need to take place that include new information systems, the development of new procedures, and mechanisms for resolving conflict. But more important, many interested parties react both positively and negatively to what they experience of the program. These reactions, if sufficiently strong, can require changes in the program, both to ensure its continual survival and to improve its capacity to meet the needs for which it was intended.

Finally, resources must be obtained and managed in a way that supports the program as it was designed if that design is to have a reasonable chance of being tested. But often resources are limited or inconsistent, producing a need to modify the program. Often the response is to do less, but sometimes the wise leader sees ways to reengineer the program so that its vision is not violated. Recently, we have seen managers of a group of delinquency prevention programs search for new sources of funding as their start-up grants were coming to an end. Because the new sources of funding were attached to goals different from those that stimulated development of the programs, program personnel have had to redefine their goals, adding educational and mental health components that would otherwise not have been central to their mission.

As this discussion indicates, we recognize both the management and adaptive components of implementation. In the sections that follow, we emphasize the adaptive side, owing to its importance and the dearth of information available in the literature. Moreover, we believe that the management side of implementation is less complex; mutual adaptation requires sensitivity, patience, willpower, and luck.

The Role of
Adaptation in Increasing the Fit

Programs change over time. Not only is there continual reshaping of a program design before it is put into action, but programs continue to change following the point at which "the tire meets the road." It is this change in attributes of a program that makes components of a program design poor predictors of program success. Moreover, it has been observed that the same program design can produce drastically different results in different settings, thus supporting the conclusion that context is critical to outcome. In addition, users of innovations, rather than being passive participants in the implementation process, directly affect how the innovations are used, adapting the innovations to existing organizational structures and norms and using them to serve their own purposes.

But it is not only innovations that undergo change during the implementation process: The organization within which the innovation is used also undergoes change. As Cochran (1992) notes with respect to ISP programs, ISP is not installed in a vacuum; rather, this innovation must be accepted by a living system in which the balance is necessarily disrupted. With regard to the Texas ISP program, Markley (1989) notes that when program management personnel changed, line staff became "demoralized." Their commitment to the program was dependent on the leadership provided by a few individuals. Other common disruptions include the transfer of personnel to a new program, the hiring of outsiders (new staff) to staff the new program, and the requirement that staff acquire new skills to continue doing their jobs.

For example, two categories of problems of sociotechnical mismatches have been noted with regard to electronic monitoring: (a) staff in agencies with electronic monitoring systems often lack the skills to operate these systems and are rarely prepared to respond to the increased flow of information that these monitoring systems provide regarding the behavior of their clients, and (b) electronic monitoring creates additional burdens on family members, thus adding to the stress of home confinement situation (Baumer,

Maxfield, & Mendelsohn, 1993). The first of these matching problems suggests that agency officials considering adoption of an innovation that requires technical skills beyond those ordinarily possessed by agency staff must consider implications for staff training, the need to hire staff who possess relevant skills and knowledge, and the impact of staff turnover rates on the agency's capacity to replace these requisite skills. Leaders must be sensitive to the tensions produced by these changes.

Berman (1981) and McLaughlin (1976) have both noted that as implementation of an innovation changes behavior in the organizational setting, responses of the setting require adaptation of the innovation for the implementation process to succeed. As Ellickson and Petersilia (1983) observe, this process of mutual adaptation implies that the same innovation can look very different across different settings. The crucial point to be made is that unless a program is carefully tailored to the setting in which it is to be used, successful implementation is unlikely.

An excellent example of this kind of tailoring of the innovation can be seen in the approach that the Center for Alternative Sentencing and Employment Services (CASES) in New York City has taken to ensure that its clients fit their target population: jail-bound rather than probation-bound offenders. Data on sentencing in New York revealed that sentencing practices differed across the five boroughs. Judges in Queens, for example, require fewer misdemeanor offenses than do those in Manhattan before sentencing an offender to serve significant jail time. To prevent use of CASES Community Service Sentencing Project (CSSP) as a replacement for probation, criteria for accepting offenders into CSSP are adjusted to sentencing patterns at the borough level (Neises, 1993).

Not only does tailoring itself promote effective adaptation, but structural characteristics of organizations also affect the capacity of a program to adapt. Yin (1982), for example, argues that decentralization of program control greatly enhances its adaptability by permitting personnel at different sites to develop the program at their own pace and allowing the program to adapt to the idiosyncrasies of each site in ways that improve chances for successful implementation. In much the same vein, Gareth Morgan's (1986) metaphor of "organizations and brains" suggests further that this multiple-site decentralized approach leads to increased chances for learning about the potential of the innovation. It may be that an innovation is more effective under some conditions than under others, but it may also be the case that different modes of adaptation make it possible for an innovation to adapt to a variety of organizational environments.

An adaptive strategy is not without its drawbacks, however (Gurney, 1982; Majone & Wildavsky, 1979; Musheno, Palumbo, Maynard-Moody, & Levine, 1990). As Musheno et al. (1990) observe, "successful implementation of policies, like community corrections, requires a delicate balance between the essential but somewhat contradictory processes of faithful adoption and constructive adaptation" (p. 251). It is rarely the case that the system that is expected to adopt a new innovation is prepared for adoption without modification of the innovation. At the same time, adaptation can severely distort the innovation so that its original purposes are lost. Musheno et al.'s (1990) study of community corrections in Colorado, Connecticut, and Oregon—states in which adoption occurred—demonstrates the impact of system structure on successful adaptation (adoption without distortion of goals).

A high level of commitment to community corrections was found in Colorado, a state in which community corrections is highly decentralized; services are provided by private, nonprofit organizations; and coordination of services is performed by local advisory boards. This structure provided street-level workers with direct access to decision making and fostered local-level adaptation. Street-level implementation is critical: It is at this level that programs and policies are translated into actions that produce the outcomes being sought. The key difference among the three states studied by Musheno et al. (1990) was that in Oregon, where control was exercised by county bureaucracies, support and involvement at the street level was considerably weaker than was the case in Colorado. The consequence for Oregon was a lower rating of success for community corrections among those persons interviewed than was found in Colorado.

Three other elements of a successful strategy are noted by Ellickson and Petersilia (1983, pp. 54-56). First, broad participation and flexible problem solving were frequently linked with implementation strategies that included an evolutionary implementation process—that is, program staff began with modest attempts to demonstrate the value of the innovation. The value of beginning small is that credibility can be established before resources are invested heavily, thus attracting a wider range of support. A second element is "generation of craft knowledge," by which Ellickson and Petersilia (1983) mean the purposeful accumulation and use of knowledge about how to operate within the program's particular organizational environment. This development of knowledge about how to gain support from specific actors in the system and about mistakes to avoid greatly enhances the capacity of program staff to exploit the program design.

A third corollary of broad participation and flexible problem solving is to approach both planning and communication as ongoing activities. The effects of initial planning and communication quickly erode as time goes on, and for program activities continually to be responsive to new information and supported by key persons whose priorities are likely to shift over time, continual involvement in shaping the program and in maintaining relationships is necessary.

Writers on implementation have often overlooked the need to formulate goals that do not overly constrict creative approaches to program design and implementation (Faust, 1993; McGarry, 1990; Schrantz, n.d.). We are often told that clearly stated goals increase the likelihood of successful implementation. Although it is true that clarity with respect to goals and the technologies selected to achieve those goals is desirable, adaptability is also needed during the planning and action stages to maximize acceptability of the innovation and the fit between the goals of the innovation and the needs of the system in which it is to be enacted.

Clarifying and Shaping Goals

Perhaps the most frequent implementation issue mentioned in the literature is goal clarity. Lack of specificity about goals leads to confusion, conflict, co-optation, inappropriate decisions, and an inability to assess the success or failure of a policy or program (see, e.g., Casper & Brereton, 1984; Kelling et al., 1986; MacKenzie et al., 1993). Some writers on implementation argue that goal fuzziness is functional (Nakamura & Smallwood, 1980). Some stakeholders may prefer not to know how to achieve the goals of a policy; in other cases, goal fuzziness is useful in supporting the development of coalitions among stakeholders with opposing views. As we have seen in the case of many community corrections programs, individuals with widely different goal preferences can support the same program for different reasons.

Goal clarity, however, does not necessarily come about prior to adoption of an innovation: Clarification of goals is a component of the implementation process in which goals that are relevant to felt needs are permitted to shape the program (Ellickson & Petersilia, 1983; McLaughlin, 1976; Nakamura & Smallwood, 1980). In other words, although the implementation process begins with some direction as to desired outcomes of using an innovation, the needs and preferences of those persons who will participate in implementing an innovation must be incorporated into the goals of the program through which the innovation is being implemented. Policy analysts, for example, have discovered that judges are often reluctant to impose fines under a tariff system due to their focus on retribution and their desire to be fair (Hillsman, 1990). By accommodating the values of judges through the use of day fines, greater fairness has been achieved, the use of fines has increased, and the collection of fines has become more predictable.

Restitution, like fines, can be adapted to a variety of aims, organizational structures, and decision points. It can serve as a means of repaying victims, as a means of reintegration, as part of a treatment program, and as a way to reduce the use of incarcerative sentences; it can be administered by a state planning agency, a probation agency, a pretrial services agency, a parole board, or a district attorney's office, among others. Furthermore, it can be installed at various decision points, including a point immediately before charging, prior to trial, as part of a sentence, at the point at which release from prison is being considered, and at the parole revocation hearing. But although restitution can serve a variety of purposes, it cannot do all of these things at the same time. Consequently, careful and continual planning is needed to ensure that its use is consistent within a manageable and well-understood design.

Consider the differences described between Oregon's Repay restitution program and the Connecticut program reported by Harland et al. (1979). Oregon's was without doubt the program that was best developed in that its goals were simple and straightforward, its policies and procedures were well developed and widely understood, and the operational style of clarification and negotiation was unobtrusive and nonthreatening to decision makers at all levels of the organization. First, this program had only one goal, compensation of victims, a goal that was widely supported. Furthermore, because the program was located in the office of the district attorney, access to case files, including police reports that were the usual starting point for loss investigations, was not a problem. Intercepting case files proactively, early in the prosecution of a case, allowed Repay staff to conduct the necessary eligibility screening and complete the loss assessments as planned. The program did not have to depend on the prosecuting attorney or any other external authority to initiate its involvement in the restitutive process, because all case files were screened by program staff, who made their own decisions about which cases to investigate. Finally, being part of the district attorney's office ensured program staff easy access to prosecuting attorneys and gave the appearance to victims and other sources of information that they were part of the prosecution team.

In Connecticut, one finds a very different picture in terms of adapting a program to the needs and goals of the larger system (Harland et al., 1979). Much of the problem with this program stemmed from its isolation from the mainstream of the state criminal justice system, both physically and professionally. Program offices were located in Hartford, separate from the Hartford courts themselves, and obviously quite removed from the courts in other counties. Physical distance clearly contributed to problems with the program: Most simply, it impeded the effective spread of information about the program; just to remind judges of its existence required special effort. Judges who were interviewed by Harland and his colleagues (1979) were barely aware of the program. They had certainly never been presented with clear rationales for restitution and they seemed to be inclined to continue sentencing as they always had. The single biggest problem faced by this program was its failure to accommodate the bargaining practices of the district attorney's office. It appears that the program director had not seen the goals of the prosecutor as relevant.

A lack of fit among program goals and needs and priorities in the larger system, poorly communicated procedures, and failure to integrate program procedures with those of the adopting system are ways in which innovations often meet their demise. Undoubtedly, the complexity of both goals and procedures, the compatibility of program goals and those of key actors of the system, and the intrusiveness of proposed procedures have much to do with the success of attempts to clarify goals. At the same time, innovations are often adopted with so little planning that potential goals they might serve are not considered.

A more insidious picture of goal-related problems is painted by Corbett and Marx (1992). Although electronic monitoring can be useful as an intermediate sanction, these authors express concern that the stated goals of an innovation like electronic monitoring can be "supplemented privately or eclipsed by additional, even contrary objectives" (p. 89). Revisions of goals after adoption can, do, and should occur, but there is no excuse for abandoning responsibility for the original purposes of an innovation. It is the role of leaders responsible for operation of the program to continue to work with external stakeholders after initiation of the program. Leaders need to shape opinion by providing stakeholders with relevant information, bringing problems to their attention, and engaging with them in efforts to solve those problems—keeping the benefits of the program on the table whenever possible.

Implementation Practices That
Decrease the Likelihood of an Adequate Fit

Negative implementation outcomes can occur when leaders lose control over the goals of a program or when program goals are overstated to gain support from the larger political environment. The fact is that the advantages of community corrections over incarceration may be ambiguous in recidivism rates and even cost, but when innovations are oversold, stakeholders rightfully feel deceived, and support may be withdrawn (see McGarry, 1990). The benefits of clearly articulated, realistic goals are many, and from an implementation perspective, clarity and realism help to guarantee development of a solid base of support.

An added problem occurs when proponents of an innovation claim that their innovation can serve a wide range of goals. Trying to satisfy constituents who represent different preferences and priorities often results in goal statements that are bound to produce disappointment for many of them. Clear, Flynn, and Shapiro (1987) note with humor the range of promises attached to intensive probation services: "Advocates of IPS programs are not humble in the claims they made for these programs. Commonly, IPS is expected to reduce prison crowding, increase public protection, rehabilitate the offender, demonstrate the potential of probation, and save money. Even a skeptic is bound to be impressed" (p. 32). Petersilia and Turner (1993a) found in their evaluation of 14 ISP programs that the primary purposes of intensive supervision probation are rarely achieved:

- The programs did not alleviate prison crowding and may have increased it in some states.
- They cost considerably more than is generally realized.
- They were no more effective than routine probation and parole in reducing recidivism. In fact, the authors conclude, an increase in emphasis on public safety is likely to add significantly to the cost of community corrections programs generally. They find that ISP programs succeed in adding punitiveness to ordinary probation programs but also argue that the potential benefits of adding rehabilitative components to ISP programs are considerable.

This tendency to pile on more goals to obtain support can be countered in three ways: (a) by specifying the theory of causal processes that link program outputs to program outcomes, (b) by permitting goals to take shape as experience with the program develops information about the program's capacities, and (c) by making goal setting an explicit activity of a stakeholder group. First, providing information on causal theories that underlie the program design forces frivolous theoretical arguments to the surface. Once exposed, they are easily dismissed. Second, we are not always aware of the potential outcomes, positive or negative, of a program until it has had a chance to produce. Although some aims are specified in advance, especially those that are need driven, other goals may begin to compete with and help to clarify earlier goal statements once the system begins to experience the program's benefits. Finally, goal setting is most effective when it is the subject of open, information-rich negotiation among groups of stakeholders.

Targeting

Related to the need to specify goals is the notion that matching programs to members of the correct target population increases the chances of successful goal achievement. Critics of community corrections have noted a number of unintended negative consequences of developing new technologies for keeping offenders in the community. Most notable is the failure of community corrections to keep offenders out of prison while increasing the level of sanction for many offenders who would otherwise have experienced only minimal supervision. This "net widening" has forced community corrections to produce more careful screening procedures and accept compromises. Compromises with respect to targeting, however, add complexity to a program, dilute program goals, and confound attempts to explain program outcomes.

Community corrections programs are more likely to demonstrate their potential if the population for which they are designed is clearly specified and they in fact deliver services to that target population and not to populations outside the target. CASES, a private agency providing intermediate sanctions for the courts in New York City, provides an excellent example of clear targeting. Its two programs, the Community Services Sentencing Project (CSSP) and the Court Employment Project (CEP), are designed for different target populations and the criteria used to identify appropriate clients are disseminated carefully to judges, prosecutors, defenders, and other service providers. Quite naturally, pressure is occasionally placed on court representatives to take inappropriate cases, but CASES staff have taken the position that the credibility of their program rests on being rigid about eligibility criteria (E. Neises, personal communication, September 28, 1993).

It is unfortunate that for several studies targets have shifted after adoption of a community corrections program, usually in the direction of the less serious offender. In Arizona, an electronic monitoring program enacted through legislation was undermined by the Board of Pardons and Parole through redefinitions of eligibility that placed less serious offenders in the program (Palumbo, Clifford, & Synder-Joy, 1990). One of the ways that this target shifting occurs is when program officials find that referring agencies are reluctant to send them cases and case flow is insufficient to support the program. Under these circumstances, less serious cases are taken to keep the program alive (Clear & Hardyman, 1990).

We maximize the level of complexity of a program when goals are fuzzy or incompatible or hidden, or when target populations are not specified. But it is sometimes the case that multiple goals must be accommodated, and under these conditions target shifting can easily occur. The report by MacKenzie et al. (1990) on Louisiana's shock incarceration program underscores the complexity issue, describing ways in which complexity was handled and the benefits of complex procedures. Louisiana officials adopted a three-stage selection process that permitted organizations with different goals to interact around cases. Although this selection system defied the conventional wisdom regarding the negative impact of procedural complexity on implementation, its effectiveness in achieving consensus was due to frequent planning meetings and seminars as well as regular correspondence focused on the program's goals. As the final selection decision was made by the department of corrections, the program effectively guaranteed that offenders placed in the program were among those headed for prison.

The Importance of Commitment:
Up, Down, and Sideways

Commitment at the Top

Most critical to moving the development of a program forward with a clear sense of direction is *leadership*. Leaders are not necessarily good managers (see Zaleznik, 1992), but a good leader keeps the process of development moving forward, looking for opportunities, avoiding pitfalls, and generating excitement in others. This point is emphasized in Petersilia's (1990a) nine conditions of successful implementation and has received extensive support throughout the change literature. Often, it is the presence of vision and commitment in one individual that enables a program to survive and develop in the face of resource constraints, political squabbles, and internal resistance, and it is this kind of commitment that breeds commitment in others. This kind of leadership is most effective when it resides at the top of the organization.

Ideally, leadership from the top drives the development and implementation of new programs. As Petersilia (1990a) found, those jurisdictions in which chief probation officers and program managers shared a sense of commitment to ISP programs experienced greater success than those in which commitment at either level was lacking. It is not always the case, however, that top administrators provide the kind of leadership that supports the implementation of new ideas. Such weaknesses in a system imply the need for those individuals committed to the program to develop strategies that cross agency boundaries and seek support from parallel agencies, such as courts and prosecutors. Preferably, this strategy can be used in a way that *includes* the top administrator.

It is often the case that agency administrators are in situations that lead them to fear innovation. Political environments characterized by conflict and dishonesty are dangerous to heads of agencies and often lead to impotence and an avoidance of planning. By finding ways to distribute the risk among agencies and peers of the agency administrator, program innovators can free the administrator to consider making a change.

Street-Level Commitment

We have made mention above of the importance of street- or line-level commitment to a program or policy. The lack of attention to those who will implement an innovation is sometimes shocking. Grau's (1981) account of attempts in a probation department to implement a community resource brokerage (CRB) model describes an initial effort by the chief probation officer to convince his staff through logical argument to adopt this new way of conducting their work. Efforts of the officers to resist this change in the nature of their job included proposal writing, open criticism, and continuation of traditional caseload activity. The resulting mutual rejection culminated in the resignation of the chief.

In 1987, Texas was under federal court order to reduce its prison population. Under pressure by threat of severe fines ($800,000 per day), the Texas Board of Pardons and Paroles was given 48 hours to develop an intensive probation supervision (IPS) concept paper (Markley, 1989). After acceptance of the IPS concept, the agency was "awarded" an additional 30 days to implement the program. Included in the program design was an agreement with RAND to conduct an evaluation of the program. Though the literature generally promotes the ideal that evaluation should, indeed, be part of program design and implementation (and that this is rarely done), the Texas case is an example of how this "ideal" could lead to several associated problems.

The evaluation design of the Texas IPS program included a random assignment method for obtaining the experimental and control groups (Markley, 1989). Markley notes that caseload officers grew frustrated when 50% of their referrals to the IPS program did not in fact enter the program. (Obviously, the other 50% made up the control group.) Caseload officers were not making referrals, despite a requirement to do so. Markley (1989) goes on to state that "developers of future programs must be aware that the more rigorous the evaluation methodology, the more rigorous the implementation problems" (p. 54).

Surprisingly, there still remains in many agencies a perception that line people should obey orders or get out (Markley, 1989). This view can be seen in a recently published work by Watts and Glaser (1992) in which the authors describe an attempt by the County of Los Angeles Probation Department to implement a program of house arrest with electronic monitoring. From an implementation perspective, this case study portrays a process that seems to us naive, given the wealth of knowledge about implementation and human resources management. The authors, who were asked to evaluate this program, wisely chose to assess the output of the program first and concluded that resistance to change on the part of supervising officers was due to a lack of incentives combined with a perception that this new type of case required more work. They found that resistance was particularly great when these line staff, "who regard themselves as professionals with considerable autonomy in case decisions, are not consulted on the proposed change in advance by the higher officials who initiate it" (p. 82). It is important to keep in mind that consultation is not the same as having a vote. No one is advocating that administrators give away their authority; rather, there is good reason to provide leadership and encourage maximal use of everyone's creative energy.

In the case of Georgia's ISP program, commitment from line staff was generated in three ways: (a) by enlisting officers on a voluntary basis, (b) by involving officers in the process of developing the program, and (c) by investing heavily in relevant training (Neises, 1990). Prospective officers were informed that because the program was to be funded by means of supervision fees and their current positions would be filled by new staff, there was an element of risk involved in joining. Moreover, no increases in salary were put forward as incentives. Instead, the program itself and the opportunity to help develop something new served as incentive for participation. Because the training was relevant to the intense direct contact officers would have with offenders on their caseloads, understanding of and commitment to the job was further enhanced.

The nature of support provided to line staff to maximize their commitment to a new program is rarely addressed, and yet it should be obvious that some types of support foster commitment more than others. Two types of support have been associated with failure: highly detailed program designs (Ellickson & Petersilia, 1983; Williams, 1976) and technical assistance (McLaughlin, 1976).

The temptation to overplan is difficult for some leaders to resist. Although line staff need direction, they are also more likely to become committed to a program if they are permitted to use their creative energies in developing their own roles and shaping the program to fit unanticipated problems. Central to McLaughlin's (1976) argument is that planning is continuous and requires input and communication with all participants. Even the best plans cannot anticipate everything that will come up during change. This makes rigid plans problematic for one simple reason: Plans cannot attempt to account for all possible contingencies, yet the attempt to do so, ironically, results in the lack of preparedness in dealing with problems. Ellickson and Petersilia (1983) also stress this point. They found that lengthy, detailed planning processes lead to a design that is "difficult to modify because of the energy already invested in it" (p. 56). They found that the programs that were most open to change and adaptation were the programs that tended to be more successfully implemented.

Good programs excite line staff. They create a locus of aspiration for staff that causes them to push the potential of the program toward its limits. This enthusiasm at the street level is often the kind of information that draws external stakeholders into greater levels of participation.

External Stakeholder Commitment

Because resources and interagency relationships are controlled at the top of an organization, the likelihood of successful implementation of an innovation developed at midlevels of an organization is limited, unless top leaders and other stakeholder groups are brought into the planning process early enough to have some degree of control over the shape of the innovation when applied at the local level. In one restitution program cited by Harland et al. (1979), necessary support from the common pleas courts and superior courts had never been established. Moreover, it was discovered that prosecutors refused to release information over the phone regarding victims, a procedure made necessary by the physical isolation of the program from the courts. In Georgia, on the other hand, implementation was conducted on a trial basis only in jurisdictions familiar with and sold on restitution. Demands of judges and prosecutors were integrated into the proposal from the beginning so that integration of the programs into existing patterns of operation was greatly simplified (Harland et al., 1979).

Georgia officials also encountered problems initially in attempting to adopt a program of intensive supervision probation (ISP) that stemmed from a planning process in which judges, as a key constituent group, were not included (Neises, 1990). Judges rejected random assignment of cases to experimental and control groups, a requirement of the funding agency and, consequently, referred very few cases to ISP. In a second attempt to implement ISP, Vince Fallin, deputy commissioner of the Georgia Department of Corrections (GDC), and others in the probation division took seriously the need to have support from judges. By means of a written survey to judges—which included the question, "What would a program in the community have to look like to get judges to use it as a sentencing option?"—Fallin and his colleagues were able to accommodate themes from the responses received into the program design, thereby increasing the level of commitment to the program.

It is important not to underestimate the political cost of commitment to a new policy or program. Stakeholders, especially those occupying top positions in the criminal justice system, can ill afford to back a poorly conceived program or a program for which support from other key actors cannot be obtained. The less popular the innovation, the more time it will take to reach the point where commitment is sufficient to go forward with enactment of a program design. Moreover, the adaptation literature warns us that if imple-

mentation of a policy is assumed to be temporary, system leaders will seek to
co-opt the policy, thus neutralizing its impact.

Commitment is further served by providing stakeholders opportunities to
see firsthand a program model in action. Demonstration projects often serve
this purpose. Both Rothman, Erlich, and Teresa (1976) and Petersilia (1990a)
note the advantages of innovations that can be tried on a pilot basis before
significant resources are encumbered. But it is also possible to show stakeholders existing programs in other locations. Mark Steward, director of
Missouri's Division of Children and Youth Services, took a group of juvenile
court judges to Massachusetts to provide these critical stakeholders, who were
somewhat resistant to some of the community programs being suggested, the
opportunity to see firsthand the kinds of programs they were being asked to
support (Steward, personal communication, June 1992). The result was en-
thusiastic support for a significant shift in resources away from institutional
placements to community-based programs.

One needs to be cautious about demonstration projects, however. As Toch
and Grant (1991) argue, demonstration projects often portray innovations in
their best light, exaggerating their potential. Under more normal circumstances, in which resources and support are less generous, these same innovations can look much less attractive. One solution to this biased view of an
innovation is to test it in several sites simultaneously. Not only do multiple-
site demonstrations provide a more realistic picture, assuming that they are
not overwhelmed with resources, they also facilitate learning about interactions between the innovation and different types of settings.

Commitment is a matter of choice. It will often be the case that those
persons whose choices we wish to influence do not relate to our work or our
values. It behooves the innovator to learn how to relate to the work and value
systems of these constituents so that communication around goals and strategies and the kinds of support being requested are spelled out in terms that
appeal to the interests of the constituents.

Communication Strategies That
Increase Commitment and Facilitate Adaptation

Constituent identification and communication are central to any implementation strategy. Unless innovators can articulate a clear need for a program,

provide potential opponents with access to information, and provide opportunity for discussion of concerns among those who can affect the program's success, successful implementation is unlikely. Ellickson and Petersilia (1983) argue that a key condition of successful implementation is a felt need for the innovation. They were particularly sensitive to situations in which proposed programs reflected opportunism rather than response to system needs. Similarly, Byrne et al. (1989) found that success in implementing ISP programs was facilitated by the presence of clearly articulated goals that bore a relationship to expressed community needs at the local level. We can further stipulate that this need should be felt by a large constituency. This idea of a felt need goes to the very center of the marketing concept that products are generated to meet the needs of customers.

Most efforts to sell community corrections to stakeholders and to the public begin with information on the cost of incarceration and the impact that rising costs are having on other services. Taxpayers, legislators, and budget officials are all sensitive to cost arguments (we do not mean to imply that these groups are discrete), but cost arguments alone have limited utility in an environment in which fear of crime is fed daily by the news and entertainment media. Governor Castle (1991) reports that in Delaware cost arguments were raised to generate support for implementation of a new sentencing system, but other information was introduced as well, including the following:

- Descriptions of successful community corrections programs in other jurisdictions
- The fact that not all serious offenders were incarcerated under the current system
- The proposal under the new system that serious offenders would be incarcerated

Central to recent marketing strategies in the area of community corrections has been the idea that intermediate punishments are in fact painful. Some programs, such as house arrest or house arrest with electronic monitoring, apparently fit the bill (Petersilia, 1990). Even more to the point, Morris and Tonry's (1990) work in the area of intermediate punishments provides evidence that community correctional programs can be conceived of as equal to prison in the amount of pain inflicted.

Because not all constituents readily accept the relevance of an innovation to the needs that they perceive, mechanisms of information exchange are needed. In Georgia, Vince Fallin, together with Larry Anderson, the Probation

Division's Diversion Program Coordinator, understood that questions regarding ISP would not necessarily be directed to them or to their own staff. Instead, concerned constituents would more likely contact officials with whom they were familiar but who might not be involved in the ISP effort. Neises (1990) reports that Fallin and Anderson developed a strategy of developing "a decentralized network of program advocates." These advocates were officials believed likely to be those who would be called for information on the ISP program. According to Neises (1990),

> A luncheon for those named by the chiefs was held in each of the thirteen pilot circuits, with approximately fifty or sixty people attending in each location. Local press coverage was arranged to spread word of the program throughout the community. The GDC's guests watched a film about probation practices and goals in Georgia, and the overcrowding morass and its effect on the system were explained. The meeting was concluded with an open forum, allowing people to discuss their views and concerns. Thus in some sense, by drawing in all the relevant local stakeholders, the department's management strategy advanced the democratic process. (p. 26)

When implementing the home confinement program, Georgia Department of Corrections personnel reportedly spent an hour with each judge in each appropriate circuit explaining the methods and advantages of home confinement. This was done even though there was little opposition to this innovation so that judges understood and supported the program.

To maintain a level of constituent support consistent with program needs, effective implementation also involves feeding users of a program information relevant to *their* needs. We can identify three types of information that should be generated and disseminated on a regular basis: (a) program descriptions, (b) feedback to decision makers on individual cases, and (c) information on program performance. Often, considerable selling of a program occurs up front. To obtain referrals, judges, probation officers, prosecutors, and others who control the dispositions of cases are provided with detailed program descriptions. This up-front educational effort is insufficient, however, for those decision makers who are not actively involved in the continual shaping of the program. Staff turnover, faulty retention of information, and changes in the program design all contribute to a decline in the effect of educational efforts.

In particular, judges and probation officers who play a role in decisions about what cases are connected with what programs have an interest in what happens to cases during program participation. Without case-level feedback, these decision makers have little information on which to base future sentencing decisions. Moreover, even when case reviews are not required, these decision makers may believe that they have a right to this information. In New York City, CASES staff provide judges with written feedback on cases every 2 months. Additional oral reports are made on request (E. Neises, personal communication, September 28, 1993). In addition, CASES court representatives are in court every day, interacting with judges, prosecutors, and defense attorneys about the appropriateness of different cases. This level of interaction helps to guarantee that these key constituents are aware of the CASES programs and that information relevant to CASES administrators reaches the appropriate persons.

In a recent process evaluation with several juvenile diversion programs in Pennsylvania, we heard several program staff members in one location complain that referrals from probation had fallen off. These staff members were unable to explain this change in probation officer behavior. By means of focus groups with two groups of probation staff, we learned that despite the educational efforts of the program at the point of unveiling, a significant number of officers knew little or nothing about the program. Either they had missed the program presentations or they were new to the agency. Probation officers who participated also expected that program staff would keep them informed about the outcomes of cases they referred. Because this was not the case, they simply ceased making referrals.

Continued support from some constituents also requires information on program productivity and cost. Typically, those who are watching budgets request this information, but officials of agencies providing services to the same or other groups of offenders are continually making judgments about what programs to support, and the playing field does not remain constant. An appropriate analogy is that of an investor who is assessing the value of a business in which he or she owns stock. The question is likely to be raised whether or not the program is living up to its promises in terms of numbers of cases served, cost of services, and program output (actual service activities relative to those advertised).

Evaluation research plays an important role in communication about a program (Castle, 1991). Research data can be used to advertise the relative benefits of an innovation as well as to develop additional sources of funding. Although we have emphasized output information in this chapter, outcome data are of interest to everyone. The strategic use of this information to maintain a base of support should be a component of the implementation strategy. This means not only generating outcome data but disseminating findings in readable form to a wide audience. In her report on the Georgia Department of Corrections, Neises (1990) writes the following:

> Integration of many communication functions at the local level has enhanced stakeholders' understanding of intermediate sanctions and their confidence in staff. Recognition of communication as an on-going program maintenance activity, rather than a sporadic effort to be made each time a program is up for re-authorization, may have forestalled disenchantment with the concept of alternatives and led to further expansion of Georgia's sentencing options. (p. 34)

It is important, too, that staff within an agency be regarded as a market segment with respect to being recipients of performance information. Their continued support is vital and their credibility in the organization's political environment is enhanced by their capacity to speak intelligently on behalf of one of their own programs.

Of all the problems associated with implementation failure over which innovators have control, the absence of feedback networks is one of the most serious. Building and maintaining support, creating opportunities for replication, and increasing the capacity of a program to achieve its goals all depend on frequent dissemination of valid information.

Developing Necessary Resources

Undoubtedly, commitment from the top facilitates access to resources necessary to support a new program or a program that was initiated with external funds, but budget woes continue to plague the development of community corrections. Most critical, the growth in the use of imprisonment and in the number of prison beds has sucked the system dry. Much of the innovation in the past few years in this area has occurred through an adaptation to decreasing resources.

A major reengineering of probation has occurred through the proliferation of risk and needs assessment tools. This innovation, discussed in detail by Jim Bonta (Chapter 2) and Peter Jones (Chapter 3), has enabled probation managers to adjust caseloads so that offenders who present the highest risk to public safety receive the greatest amount of attention, to rationalize budgets to demonstrate more precisely the level of funding needed by the department, and to link offenders with services not provided directly by probation departments. This restructuring of personnel is paralleled by the development of technologies that reduce demands on personnel.

In New York City, for example, low-risk probationers will soon be contacting the probation department electronically by means of kiosks located at probation offices. Much like bank card machines, these kiosks provide for identification of the probationer and the exchange of information through a video screen. Similarly, electronic monitoring, now used in many jurisdictions around the country, eases the demand on human resources. These technological developments represent well the concept of mutual adaptation: The goals of community corrections can remain constant while the means change in response to a steady decline in resources that threatens the capacity of agencies to continue the level of output consistent with their program goals.

Other responses to funding constraints focus on generating additional resources. Finn and Parent (1990) describe how probation departments in Texas have adopted supervision fees, requiring offenders to pay a portion of the cost of supervision. Clearly, the adoption of an ISP means that the per-probationer cost of supervision will increase for the portion of the probation population that receives these more intensive services. Forcing offenders to pay a portion of the cost not only makes adoption of the innovation more palatable to budget-conscious stakeholders, it provides a way of rethinking the goals of intensive probation. In paying these supervision fees, the offender becomes more customerlike, albeit unwillingly. One could argue that the quality of service matters more to those who pay for a service than to those who merely receive the service.

Another growing source of resources is the private sector. Public-private ventures have been common in prison settings for many years, and private correctional agencies, both institutional and community based, have supplanted and added to public services in many locations. Our focus here is not on the merits of private sector correctional operations; rather, we note the growth in efforts to engage business and community organizations in supporting community corrections. It is important to emphasize that the private sector has more to offer than just money.

In 1992, Michael Schumacher, chief probation office of the Orange County, California, Probation Department, was concerned that the public knew little about the programs of his department and thus was not in a position to support new initiatives. He and his colleagues decided to reach out to the community for assistance, and through approaching community leaders for help in building community awareness, the Probation Community Action Association (PCAA) was born.

The PCAA grew out of a request for help in making the public aware of the programs, activities, and innovative ideas of a public agency in which staff had embarked on a period of systematic restructuring of their way of doing business. Moreover, the department was in the midst of developing a new approach to preventing recidivism. Schumacher and his colleagues asked more than 60 corporate and community leaders with whom they were familiar to help—not with their money but with their skills and creative ideas. Recognizing that business leaders represent only one segment of the community and that most were white, leaders of grassroots community organizations were also asked to join in this community awareness effort.

The PCAA has produced an innovation that is worth noting: A nonprofit organization has been formed to raise funds from private sources to support a multiagency endeavor. Corporations are being asked to make 5-year contributions to PCAA of large amounts of money that will be placed in an endowment fund, the profits of which will be spent on this new program but not the principle. At the end of 5 years, or at the request of the corporation, the principle will be returned. An additional use of these funds will be to obtain matching funds from government sources.

The search for resources, of course, has its downside. Why the proliferation of electronic monitoring and boot camps with so little evidence that they achieve meaningful goals (Byrne & Pattavina, 1992)? The answer is simple: money. When government funding agencies advertise the availability of large sums of money for adopting a new innovation or replicating an exemplary program, among those that come running are officials from agencies that have made no investment in assessing needs, planning strategically, or developing a direction for program development. These are the opportunists that Ellickson and Petersilia (1983) spoke of in connection with failed implementation efforts. It is indeed unfortunate that federal funding agencies overdefine the goals and strategies of community corrections, thus suppressing need-related, creative development and adaptation to local political environments.

Conclusion

We have emphasized the idea that implementation is an ongoing process of adaptation, negotiation, and communication. To maximize the mutual fit between a program or policy and the environment within which it is initiated and allowed to develop, both the innovation and the environment must change. But the process of change cannot be allowed to drift out of control or it will damage the system as a whole. It is for this reason that we have also emphasized the need for a larger, shared vision of corrections, developed at the local level, that guides the process of mutual fitting.

In her article on survival conditions for ISP, Joan Petersilia (1990a) writes the following:

> If there is a single, most critical message for future innovators in this discussion, it could be summed up thus: Unless a community recognizes or accepts the premise that a change in corrections is needed, is affordable, and does not conflict with its sentiments regarding just punishment, an innovative project has little hope of surviving, much less succeeding. (p. 144)

To sell community corrections more effectively and guide the development of programs that are implemented well, we need a vision of corrections based on ideals or a preferred future. Continued growth of imprisonment in the face of the power of budgetary constraints demonstrates clearly the power of a vision, albeit a negative one. Putting bad people away behind walls and bars is a vision with wide appeal. Our inability to create and sell a different, credible, and powerful vision of criminal justice is the greatest obstacle in the United States to developing a more humane and constructive system of corrections. Community corrections means many things—more of the same, alternatives to something we don't like, new technologies, punitive measures that are as painful as prison, and so on. What is lacking is a larger vision of what corrections can look like without large numbers of men and women behind bars. With such a vision, implementation of community corrections could be placed in the context of a strategy that would drive development of a more just and humane criminal justice system. Without that vision, some of our innovations that are successfully implemented will serve only to reinforce the system as we know it.

The proliferation of community corrections programs, whether characterized as alternatives to incarceration, intermediate sanctions, or intermediate punishments, has occurred in a vision vacuum. What many innovators have provided, through the development of new technologies and the occasional effective implementation of new technologies, are some of the elements that might be included in a new vision of corrections, but as a group, these innovations have not been plugged into a larger paradigm. In other words, we are coming to believe that correctional programs in the community are superior to prison, but we lack the capacity to articulate why, except with regard to some minor offenders under some circumstances. Successful implementation depends on our ability to articulate in terms that others can understand the advantages of a different kind of correctional system. The current literature on community corrections is coming to accept the centrality of punishment as an aim of corrections. Morris and Tonry's (1990) book on intermediate punishments has influenced the language of community corrections as well as the goals that are put forward. Recently, Lurigio and Petersilia (1992) noted that although the revival of interest in intensive supervision probation (ISP) was stimulated by the outcries over prison overcrowding, ISP as a technology is credible from a theoretical perspective: It serves the goals of deterrence and incapacitation. But although implementation is served well by this move toward finding common ground with legislators and others, the new vision of corrections is becoming more complex as policymakers debate the potential of community corrections.

Improving Corrections Policy

The Importance of Researchers
and Practitioners Working Together

Joan Petersilia

This book grew out of one of the most exciting corrections conferences recently held in the United States—What Works in Community Corrections: A Consensus Conference, sponsored by the International Association of Residential and Community Alternatives (IARCA), in Philadelphia, November 3 through November 6, 1993. Conference organizers commissioned papers from leading researchers, asking each of them to summarize what was known about their assigned topic in the "What works?" debate and to identify relevant policy and program implications of their findings.

Each author did an admirable job, as the foregoing chapters attest, and the effectiveness of community corrections programs was well assessed. But more important than the details found in the individual chapters was the consensus that emerged from all of the authors (and conference attendees) concerning priorities. When all was said and done, there was a strong sense that the biggest challenge for corrections was not to design more and better research studies but, rather, for more productive relationships between "those who study" and "those who do." It was agreed that improvements in corrections policy and practice are more likely to emerge if researchers and practitioners work more closely together—identifying key research questions, selecting sites to test model programs, interpreting findings, and devising more realistic and politically sensitive policy solutions.

Collaborations between researchers and practitioners are obviously important in all policy areas, but they seem particularly critical in the area of corrections. The U.S. approach to corrections policy remains in disarray. A justifiable perception exists that federal, state, and local governments are largely paralyzed in their efforts to develop a sound corrections strategy. As a result, corrections is not being directed by those who are most knowledgeable about it; instead, policies appear driven by public opinion, fear, and political hype. One has only to witness the current adoption of "three strikes and you're out" mandates to be convinced that public opinion, rather than class knowledge, is driving crime policy.

Community-based sentencing programs are going through particularly difficult times right now. Both public and policymakers are frustrated with levels of violent crime and they are demanding harsh punishment—which in their minds equates with prison. The growth in prison populations means that fewer dollars are available for positive programming in community corrections. Yet experts believe that the criminal justice system's best hope of forestalling crime in the long run comes from community-based sanctions, not incarceration (Reiss & Roth, 1994). Producing scientific evidence to "prove" this and getting the relevant information into the public debate are exceedingly difficult. The prospects, however, are significantly enhanced if practitioners and researchers create stronger, more vocal alliances.

As Francis Hartmann (1994) noted in his conference summary, one reason corrections has taken the course it has is that policymakers have not taken the time to articulate what they are doing, evaluate their effectiveness, and take a proactive stance in educating the public about appropriate directions. Without this information, the public and, in turn, elected officials, act instead on information garnered from politicians and the media. Public opinion can be influenced by professional leadership, but there has to be a message, a plan, and a policy that is clearly articulated and readily understood.

Although there is widespread agreement that developing good relationships between academics and practitioners is important, bringing such relationships about in practice is exceedingly difficult. Academics deal mostly with understanding the problem, whereas practitioners and policymakers focus mostly on solutions. Academics have the luxury of considering options out of context, but policymakers must weigh the empirical results against political and economic constraints. Both groups agree that research must be good, credible, timely, and relevant. Researchers, however, place more emphasis on the first two, policymakers on the later two—hence there exists a natural tension.

Fortunately, researchers and practitioners have collaborated on a number of important projects in corrections, and from those efforts many valuable lessons can be gleaned. Researchers and practitioners have developed risk-need classification instruments for probation and parole, bail and sentencing guidelines, and recidivism prediction instruments for prison release, among others (Clear & Braga, 1995). Program evaluations have been informative on the effectiveness of intermediate sanctions, work and education programs, juvenile justice, aftercare services, and so on (Blumstein & Petersilia, 1994). These experiences have taught us some valuable lessons about creating partnerships for the purpose of informing public policy.

Creating a Collaborative Framework

It is clear that we need to create many more occasions where academics and practitioners meet to try to understand each other. But more than that, practitioners need to be involved at the outset in shaping the research agenda and deciding which topics should be given research priority. They are often left out or given a minor role in setting research priorities. In an ideal world, I believe practitioners should identify the pressing questions, researchers should design appropriate methodologies for answering those questions, and together they should interpret findings and suggest policy implications. When researchers or funders alone set research priorities, the relevance of research to operational needs and problems is often not adequately considered. Practitioners need to be involved in reviewing research proposals, providing sites for experiments, and disseminating research results. They also need to be consulted in deciding how programs will be evaluated and which outcome measures will be used to judge program effectiveness, whether it be recidivism, social indicators, family functioning, or whatever.

Creating collaboration cannot be left to informal arrangements among researchers, policymakers, and practitioners. All three must cooperate with funding agencies to develop a model for embodying and formalizing this collaborative framework. The model should include the following:

- Developing a forum for involving the policy community and researchers in continuing dialogue over research questions; interim findings; final results; and implications for policy, practice, and new research. Both the American Correctional Association (ACA) and the American Probation and Parole Association (APPA) have recently established working committees toward these ends.

- Organizing regularly convened conferences that bring members of the research and policy communities together to discuss emerging problems, eliciting their responses to results and helping them use the results in policy and practice. The IARCA conference serves as an exemplary example in this regard.

Once policy-relevant studies are produced, we need to disseminate and report the research results more effectively. The notion that a researcher writes a report with some recommendations and then a decision maker regards it, chooses a course of action, and implements it has been shown to have little applicability to real-world policy making. Light and Newman (1992) confirm that it does not work this way for corrections managers, even though they are anxious to use research findings. Research findings seldom enter into corrections managers' normal reading materials—which are instead newsletters, digests, staff reports, and the popular media. And as Light and Newman correctly observed, "If social science research is to be used, it must first enter the awareness of potential users" (p. 229).

It is now understood that research ideas must be part of the day-to-day interactions decision makers encounter. If the decision maker finds enough consistency pointing in a particular direction, he or she makes a decision and finds its implementation influenced by the fact that staff (and those he or she interacts with) have regarded the same sources and think of the problem in the same terms. Thus, dissemination is critically important, and research findings must be persuasively and engagingly communicated to the policy community to build knowledge about a problem in a common framework over the long term. Dissemination must be an ongoing process, rather than stopping with the production of the final report or journal article.

The dissemination problem is rather easy to fix, but it requires the researcher to envision a larger sense of constituency. This means that researchers must accept that their writings are designed more to influence policy than to impress their colleagues. It means that researchers must expend effort creating readable publications—not only for those who must consider the findings and recommendations but for the media and the general public as well. It means that researchers must take seriously the responsibility to make the practical implications of their findings clear, by giving the same explicit attention to the implications of the research as they currently do to reporting data and methods. It may also mean revising (and republishing) the results in several different formats (e.g., policy briefs, trade journals, and newspaper editorials). And most important, it means having face-to-face meetings with decision makers, who seldom wish to read even the most policy-oriented documents and prefer collaborative discussions rather than formal academic-style presentations. In short, we who are researchers must accept that until we inform the public of what we learn, our work is unfinished.

A couple of ongoing efforts are attempting to accomplish these aims. *Federal Probation* now includes in each quarterly publication a review of corrections research that is judged to have practical relevance. And recently, *The Prison Journal* has expanded and changed direction to focus more specifically on disseminating research on incarceration and alternative sanctions.

The dissemination vehicle is not the only problem. Researchers tend to shy away from suggesting policy and program implications because they fear the specters of "advocacy" and subjectivity. Credible policy research, however, must include at least a discussion of alternative policies and their possible consequences or a statement that the evidence is not sufficient to support any policy advice. Explanation of the meaning and implications of a study's findings does not constitute advocacy, nor does it violate scientific objectivity, as long as the findings and analysis lead logically to the conclusions and implications drawn.

Even when a readable, policy-relevant document has been produced and discussed with practitioner audiences, the collaborative framework remains woefully incomplete. Researchers need to help practitioners understand and apply the research findings. Criminal justice agency staff may consider research results and implications potentially useful in their jurisdictions, but they need direct and practical help to adapt policies and programs to their particular situation. Many practitioners have noted that research results are not at all self-implementing, and researchers should provide more education and training follow-up. The National Institute of Corrections (NIC) has been tremendously helpful here. It provides small technical assistance grants to agencies and researchers who wish to work together on implementing program or policy recommendations. It also funds ongoing larger programs of technical assistance and training to assist state and county agencies and interagency teams throughout the country to develop and enhance program and policy development capacity and skills.

Equally important, practitioners need to help researchers understand the usefulness and practicality of their recommendations once contextual matters are considered. Richard Nathan (1988) notes that researchers often fail to recognize that the relationship between social science and policy should be a two-way street: *"The conduct of applied social science research is not only a matter of what social science can do for the real world. It is also and very much a matter of what the real world can do for social science* [emphasis in original]."

We must also strive to conduct higher-quality corrections research, using larger samples and experimental research designs. Corrections research, for the most part, remains badly flawed. Important topical issues have not been addressed, and most of the existing studies are of poor quality. A major reason for this is the nature of the research itself. The vast majority of corrections research is descriptive, not evaluative. Yet policymakers and practitioners typically want answers to the question, Did the program work? Answering that question requires credible program evaluations, which are rare in criminal justice. Even when program evaluations are attempted, researchers and practitioners often fail to create adequate control groups. In other words, they end up comparing apples with oranges, and the conclusions remain ambiguous at best.

The proliferation of this type of research has strained the relationships between researchers and practitioners. Practitioners who cooperate with researchers often expect that the final research report will provide a clear assessment about the program's effectiveness. This expectation is seldom realized, and practitioners are often left frustrated by the research enterprise, judging research results vague and complicated and the implications so couched in caveats as to be of little practical value.

Researchers are not entirely to blame for this situation. They know that it is nearly impossible to assess program effectiveness unless one engages in more active research, in which the researcher manipulates the assignment of cases into comparison groups so that the two study groups are equivalent in all aspects except that one group is given a treatment and the other group is not. Any subsequent changes observed in these groups can then be attributed with a high degree of confidence to the differences in treatments. Researchers have been calling for such experiments in recent years, and practitioners should cooperate. Yes, implementing such experiments requires agency staff time, resources, and energy, but once completed, these experiments will provide more solid and credible information on the effects of correctional interventions on offender behavior.

Perhaps most important, researchers need to help program administrators understand more about the conduct of research. It should be acknowledged at the outset that it is hard to find statistically significant effects of corrections programs. We implement rather small interventions to correct what are almost intractable social problems, and money does not often permit a large number of persons to be involved, with the result that huge effects need to be produced before statistically significant findings can be found. Not understanding this situation often causes a great deal of frustration to program operators who "know that the program works." It may well work on an individual basis, but for it to be statistically confirmed, large samples and relatively large effects must be demonstrated. Let's take an example to illustrate. Suppose a probation population has an average 50% recidivism rate and a program manager believes that a new employment assistance program can reduce that rate to 30%. To evaluate that program scientifically, the manager would need to assign about 150 probationers randomly to the two programs during the study period. Often, the necessary-sized samples cannot be obtained, and hence the evaluation fails to show statistical significance. Researchers need to educate policymakers as to the futility of conducting program evaluations with small sample sizes—they will invariably show "no effect," further frustrating program managers.

But even "no effect" research findings need not be threatening to the program administrator who is comfortable with data and its proper usage. Research should *contribute* to policy and practice, but is not meant to provide the sole or even primary basis for it. In other words, research findings are meant to inform policy, not make it.

Research is not and cannot be an unambiguous guide to policy. Though a useful source of knowledge, research usually makes statements about relationships between two or more phenomena (such as the relationship between intensive supervision and recidivism). The fact that X produces a change in Y is not, in itself, sufficient grounds for a policy decision about Y; nor is the evidence that a change in X does not have any effect on Y sufficient grounds for abandoning an intervention on X.

An example may clarify the point. Susan Turner and I recently completed evaluating a 14-site randomized experiment to test the effectiveness of intensive supervision probation and parole (Petersilia & Turner, 1993c). The research solidly demonstrated that increasing supervision to offenders did not reduce recidivism. But that finding by itself does not provide compelling grounds for disbanding intensive supervision probation and parole (ISP). There are moral, justice, and economic issues that must be considered, along with the research findings. It is quite possible that ISP is justified, regardless of impact on recidivism, for purposes of proportionality in sentencing, cost savings, or myriad other organizational and bureaucratic goals. Judgments about whether or not a program should be continued are, in the final analysis, not solely scientific judgments. Understanding this subtle difference puts the astute practitioner—not the researcher—clearly in the driver's seat when it comes to interpreting research for policy's sake.

Researchers have the responsibility to provide *policy-relevant* information to administrators debating ISP program design and continuation, but it is the program administrator's responsibility to derive *policy prescriptions,* based on the research as well as other considerations. In the first instance, I am fulfilling my policy analyst role; if I engage in the latter, I am an advocate. Both the researcher and administrator have distinct responsibilities in the policy process, and if each of us takes those responsibilities seriously, we will establish a cumulative body of information about what works in criminal justice.

Whether or not the door remains open after studies with "no effects" are produced depends on the working relationship established between the researcher and the host agency and how conversant the administrator is with the appropriate use of research findings. It is *not* that researchers have the advice and practitioners need to listen. Rather, we are mutually dependent on—and potentially mutually beneficial to—one another. The practitioner community exercises control of the "laboratory" and continually generates policies and practices that must be evaluated and tested to determine their scientific merit and practical consequences.

Concluding Remarks

Some have suggested that the current crisis in corrections may be a blessing in disguise, because it has forced those in the field to begin to define exactly what they do, with whom, and to what effect. It need not be a daunting challenge. As practitioners and researchers, together we possess the necessary expertise to engage the U.S. public in more informed debates concerning crime control. But we have not chosen to use our expertise effectively, and, perhaps most important, we have not joined forces to create a united voice for correctional change.

We cannot afford to shy away from this challenge. The crime debates and decisions will continue, with or without our input; and I believe we have a strong obligation to place our best scientific information into the hands of those who make justice-related decisions. As corrections experts, we know more about the issues, have the best data available, can analyze it in responsible ways, and convey the caveats better than those who are now doing it and often seem to be "flying by the seat of their pants." Crime is too important to leave science or practical experience out of it. Neither can alone provide all of the answers, but a joined voice could serve to shift the crime debate away from ideological positions and toward one grounded in science and practical experience.

The interaction between practitioners and researchers at the conference from which this book developed was widely reported in both camps to have been stimulating and encouraging for the future. By the time this book is published, a follow-on conference will have been held in Seattle, Washington, extending the dialogue and inquiry into related subtopic areas of interest to those charged with making community corrections work in the future. Still further national gatherings are anticipated around the same theme in subsequent years. If the quality of presentation and interaction is as high and if the expected spin-offs into more ongoing practitioner-researcher collaboration at the local level materialize, at least the focus on what works will be sustained. If we do not lose track of the question, we will perhaps be less satisfied to continue doing business in an answerless vacuum.

References

Ackoff, R. (1984). *Creating the corporate future.* New York: John Wiley.

Administrative Office of the Courts. (1992). *New Jersey intensive supervision program: Progress report.* Trenton, NJ: Author.

Alkin, M. (1990). *Debates on evaluation.* Newbury Park, CA: Sage.

Altschuler, D., & Armstrong, T. (1990). *Intensive community-based aftercare programs: Assessment report.* Washington, DC: Office of Juvenile Justice and Delinquency Prevention.

Anderson, J. E. (1951). Review of unraveling juvenile delinquency. *Journal of Criminal Law, Criminology, and Police Science, 41,* 745-748.

Andrews, D. (1982). *The Level of Supervision Inventory (LSI): The first follow-up.* Toronto: Ministry of Correctional Services.

Andrews, D., & Bonta, J. (1994). *The psychology of criminal conduct.* Cincinnati, OH: Anderson.

Andrews, D., Bonta, J., & Hoge, R. (1990). Classification for effective rehabilitation: Rediscovering psychology. *Criminal Justice and Behavior, 17,* 19-52.

Andrews, D., & Kiessling, J. (1980). Program structure and effective correctional practices: A summary of the CaVIC research. In R. Ross & P. Gendreau (Eds.), *Effective correctional treatment* (pp. 441-463). Toronto: Butterworths.

Andrews, D., Kiessling, J., Mickus, S., & Robinson, D. (1985). *The Level of Supervision Inventory: Risk/needs assessment in community corrections.* Unpublished manuscript, Department of Psychology, Carleton University, Ottawa.

Andrews, D., Kiessling, J., Robinson, D., & Mickus, S. (1986). The risk principle of case classification: An outcome evaluation with young adult probationers. *Canadian Journal of Criminology, 28,* 377-384.

Andrews, D., & Robinson, D. (1984). *The Level of Supervision Inventory: Second report.* Report to Research Services (Toronto) of the Ontario Ministry of Correctional Services.

Andrews, D., & Wormith, J. (1989). Personality and crime: Knowledge destruction and construction in criminology. *Justice Quarterly, 6,* 289-309.

Andrews, D., Zinger, I., Hoge, R., Bonta, J., Gendreau, P., & Cullen, F. (1990). Does correctional treatment work? A clinically-relevant and psychologically-informed meta-analysis. *Criminology, 28,* 369-404.

Arbuthnot, J., & Gordon, D. (1986). Behavioral and cognitive effects of a moral reasoning development intervention of high-risk behavior disordered adolescents. *Journal of Consulting and Clinical Psychology, 54,* 208-216.

Argyris, C., Putnam, R., & Smith, D. (1985). *Action science.* San Francisco: Jossey-Bass.

Arling, G., & Lerner, K. (1981). *CMC—Strategies for case planning and supervision* (Model Probation and Parole Management Project). Washington, DC: National Institute of Corrections.

Armstrong, T. (1988). National survey of juvenile intensive probation supervision: Parts 1 & 2. *Criminal Justice Abstracts, 20*(2, 3), 342-348, 497-523.

Armstrong, T. L. (1991). Introduction. In *Intensive interventions with high-risk youths: Promising approaches in juvenile probation and parole.* Monsey, NY: Criminal Justice Press.

Austin, J., & Hardyman, P. (1991). *The use of early parole with electronic monitoring to control prison crowding: Evaluation of the Oklahoma Department of Corrections pre-parole supervised release with electronic monitoring.* San Francisco: National Council on Crime and Delinquency.

Automotive Transportation Center. (1990). *A survey of home detention programs in Indiana.* Indianapolis, IN: Author.

Aziz, D., Korotkin, P., & MacDonald, D. (1990). *Shock incarceration program follow-up study, August 1990.* Albany: New York Department of Correctional Services.

Aziz, D., Korotkin, P., & MacDonald, D. (1991). *Shock incarceration program follow-up study, May 1991.* Albany: New York Department of Correctional Services.

Baer, J., Baumgartner, W., Hill, V., & Blahd, W. (1991). Hair analysis for the detection of drug use in pretrial, probation, & parole populations. *Federal Probation, 55*(1), 3-10.

Baird, J. (1981). Probation and parole classification: The Wisconsin model. *Corrections Today, 43,* 36-41.

Baird, J., Heinz, R., & Bemus, B. (1979). *The Wisconsin case classification/staff deployment project.* Madison, WI: Bureau of Community Corrections.

Baird, S. (1973). *Juvenile parole prediction studies.* Joliet: Illinois Department of Corrections, Division of Research and Long Range Planning.

Baird, S. (1984, July). *Classification of juveniles in corrections: A model systems approach.* Unpublished monograph. Madison, WI: Isthmus Associates.

Baird, S. (1991). Intensive supervision programs for high-risk juveniles: Critical issues in program evaluation. In T. Armstrong (Ed.), *Intensive intervention with high risk youths: Promising approaches in juvenile probation and parole* (pp. 295-316). New York: Criminal Justice Press.

Baird, S., Storrs, G., & Connolly, H. (1984). *Classification and case management for juvenile offenders: A model systems approach.* Washington, DC: A. D. Little.

Baird, S., & Wagner, D. (1990). Measuring diversion: The Florida Community Control Program. *Crime & Delinquency, 36,* 112-125.

Ball, R., Huff, C., & Lilly, J. (1988). *House arrest and correctional policy: Doing time at home.* Newbury Park, CA: Sage.

Bangert-Drowns, R. (1992). Review of developments in meta-analytic method. In A. Kazdin (Ed.), *Methodological isues and strategies in clinical research* (pp. 439-467). Washington, DC: American Psychological Association.

Barkwell, L. (1980). Differential probation treatment of delinquency. In R. Ross & P. Gendreau (Eds.), *Effective correctional treatment* (pp. 281-297). Toronto: Butterworths.

Barton, C., Alexander, J., Waldron, H., Turner, C., & Warburton, J. (1985). Generalizing treatment effects of functional family therapy: Three replications. *American Journal of Family Therapy, 13,* 16-26.

Barton, W., & Butts, J. (1990). Viable options: Intensive supervision programs for juvenile delinquents. *Crime & Delinquency, 36,* 238-256.

Basta, J., & Davidson, W. (1988). Treatment of juvenile offenders: Study outcomes since 1980. *Behavioral Sciences and the Law, 6,* 355-384.

Baumer, T., Maxfield, M., & Mendelsohn, R. (1993). A comparative analysis of three electronically monitored home detention programs. *Justice Quarterly, 10,* 121-142.

Baumer, T., & Mendelsohn, R. (1991, November). *Comparing methods of monitoring home detention: The results of a field experiment.* Paper presented at the meeting of the American Society of Criminology, San Francisco.

Baumer, T., & Mendelsohn, R. (1993). *A cautionary tale about electronically monitored home detention.* Paper presented at the Electronically Monitored Home Confinement Conference at Simon Fraser University, Canada.

Baumer, T., Mendelsohn, R., & Rhine, C. (1990). *Executive summary—The electronic monitoring of non-violent convicted felons: An experiment in home detention.* Washington, DC: National Institute of Justice.

Beamon, A. (1991). An empirical comparison of meta-analytic and traditional reviews. *Personality and Social Psychology Bulletin, 17,* 252-257.

Beck, J., & Klein-Saffran, J. (1989). *Community control project* (Report No. 44). Washington, DC: United States Parole Commission.

Belenko, S., & Mara-Drita, I. (1988). *Drug use and pretrial misconduct: The utility of pre-arraignment drug tests as a predictor of failure-to-appear: Preliminary report.* New York: New York City Criminal Justice Agency.

Belenko, S., Mara-Drita, I., & McElroy, J. (1992). Drug tests and prediction of pretrial misconduct: Findings and policy issues. *Crime & Delinquency, 38,* 557-582.

Bernsten, K., & Christiansen, K. (1965). A resocialization experiment with short-term offenders. *Scandinavian Studies in Criminology, 1,* 35-54.

Berman, P. (1981). Thinking about programmed and adaptive implementation: Matching strategies to situations. In H. Ingram & D. Mann (Eds.), *Why policies succeed or fail* (pp. 205-227). Beverly Hills, CA: Sage.

Berman, P., & McLaughlin, M. (1975). *Federal programs supporting educational change: The findings in review* (IV, R-1589/4-HEW). Santa Monica, CA: RAND.

Berk, R. (1983). An introduction to sample selection bias in sociological data. *American Sociological Review, 48,* 386-398.

Blomberg, T. G. (1980). Widening the net: An anomaly in the evaluation of diversion programs. In M. W. Klein & K. Teilman (Eds.), *Handbook of criminal justice admninistration.* Beverly Hills, CA: Sage.

Blumstein, A., & Cohen, J. (1973). A theory of the stability of punishment. *Journal of Criminal Law and Criminology, 64,* 198-206.

Blumstein, A., Cohen, J., Martin, S., & Tonry, M. (Eds.). (1983). *Research on sentencing: The search for reform.* Washington, DC: National Academy Press.

Blumstein, A., Cohen, J., Roth, J., & Visher, C. (Eds.). (1986). *Criminal careers and "career criminals."* Washington, DC: National Academy Press.

Blumstein, A., & Petersilia, J. (1994). *NIJ and its research program.* Washington, DC: National Institute of Justice, U.S. Department of Justice.

Bonta, J. (1993). *Everything you wanted to know about electronic monitoring and never bothered to ask.* Ottawa: Ministry Secretariat, Solicitor General Canada.

Bonta, J., & Motiuk, L. (1985). Utilization of an interview-based classification instrument: A study of correctional halfway houses. *Criminal Justice and Behavior, 12,* 333-352.

Bonta, J., Parkinson, R., Pang, B., & Barkwell, L. (1994). *Toward a revised Manitoba offender classification system* (Report available from Corrections Research, Ministry Secretariat, Solicitor General Canada, Ottawa).

Borduin, C. (in press). Innovative models of treatment and service delivery in the juvenile justice system. *Journal of Clinical Child Psychology.*

Bottomly, A. (1973). Parole decisions in a long-term closed prison. *British Journal of Criminology, 13,* 26-40.

Braithwaite, J. (1989). *Crime, shame and reintegration.* Cambridge, UK: Cambridge University Press.

Brennan, T. (1987). Classification: An overview of selected methodological issues. In D. Gottfredson & M. Tonry (Eds.), *Prediction and classification: Criminal justice decision making* (pp. 201-248). Chicago: University of Chicago Press.

Brill, R. (1978). Implications of the conceptual level matching model for treatment of delinquents. *Journal of Research in Crime and Delinquency, 15*(2), 229-246.

Britt, C., Gottfredson, M., & Goldkamp, J. (1992). Drug testing and pretrial misconduct: An experiment on the specific deterrent effects of drug monitoring defendants on pretrial release. *Journal of Research in Crime and Delinquency, 29,* 62-78.

Brody, S. (1976). *The effectiveness of sentencing: A review of the literature* (Home Office Research Report No. 35). London: Her Majesty's Stationery Office.

Brown, M., & Roy, S. (1995). Manual and electronic house arrest: An evaluation of factors related to failure. In J. Smykla & W. Selke (Eds.), *Intermediate sanctions: Sentencing in the '90s* (pp. 37-53). Cincinnati, OH: Anderson.

Burgess, E. (1928). Factors determining success or failure on parole. In A. Bruce, A. Harno, E. Burgess, & J. Landesco (Eds.), *The workings of the indeterminate-sentence law and the parole system in Illinois.* Springfield, IL: State Board of Parole.

Burton, V., Marquart, J., Cuvelier, S., Alarid, L., & Hunter, R. (1993). A study of attitudinal change among boot camp participants. *Federal Probation, 57*(3), 46-52.

Byrne, J. (1990). The future of intensive probation supervision and the new intermediate sanctions. *Crime & Delinquency, 36,* 6-41.

Byrne, J., & Kelly, L. (1989). *Restructuring probation as an intermediate sanction: An evaluation of the implementation and impact of the Massachusetts Intensive Probation Supervision Program: Final report.* Washington, DC: National Institute of Justice, Research Program on the Punishment and Control of Offenders.

Byrne, J., Lurigio, A., & Baird, C. (1989). The effectiveness of the new intensive supervision programs. *Research in Corrections, 2*(2), 1-48.

Byrne, J., Lurigio, A., & Petersilia, J. (Eds.). (1992). *Smart sentencing: The emergence of intermediate sanctions.* Newbury Park, CA: Sage.

Byrne, J., & Pattavina, A. (1992). The effectiveness issue: Assessing what works in the adult community corrections system. In J. Byrne, A. Lurigio, & J. Petersilia (Eds.), *Smart sentencing: The emergence of intermediate sanctions* (pp. 281-303). Newbury Park, CA: Sage.

Camp, G., & Camp, C. (1993a). *The corrections yearbook: Adult corrections.* South Salem, NY: Criminal Justice Institute.

Camp, G., & Camp, C. (1993b). *The corrections yearbook: Probation and parole.* South Salem, NY: Criminal Justice Institute.

Casper, J., & Brereton, D. (1984). Evaluating criminal justice reforms. *Law and Society Review, 18,* 121-143.

Castle, M. (1991). Alternative sentencing: Selling it to the public. *NIC Research in Action.* Washington, DC: Department of Justice, Office of Justice Programs.

Challinger, D. (1974). A predictive device for parolees in Victoria. *Australian and New Zealand Journal of Criminology, 71,* 102-106.

Chandler, M. (1973). Egocentrism and antisocial behavior: The assessment and training of social perspective-taking skills. *Developmental Psychology, 44,* 326-333.

Cialdini, R. (1993). *Influence: Science and practice.* New York: HarperCollins.

Clear, T. (1994). *Harm in American penology: Offenders, victims, and their communities.* Albany: SUNY.

Clear, T., & Braga, A. (1995). Community corrections. In J. Q. Wilson & J. Petersilia (Eds.), *Crime.* San Francisco: Institute for Contemporary Studies.

Clear, T., & Byrne, J. (1992). The future of intermediate sanctions: Questions to consider. In J. Byrne, A. Lurigio, & J. Petersilia (Eds.), *Smart sentencing: The emergence of intermediate sanctions* (pp. 319-331). Newbury Park, CA: Sage.

Clear, T., Flynn, S., & Shapiro, C. (1987). Intensive supervision in probation: A comparison of three projects. In B. McCarthy (Ed.), *Intermediate punishments: Intensive supervision, home confinement, and electronic surveillance* (pp. 31-51). Monsey, NY: Criminal Justice Press.

Clear, T., & Hardyman, P. (1990). The new intensive supervision movement. *Crime & Delinquency, 36,* 42-60.

Clements, C. (1986). *Offender needs assessment.* College Park, MD: American Corrections Association.

Cochran, D. (1992). The long road from policy development to real change in sentencing practice. In J. Byrne, A. Lurigio, & J. Petersilia (Eds.), *Smart sentencing: The emergence of intermediate sanctions* (pp. 307-318). Newbury Park, CA: Sage.

Coffee, J., & Tonry, M. (1983). Hard choices: Critical trade-offs in the implementation of sentencing reform through guidelines. In M. Tonry & F. Zimring (Eds.), *Reform and punishment.* Chicago: University of Chicago Press.

Cohen, J. (1988). *Statistical power analysis for the behavioral sciences.* Hillsdale, NJ: Lawrence Erlbaum.

Collingwood, T., Douds, A., & Williams, H. (1980). Juvenile diversion: The Dallas Police Department Youth Services Program. In R. Ross & P. Gendreau (Eds.), *Effective correctional treatment* (pp. 93-100). Toronto: Butterworths.

Cook, T., Cooper, H., Cordray, D., Hartman, H., Hedges, L., Light, R., Louis, T., & Mosteller, F. (Eds). (1992). *Meta-analysis for explanation: A casebook.* New York: Russell Sage.

Copas, J. (1985). Prediction equations, statistical analysis, and shrinkage. In D. Farrington & R. Tarling (Eds.), *Prediction in criminology* (pp. 232-255). Albany: SUNY.

Copas J., & Tarling, R. (1984). *Some methodological issues in making predictions.* Paper prepared for the National Academy of Sciences Panel on Research in Criminal Careers.

Corbett, R., & Marx, G. (1992). Emerging technofallacies in the electronic monitoring movement. In J. Byrne, A. Lurigio, & J. Petersilia (Eds.), *Smart sentencing: The emergence of intermediate sanctions* (pp. 85-100). Newbury Park, CA: Sage.

Craig, M., & Glick, S. (1963). Ten years' experience with the Glueck social prediction table. *Crime & Delinquency, 9,* 249-261.

Cullen, F., & Gendreau, P. (1989). The effectiveness of correctional rehabilitation: Reconsidering the "nothing works" debate. In L. Goodstein & D. MacKenzie (Eds.), *American prisons: Issues in research and policy* (pp. 23-44). New York: Plenum.

Cullen, F., & Gilbert, K. (1982). *Reaffirming rehabilitation.* Cincinnati, OH: Anderson.

Cullen, F., Maakestad, W., & Cavender, G. (1987). *Corporate crime under attack: The Ford Pinto case and beyond.* Cincinnati, OH: Anderson.

Cullen, F., Skovron, S., Scott, J., & Burton, V. (1990). Public support for correctional rehabilitation: The tenacity of the rehabilitative ideal. *Criminal Justice and Behavior, 17,* 6-18.

Cullen, F., & Wright, J. (in press). The future of corrections. In B. Maguire & P. Radosh (Eds.), *The past, present, and future of American criminal justice.* New York: General Hall.

Currie, E. (1985). *Confronting crime: An American challenge.* New York: Pantheon.

Currie, E. (1989). Confronting crime: Looking toward the twenty-first century. *Justice Quarterly, 6,* 5-25.

Currie, E. (1993). *Reckoning: Drugs, the cities, and the American future.* New York: Hill & Wang.

Davidson, W., Gottschalk, R., Gensheimer, L., & Mayer, J. (1984). *Interventions with juvenile delinquents: A meta-analysis of treatment efficacy.* Washington, DC: National Institute of Juvenile Justice and Delinquency Prevention.

Davidson, W., Redner, R., Blakely, C., Mitchell, C., & Emshoff, J. (1987). Diversion of juvenile offenders: An experimental comparison. *Journal of Consulting and Clinical Psychology, 55,* 68-75.

Davis, S. (1986a). *Evaluation of the first year of expanded house arrest: October 1, 1984 through September 30, 1985.* Oklahoma City: Oklahoma Department of Corrections.

Davis, S. (1986b). *Previous incarcerations and house arrest placement outcome.* Oklahoma City: Oklahoma Department of Corrections.

Davis, S. (1987). *Evaluation of the second year of expanded house arrest: October 1, 1985 through September 30, 1986.* Oklahoma City: Oklahoma Department of Corrections.

Dawes, R. (1975). Case by case versus rule-generated procedures for the allocation of scarce resources. In M. Kaplan & S. Schwartz (Eds.), *Human judgment and decision processes in applied settings* (pp. 83-96). New York: Academic Press.

DeJong, W., & Franzeen, S. (1993) On the role of intermediate sanctions in corrections reform: The views of criminal justice professionals. *Journal of Crime and Justice, 16,* 47-73.

Dembo, R., Williams, L., Wish, E., & Schmeidler, J. (1990). Urine testing of detained juveniles to identify high-risk youth. In *Research in brief.* Washington, DC: National Institute of Justice.

Dickey, W. (1994). *Evaluating boot camp prisons.* Washington, DC: Campaign for an Effective Crime Policy.

DiIulio, J. (1987). *Governing prisons: A comparative study of correctional management.* New York: Free Press.

DiIulio, J. (1991). *No escape: The future of American corrections.* New York: Basic Books.

Doble, J., & Klein, J. (1989). *Prison overcrowding and alternative sentences: The views of the people of Alabama.* New York: Public Agenda Foundation.

Duffee, D., & Duffee, B. (1981). Studying the needs of offenders in prerelease centers. *Journal of Research in Crime and Delinquency, 18,* 232-253.

Duncan, O., Ohlin, L., Reiss, A., & Stanton, H. (1953). Formal devices for making selection decisions. *American Journal of Sociology, 58,* 573-584.

Durham, A. (1993). Public opinion regarding sentences for crime: Does it exist? *Journal of Criminal Justice, 21,* 1-11.

Eagly, A., & Chaiken, S. (1993). *The psychology of attitudes.* Fort Worth, TX: Harcourt, Brace, Jovanovich.

Ellickson, P., & Petersilia, J. (1983). *Implementing new ideas in criminal justice.* Santa Monica, CA: RAND.

Elliott, D., Huizinga, D., & Menard, S. (1989). *Multiple problem youth: Delinquency, substance abuse, & health problems.* New York: Springer-Verlag.

Elmore, R. (1982). Backward mapping: Implementation research and policy decisions. In W. Williams (Ed.), *Studying implementation: Methodological and administrative issues* (pp. 18-35). Chatham, NJ: Chatham House.

Ervin, L., & Schneider, A. (1990). Explaining the effects of restitution on offenders: Results from a national experiment in juvenile courts. In B. Galaway & J. Hudson (Eds.), *Criminal justice, restitution, and reconciliation* (pp. 18-35). Monsey, NY: Criminal Justice Press.

Erwin, B. (1986). Turning up the heat on probationers in Georgia. *Federal Probation, 50*(2), 17-24.

Everitt, B. S. (1993). *Cluster analysis.* London: Edward Arnold.

Fagan, J., Forst, M., & Vivona, T. (1988). *Treatment and reintegration of violent juvenile offenders.* San Francisco: URSA Institute.

Fallen, D., Apperson, C., Hall-Milligan, J., & Aos, S. (1977). *Intensive parole supervision: Report.* Washington, DC: Department of Social and Health Services.

Farrington, D. (1983). *Further analysis of a longitudinal survey of crime and delinquency.* Washington, DC: National Institute of Justice.

Farrington, D. (1985). Predicting self-reported and official delinquency. In D. Farrington & R. Tarling (Eds.), *Prediction in criminology* (pp. 150-173). Albany: SUNY.

Farrington, D., & Tarling, R. (Eds.). (1985). *Prediction in criminology.* Albany: SUNY.

Faust, D. (1993). Bringing the process home: Making it work in your agency. In P. McGarry & M. Carter (Eds.), *The intermediate sanctions handbook: Experiences and tools for policy-makers.* Washington, DC: Center for Effective Public Policy.

Fergusson, D., Donnell, A., Slater, S., & Fifield, J. (1975). *The prediction of juvenile offending: A New Zealand study.* Wellington, New Zealand: A. Shearer, Government Printer.

Feeley, M., & Simon, J. (1992). The new penology: Notes on the emerging strategy of corrections and its implications. *Criminology, 30,* 449-474.

Finckenauer, J. (1982). *Scared straight! and the panacea phenomenon.* Englewood Cliffs, NJ: Prentice Hall.

Finn, P., & Parent, D. (1990). Making the offender foot the bill: A Texas program. In *Program focus.* Washington, DC: Department of Justice, National Institute of Justice.

Fisher, F., & Kadane, J. (1983). Empirically based sentencing guidelines and ethical considerations. In A. Blumstein, J. Cohen, S. Martin, & M. Tonry (Eds.), *Research on sentencing: The search for reform* (pp. 184-193). Washington, DC: National Academy Press.

Florida Department of Corrections. (1990). *Boot camp: A twenty-five month review.* Tallahassee: Bureau of Planning, Research and Statistics.

Flowers, G., Carr, T., & Ruback, R. (1991). *Special Alternative Incarceration Project.* Atlanta: Georgia Department of Corrections.

Gabor, T. (1986). *The prediction of criminal behavior.* Toronto: University of Toronto Press.

Galaway, B. (1988). Restitution as innovation or unfulfilled promise? *Federal Probation, 52*(3), 3-14.

Garrett, C. (1985). Effects of residential treatment on adjudicated delinquents: A meta-analysis. *Journal of Research in Crime and Delinquency, 22,* 287-308.

Geismar, L., & Wood, K. (1986). *Family and delinquency: Resocializing the young offender.* New York: Human Sciences Press.

Gendreau, P. (1981). Treatment in corrections: Martinson was wrong. *Canadian Psychology, 22,* 332-338.

Gendreau, P. (1989). Programs that do not work: A brief comment on Brodeur and Doob. *Canadian Journal of Criminology, 31,* 193-195.

Gendreau, P. (in press). Offender rehabilitation: What we know and what needs to be done. *Criminal Justice and Behavior.*

Gendreau, P., & Andrews, D. (1990). Tertiary prevention: What the meta-analysis of the offender treatment literature tells us about "what works." *Canadian Journal of Criminology, 32,* 173-184.

Gendreau, P., & Andrews, D. (1994). *The correctional program assessment inventory* (5th ed.). Saint John: University of New Brunswick.

Gendreau, P., Cullen, F., & Bonta, J. (1994). Intensive rehabilitation supervision: The next generation of community corrections programs? *Federal Probation, 58*(1), 72-78.

Gendreau, P., & Goddard, M. (1995). *Community corrections in the U.S.: A decade of punishing stupidly.* Manuscript submitted for publication.

Gendreau, P., Goggin, C., & Annis, H. (1990). Survey of existing substance abuse programs. *Forum on Corrections Research, 2,* 608.

Gendreau, P., & Little, T. (1993). *A meta-analysis of the effectiveness of sanctions on offender recidivism.* Unpublished manuscript.

Gendreau, P., Little, T., & Goggin, C. (1995). *A meta-analysis of the predictors of adult offender recidivism: Assessment guidelines for classification and treatment.* Ottawa: Ministry Secretariat, Solicitor General of Canada.

Gendreau, P., Paparozzi, M., Little, T., & Goddard, M. (1993). Does "punishing smarter" work? An assessment of the new generation of alternative sanctions in probation. *Forum on Corrections Research, 5,* 31-34.

Gendreau P., & Ross, R. (1979). Effective correctional treatment: Bibliotherapy for cynics. *Journal of Research in Crime and Delinquency, 25,* 463-489.

Gendreau, P., & Ross, R. (1981a). Correctional potency: Treatment and deterrence on trial. In R. Roesch & R. Corrado (Eds.), *Evaluation and criminal justice policy* (pp. 29-57). Beverly Hills, CA: Sage.

Gendreau, P., & Ross, R. (1981b). Offender rehabilitation: The appeal of success. *Federal Probation, 45,* 45-48.

Gendreau, P., & Ross, R. (1983-1984). Correctional treatment: Some recommendations for successful intervention. *Juvenile and Family Court Journal, 34,* 31-40.

Gendreau P., & Ross, R. (1987). Revivification of rehabilitation: Evidence from the 1980s. *Justice Quarterly, 4,* 349-407.

Genevie, L., Margolies, E., & Muhlin, G. (1986). How effective is correctional intervention? *Social Policy, 17,* 52-57.

Gensheimer, L., Mayer, J., Gottschalk, R., & Davidson, W. (1986). Diverting youth from the juvenile justice system: A meta-analysis of intervention efficacy. In S. Apter & A. Goldstein (Eds.), *Youth violence: Program and prospects* (pp. 39-57). Elmsford, NY: Pergamon.

Gibbons, D. (1965). *Changing the lawbreaker.* Englewood Cliffs, NJ: Prentice Hall.

Glass, G., McGraw, B., & Smith, M. (1981). *Meta-analysis in social research.* Beverly Hills, CA: Sage.

Glueck, S., & Glueck, E. (1950). *Unraveling juvenile delinquency.* Cambridge, MA: Harvard University Press.

Goldkamp, J. (1987). Prediction in criminal justice policy development. In D. Gottfredson & M. Tonry (Eds.), *Prediction and classification: Criminal justice decision making* (pp. 103-150). Chicago: University of Chicago Press.

Goldkamp, J., & Gottfredson, M. (1985). *Policy guidelines for bail: An experiment in court reform.* Philadelphia: Temple University Press.

Goldkamp, J., Gottfredson, M., & Jones, P. (1988). *The implementation and evaluation of bail/pretrial release guidelines in Maricopa County Superior Court, Dade County Superior Circuit Court and Boston Municipal Court* (Vol. 2). Unpublished NIJ Report, Temple University, Philadelphia.

Goldkamp, J., Gottfredson, M., & Jones, P. (1994). *Unnecessary detention or unsafe release: Exploring judicial reform of pretrial release in three major criminal courts.* New York: Plenum.

Goldkamp, J., Gottfredson, M., & Weiland, D. (1990). Pretrial drug testing and defendant risk. *Journal of Criminal Law and Criminology, 81,* 585-652.

Goldkamp, J., & Jones, P. (1992). Pretrial drug-testing experiments in Milwaukee and Prince George's County: The context of implementation. *Journal of Research in Crime and Delinquency, 29,* 430-465.

Gordon, D., & Arbuthnot, J. (1987). Individual, group, & family interventions. In H. Quay (Ed.), *Handbook of juvenile delinquency* (pp. 290-324). New York: John Wiley.

Gordon, D., Arbuthnot, J., Gustafson, K., & McGreen, P. (1988). Home-based behavioral-systems family therapy with disadvantaged juvenile delinquents. *American Journal of Family Therapy, 16,* 243-255.

Gottfredson, D. (1987). Prediction and classification. In D. Gottfredson & M. Tonry (Eds.), *Prediction and classification: Criminal justice decision making* (pp. 1-20). Chicago: University of Chicago Press.

Gottfredson, D., & Ballard, K. (1964). *Association analysis, predictive attribute analysis, and parole behavior.* Paper presented at Western Psychological Association, Portland, OR.

Gottfredson, D., Hoffman, P., Sigler, M., & Wilkins, L. (1975). Making paroling policy explicit. *Crime & Delinquency, 21,* 34-44.

Gottfredson, D., & Tonry, M. (Eds.). (1987). *Prediction and classification: Criminal justice decision making.* Chicago: University of Chicago Press.

Gottfredson, D., Wilkins, L., & Hoffman, P. (1978). *Guidelines for parole and sentencing.* Lexington, MA: D. C. Heath.

Gottfredson, M. (1974). An empirical analysis of pretrial release decisions. *Journal of Criminal Justice, 2,* 287.

Gottfredson, M. (1984). *Victims of crime: The dimensions of risk* (Home Office Research Study No. 81). London: Her Majesty's Stationary Office.

Gottfredson, M., & Gottfredson, D. (1988). *Decision making in criminal justice: Toward the rational exercise of discretion.* New York: Plenum.

Gottfredson, M., & Hirschi, T. (1990). *A general theory of crime.* Stanford, CA: Stanford University Press.

Gottfredson, S. (1987). Prediction: An overview of selected methodological issues. In D. Gottfredson & M. Tonry (Eds.), *Prediction and classification: Criminal justice decision making* (pp. 21-51). Chicago: University of Chicago Press.

Gottfredson, S., & Gottfredson, D. (1979). *Screening for risk: A comparison of methods.* Washington, DC: National Institute of Corrections.

Gottfredson S., & Gottfredson, D. (1985). Screening for risk among parolees: Policy, practice and method. In D. Farrington & R. Tarling (Eds.), *Prediction in criminology* (pp. 54-77). Albany: SUNY.

Gottfredson, S., & Gottfredson, D. (1986). The accuracy of prediction models. In A. Blumstein, J. Cohen, & C. Visher (Eds.), *Criminal careers and "career criminals"* (Vol. 2, pp. 212-290). Washington, DC: National Academy Press.

Gottfredson, S., & Taylor, R. (1983). *The correctional crisis: Prison populations and public policy.* Washington, DC: National Institute of Justice.

Gottfredson, S., & Taylor, R. (1986). Person-environment interactions in the prediction of recidivism. In R. Sampson & J. Byrne (Eds.), *Environmental criminology* (pp. 133-155). New York: Springer-Verlag.

Gottschalk, R., Davidson, W., II, Gensheimer, L., & Mayer, J. (1987). Community based interventions. In H. Quay (Ed.), *Handbook of juvenile delinquency* (pp. 266-289). New York: John Wiley.

Graham, S. (1981). Predictive and concurrent validity of the Jesness Inventory Asocial Index. *Journal of Consulting and Clinical Psychology, 5,* 740-742.

Grau, C. (1981). The limits of planned change in courts. *Justice System Journal, 6,* 84-99.

Graziano, A., & Mooney, K. (1984). *Children and behavior therapy.* Chicago: Aldine.

Greenberg, D. (1977). The correctional effects of corrections: A survey of evaluations. In D. Greenberg (Ed.), *Corrections and punishment* (pp. 111-148). Beverly Hills, CA: Sage.

Greene, J. (1988). Structuring criminal fines: Making an "intermediate penalty" more useful and equitable. *Justice System Journal, 13,* 37-50.

Greenwood, P. (1982). *Selective incapacitation.* Santa Monica, CA: RAND.

Greenwood, P., & Zimring, F. (1985). *One more chance: The pursuit of promising intervention strategies for chronic juvenile offenders.* Santa Monica, CA: RAND.

Gruenewald, P., Laurence, S., & West, B. (1985). *National evaluation of the New Pride Replication Program. Executive summary.* Walnut Creek, CA: Pacific Institute for Research and Evaluation.

Gurney, J. (1982). Prosecutorial discretion and the implementation of a legislative mandate. In M. Morash (Ed.), *Implementing criminal justice policies* (pp. 41-49). Beverly Hills, CA: Sage.

Haapanen, R. (1988). *Selective incapacitation and the serious offender: A longitidunal study of criminal career patterns.* Sacramento: California Department of Youth Authority.

Haapanen, R. (1993). *Drug testing for youthful offenders on parole: An experimental study.* Unpublished project description, California Youth Authority, Sacramento, CA.

Hagan, J. (1993). Structural and cultural disinvestment and the new ethnographies of poverty and crime. *Contemporary Sociology, 22,* 327-332.

Hann, R., & Harman, W. (1992). *Predicting general release risk for Canadian penitentiary inmates* (User Report No. 1992-07). Ottawa: Ministry Secretariat, Solicitor General, Canada.

Harland, A. (1993). Defining a continuum of sanctions: Some research and policy implications. *Perspectives, 17*(2), 6-15.

Harland, A., & Harris, P. (1984). Developing and implementing alternatives to incarceration: A problem of planned change in criminal justice. *University of Illinois Law Review, 2,* 319-364.

Harland, A., & Harris, P. (1987). Structuring the development of alternatives to incarceration. In S. Gottfredson & S. McConville (Eds.), *America's correctional crisis.* Westport, CT: Greenwood.

Harland, A., & Rosen, C. (1990). Impediments to the recovery of restitution by crime victims. *Violence and Victims, 5*(2), 127-140.

Harland, A., Warren, M., & Brown, E. (1979). *A guide to restitution programming* (Working Paper 17). Albany, NY: Criminal Justice Research Center.

Harris, M. (1983-1984). Strategies, values, & the emerging generation of alternatives to incarceration. *Review of Law and Social Change, 12,* 141-170.

Harris, P. (1994). Client management classification and prediction of probation outcome. *Crime & Delinquency, 40,* 154-174.

Hartmann, F. (1994, February). Consensus statement, IARCA Conference. *IARCA Journal on Community Corrections,* pp. 14-15.

Hathaway, S., & Monachesi, E. (1957). The personalities of pre-delinquent boys. *Journal of Criminal Law, Criminology and Police Science, 48,* 249-263.

Hathaway, S., Monachesi, E., & Young, L. (1960). Delinquency rates and personality. *Journal of Criminal Law, Criminology and Police Science, 50,* 433-444.

Havinghurst, R., Bowman, P., Liddle, G., Mathews, C., & Pierce, J. (1962). *Growing up in River City*. New York: John Wiley.

Hedges, L., & Olkin, I. (1985). *Statistical methods for meta-analysis*. New York: Academic Press.

Heinz, J., Galaway, B., & Hudson, J. (1976). Restitution or parole: A follow-up study of adult offenders. *Social Service Review, 50,* 148-156.

Hillsman, S. (1990). Fines and day fines. In M. Tonry & N. Morris (Eds.), *Crime and justice: A review of research* (Vol. 12, pp. 47-98). Chicago: University of Chicago Press.

Hindelang, M., Hirschi, T., & Weis, J. (1981). *Measuring delinquency*. Beverly Hills, CA: Sage.

Hoffman, P. (1983). Screening for risk: A revised salient factor score (SFS 81). *Journal of Criminal Justice, 11,* 539-547.

Hoffman, P., & Beck, J. (1985). Recidivism among released federal prisoners: Salient factor score and five year follow-up. *Criminal Justice and Behavior, 12,* 501-507.

Hoffman, P., Stone-Meierhoefer, B., & Beck, J. (1978). Salient factor score and releasee behavior: Three validation samples. *Law and Human Behavior, 2,* 47-63.

Hoge, R., Leschied, A., & Andrews, D. (1993). *An investigation of young offender services in the province of Ontario: A report of the repeat offender project*. Toronto: Ontario Ministry of Community and Social Services.

Holley, P., & Connelly, M. (1993). *Preliminary assessment of the Regimented Inmate Discipline Program*. Weatherford: Southwestern Oklahoma State University.

Hollin, C. (1993). Advances in the psychological treatment of delinquent behavior. *Criminal Behavior and Mental Health, 3,* 42-157.

Horst, P. (1966). *Psychological measurement and prediction*. Belmont, CA: Wadsworth.

Hudzik, J., & Cordner, G. (1983). *Planning change in criminal justice organizations and systems*. New York: Macmillan.

Hunt, D. (1971). *Matching models in education*. Toronto: Ontario Institute for Studies in Education.

Innes, C. (1993). Recent public opinion in the United States toward punishment and corrections. *Prison Journal, 73,* 220-236.

Irwin, J., & Austin, J. (1994). *It's about time: America's imprisonment binge*. Belmont, CA: Wadsworth.

Izzo, R., & Ross, R. (1990). Meta-analysis of rehabilitation programs for juvenile delinquents: A brief report. *Criminal Justice and Behavior, 17,* 134-142.

Jesness, C. (1971-1972, Winter). Comparative effectiveness of two institutional treatment programs for delinquents. *Child Care Quarterly, 1*(2), 119-139.

Jesness, C. (1975). Comparative effectiveness of behavior modification and transactional analysis programs for delinquents. *Journal of Consulting and Clinical Psychology, 43,* 758-779.

Jesness, C., Allison, T., McCormick, P., Wedge, R., & Young, M. (1975). *Cooperative Behavior Demonstration Project. Final report*. Sacramento, CA: Office of Criminal Justice Planning.

Johns, D., & Wallach, J. (1981). *Juvenile delinquency prevention: A review of evaluation studies, 1974-1979*. Sacramento: California Youth Authority.

Jolin, A. (1988). *Electronic Surveillance Program: Clackamas County community corrections, Oregon evaluation*. Oregon City, OR: Clackamas County Community Corrections.

Jolin, A., & Stipak, B. (1991). *Clackamas County Community Corrections Intensive Drug Program: Program evaluation report*. Portland, OR: Portland State University, Department of Administration of Justice.

Jolin, A., & Stipak, B. (1992). Drug treatment and electronically monitored home confinement: An evaluation of a community-based sentencing option. *Crime & Delinquency, 38,* 158-170.

Jones, P. (1991). The risk of recidivism: Evaluating the public safety component of a community corrections program. *Journal of Criminal Justice, 19,* 49-66.

Jones, P. (1993a). *The development and validation of a risk classification instrument for probation violators.* Unpublished report for New York City Department of Probation.

Jones, P. (1993b, July). *Diverting probation violators from jail? The Edgecombe Day Treatment Center, New York City.* Paper presented at the British Criminology Conference, Cardiff, Great Britain.

Jones, P., & Goldkamp, J. (1991a). The bail guidelines experiment in Dade County, Miami: A case study in the development and implementation of a policy innovation. *Justice System Journal, 15,* 445-476.

Jones, P., & Goldkamp, J. (1991b). Judicial guidelines for pretrial release: Research and policy developments in the United States. *Howard Journal of Criminal Justice, 30,* 140-160.

Jones, P., & Goldkamp, J. (1993). Implementing pretrial drug-testing programs in two experimental sites: Some deterrence and jail bed implications. *Prison Journal, 73,* 199-219.

Juvenile Justice Statistics and Systems Development Program. (1991, May). *Advisors' handbook.* Pittsburgh: National Center for Juvenile Justice.

Kass, G. V. (1980). An exploratory technique for investigating large quantities of categorical data. *Applied Statistics, 29,* 119-127.

Kaufman, P. (1985). *Meta-analysis of juvenile delinquency prevention programs.* Unpublished master's thesis, Claremont Graduate School, Claremont, CA.

Kelley, F., & Baer, D. (1971). Physical challenge as a treatment for delinquency. *Crime & Delinquency, 17,* 437-445.

Kelling, G., Edwards, S., & Moore, M. (1986). Federally funded community crime control: Urban Initiatives Anti-Crime Program. *Criminal Justice Policy Review, 1,* 59-75.

Knapp, K. (1988a, Winter). Assistance for structured sentencing projects. Next step: Nonimprisonment guidelines. *Perspectives,* pp. 8-10.

Knapp, K. (1988b). Structured sentencing: Building on experience. *Judicature, 72,* 46.

Kobrin, S., & Klein, M. (1982). *National evaluation of the deinstitutionalization of status offender programs.* Washington, DC: U.S. Department of Justice.

Kohlberg, L. (1976). Moral stages and moralization. In T. Lickona (Ed.), *Development and behavior* (pp. 31-53). New York: Holt, Rinehart and Winston.

Krisberg, B., & Austin, J. (1982). The unmet promise of alternatives to incarceration. *Crime and Delinquency, 28*(3), 374-409.

Krisberg, B., Rodriguez, O., Baake, A., Neuenfeldt, D., & Steele, P. (1989). *Demonstration of post-adjudication, non-residential intensive supervision programs: Assessment report.* San Francisco: National Council on Crime and Delinquency.

Kurz, G. A., & Moore, L. E. (1993, July). *Toward the development of "8%" problem solutions.* Unpublished research paper, Orange County Probation Department, California.

Lab, S., & Whitehead, J. (1988). An analysis of juvenile correctional treatment. *Crime & Delinquency, 34,* 60-85.

Langan, P. (1994). Between prison and probation: Intermediate sanctions. *Science, 264,* 791-793.

Larson, J. (1980). *Why government programs fail: Improving policy implementation.* New York: Praeger.

Latessa, E. (1991). *A preliminary evaluation of the Cuyahoga County adult probation department's intensive supervision groups.* Cincinnati, OH: University of Cincinnati.

Latessa, E. (1992). *Intensive supervision and case management classification: An evaluation.* Cincinnati, OH: University of Cincinnati.

Latessa, E. (1993a). *An evaluation of the Lucas County Adult Probation Department's IDU and high risk groups.* Cincinnati, OH: University of Cincinnati.

Latessa, E. (1993b). *Profile of the special units of the Lucas County Adult Probation Department.* Cincinnati, OH: University of Cincinnati.

Lawrence, P., & Lorsch, J. (1969). *Developing organizations: Diagnosis and action.* Reading, MA: Addison-Wesley.

Lee, R., & Haynes, N. (1980). Project CREST and the anal-treatment approach to delinquency: Methods and research summarized. In R. Ross & P. Gendreau (Eds.), *Effective correctional treatment* (pp. 171-184). Toronto: Butterworths.

Liebert, R., & Spiegler, M. (1990). *Personality: Strategies and issues* (6th ed.). Pacific Grove, CA: Brooks/Cole.

Light, S., & Newman, T. (1992). Awareness and use of social research among executive and administrative staff members of correctional agencies. *Justice Quarterly, 9,* 61-83.

Lillis, J. (1993, September). "Shock" prisons now used in over half DOC systems. *Correctional Compendium, 18,* 8, 12.

Lilly, J., Ball, R., Curry, G., & McMullen, J. (1993). Electronic monitoring of the drunk driver: A seven-year study of the home confinement alternative. *Crime & Delinquency, 39,* 462-484.

Lilly, J., Ball, R., & Wright, J. (1987). Home incarceration with electronic monitoring in Kenton County, Kentucky: An evaluation. In B. McCarthy (Ed.), *Intermediate punishments: Intensive supervision, home confinement and electronic surveillance* (pp. 189-203). New York: Criminal Justice Press.

Lippitt, R. (1983). Future before you plan. *The NTL manager's handbook* (pp. 374-381). United Kingdom: Tavistock, NTL Institute.

Lipsey, M. (1989). *The efficacy of intervention for juvenile delinquency.* Paper presented at the American Society of Criminology annual meeting, Reno, Nevada.

Lipsey, M. (1992). Juvenile delinquency treatment: A meta-analytic inquiry into the variability of effects. In T. Cook, H. Cooper, D. Cordray, H. Hartmann, L. Hedges, R. Light, T. Louis, & F. Mosteller (Eds.), *Meta-analysis for explanation* (pp. 83-127). New York: Russell Sage.

Lipsey, M., & Wilson, D. (1993). The efficacy of psychological, educational, and behavioral treatment: Confirmation from meta-analysis. *American Psychologist, 48,* 1181-1209.

Lipton, D., Martinson, R., & Wilks, J. (1975). *The effectiveness of correctional intervention: A survey of treatment evaluation studies.* New York: Praeger.

Little, R., & Rubin, D. (1987). *Statistical analysis with missing data.* New York: John Wiley.

Loeber, R., & Dishion, T. (1983). Early predictors of male delinquency: A review. *Psychological Bulletin, 94,* 68-99.

Loey, T. (1994, April 21). Boot camp's grads slipping back to jail. *Boston Globe,* pp. 1, 26.

Losel, F., & Koferl, P. (1989). Evaluation research on correctional treatment in West Germany: A meta-analysis. In H. Wegener, F. Losel, & J. Haisch (Eds.), *Criminal behavior and the justice system: Psychological perspectives* (pp. 334-355). New York: Springer-Verlag.

Loveless, P. (1990, November). *The impact of a home incarceration program on the offenders, the community, and the system.* Paper presented at the annual meeting of the American Society of Criminology, Baltimore, MD.

Loza, W. (1991). *Effectiveness of the Wisconsin Case Management: Strategies for use with Canadian offenders.* Unpublished doctoral dissertation, Carleton University, Ottawa.

Lundman, R. (1984). *Prevention and control of juvenile delinquency.* New York: Oxford.

Lurigio, A. J., & Petersilia, J. (1992). The emergence of intensive probation programs in the United States. In J. M. Byrne, A. J. Lurigio, & J. Petersilia (Eds.), *Smart sentencing: The emergence of intermediate sanctions* (pp. 3-17). Newbury Park, CA: Sage.

MacKenzie, D. (1990). Boot camp prisons: Components, evaluations, and empirical issues. *Federal Probation, 54*(3), 44-52.

MacKenzie, D. (1991). The parole performance of offenders released from shock incarceration (boot camp prisons): A survival time analysis. *Journal of Quantitative Criminology, 7,* 213-236.

MacKenzie, D., & Ballow, D. (1989). Shock incarceration programs in state correctional jurisdictions: An update. In *Research in action.* Washington, DC: National Institute of Justice.

MacKenzie, D., & Shaw, J. (1990). Inmate adjustment and change during shock incarceration: The impact of correctional boot camp programs. *Justice Quarterly, 7,* 125-150.

MacKenzie, D., & Shaw, J. (1993). The impact of shock incarceration on technical violations and new criminal activities. *Justice Quarterly, 10,* 463-487.

MacKenzie, D., Shaw, J., & Gowdy, V. (1993). An evaluation of shock incarceration programs in Louisiana. In *Research in brief.* Washington, DC: National Institute of Justice.

MacKenzie, D., & Souryal, C. (1993). *Inmate attitude change during incarceration: A comparison of boot camp and traditional prison.* College Park: University of Maryland.

Mainprize, S. (1993). *Social, psychological, and familial impacts of home confinement and electronic monitoring: Exploratory research findings from BC's pilot project.* Paper presented at the conference on Electronically Monitored Home Confinement, Vancouver, BC.

Majone, G., & Wildavsky, A. (1979). Implementation as evolution. In J. Pressman & A. Wildavsky (Eds.), *Implementation* (2nd ed., pp. 163-180). Berkeley: University of California Press.

Maletzky, B. (1991). *Treating the sexual offender.* Newbury Park, CA: Sage.

Maltz, M. (1984). *Recidivism.* Orlando, FL: Academic Press.

Mannheim, H., & Wilkins, L. (1955). *Prediction methods in relation to Borstal training.* London: Her Majesty's Stationary Office.

Markley, G. (1989). The marriage of mission, management, marketing and measurement. *Research in Corrections, 2*(2), 49-56.

Marshall, W., & Pithers, W. (1994). A reconsideration of treatment outcome with sex offenders. *Criminal Justice and Behavior, 21,* 10-27.

Martinson, R. (1974). What works? Questions and answers about prison reform. *Public Interest, 35,* 22-54.

Martinson, R. (1976). California research at the crossroads. *Crime & Delinquency, 22,* 178-191.

Martinson, R. (1979). New findings, new views: A note of caution regarding sentencing reform. *Hofstra Law Review, 7,* 243-258.

Matson, J., & DiLorenzo, T. (1984). *Punishment and its alternatives: A new perspective for behavior modification.* New York: Springer.

Maxfield, M., & Baumer, T. (1991). *Evaluation of pretrial home detention with electronic monitoring: Final report.* Bloomington: Indiana University.

Mayer, J., Gensheimer, L., Davidson, W., & Gottschalk, R. (1986). Social learning treatment within juvenile justice: A meta-analysis of impact in the natural environment. In S. Apter & A. Goldstein (Eds.), *Youth violence: Program and prospects* (pp. 24-38). Elmsford, NY: Pergamon.

McCord, W., & McCord, J. (1964). *The psychopath: An essay on the criminal mind.* New York: Van Nostrand Reinhold.

McCorkle, R. (1993). Research note: Punish and rehabilitate? Public attitudes toward six common crimes. *Crime & Delinquency, 39,* 240-252.

McGarry, P. (1990, Spring). Improving the use of intermediate sanctions. *Community Corrections Quarterly, 1*(3), 2-6.

McLaughlin, M. (1976). Implementation as mutual adaptation: Change in classroom organization. In W. Williams & R. Elmore (Eds.), *Social program evaluation* (pp. 167-180). San Diego: Academic Press.

Meehl, P. (1954). *Clinical versus statistical prediction.* Minneapolis: University of Minnesota Press.

Meehl, P., & Rosen, A. (1955). Antecedent probability and the efficacy of psychometric signs, patterns or cutting scores. *Psychological Bulletin, 52,* 194-216.

Megargee, E., & Bohn, M. (1979). *Classifying criminal offenders: A new system based on the MMPI.* Beverly Hills, CA: Sage.

Menzies, R., Webster, C., McMain, S., Staley, S., & Scaglione, R. (1994). The dimensions of dangerousness revisited: Assessing forensic predictions about violence. *Law and Human Behavior, 18,* 1-28.

Mieczkowski, T., Landress, H., Newel, R., & Coletti, S. (1993). Testing hair for illicit drug use. In *Research in brief.* Washington, DC: National Institute of Justice.

Miller, J. (1986). Sentencing: What lies between sentiment and ignorance? *Justice Quarterly, 3,* 231.

Ministry of Correctional Services. (1991). *An evaluation of the electronic monitoring pilot project.* Ottawa: Ministry of Correctional Services.

Ministry of Justice. (1988). *Electronic house arrest: A captivating alternative?* The Hague, Netherlands: Committee on the Electronic Monitoring of Offenders.

Mitchell, C., Zehr, J., & Butter, C. (1985a). *Intensive supervision/early release parole.* Salt Lake City: Utah Department of Corrections.

Mitchell, C., Zehr, J., & Butter, C. (1985b). *Intensive supervision/high risk parole.* Salt Lake City: Utah Department of Corrections.

Mitchell, S., & Rosa, P. (1981). Boyhood behavior problems as precursors of criminality: A fifteen year follow-up. *Journal of Child Psychology and Psychiatry, 22,* 19-33.

Molof, M. (1991). *Study of the intensive probation supervision for multiple DUI offenders in Linn County, Oregon.* Linn County, OR: Integrated Research Services.

Monahan, J. (1981). *Predicting violent behavior.* Beverly Hills, CA: Sage.

Monahan, J. (1984). The prediction of violent behavior: Toward a second generation of theory and policy. *American Journal of Psychiatry, 141,* 10-15.

Moon, M., & Latessa, E. (1993, March). *The effectiveness of an outpatient drug treatment program on felony probationers.* Paper presented at the annual meeting of the Academy of Criminal Justice Sciences, Kansas City.

Moos, R. (1975). *Evaluating correctional and community settings.* New York: John Wiley.

Morgan, G. (1986). *Images of organization.* Newbury Park, CA: Sage.

Morris, N., & Miller, M. (1985). Predictions of dangerousness. In M. Tonry & N. Morris (Eds.), *Crime and justice: An annual review of research* (Vol. 6). Chicago: University of Chicago Press.

Morris, N., & Tonry, M. (1990). *Between prison and probation: Intermediate punishments in a rational sentencing system.* New York: Oxford University Press.

Motiuk, L. (1991). *Antecedents and consequences of prison adjustment: A systematic assessment and reassessment approach.* Unpublished doctoral dissertation, Carleton University, Ottawa, Canada.

Motiuk, L. (1993). Where are we with our ability to assess risk? *Forum on Corrections Research, 5,* 14-19.

Motiuk, L., Bonta, J., & Andrews, D. (1990, June). *Dynamic predictive criterion validity in offender assessment.* Paper presented at the Canadian Psychological Association annual conference, Ottawa.

Motiuk, L., & Porporino, F. (1989). *Field test of the Community Risk/Needs Management Scale* (Research Report No. R-06). Ottawa: Correctional Service Canada.

Mueller, P. (1960). Success rates as a function of treatment assignment and juvenile delinquency classification interaction. *California State Board of Corrections Monograph, 1,* 7-14.

Musheno, M., Palumbo, D., Maynard-Moody, S., & Levine, J. (1990). Evaluating the implementation of community corrections. In D. Duffee & E. McGarrell (Eds.), *Community corrections: A community field approach* (pp. 251-268). Cincinnati, OH: Anderson.

Nakamura, R., & Smallwood, F. (1980). *The politics of policy implementation.* New York: St. Martin's.

Nathan, R. (1988). *Social science in government: Uses and abuses.* Princeton, NJ: Princeton University Press.

National Advisory Commission on Criminal Justice Standards and Goals. (1973). *Report of the Task Force on Corrections.* Washington, DC: Government Printing Office.

National Council on Crime and Delinquency. (1991). *Evaluation of the Florida Community Control Program.* San Francisco: Author.

Neises, E. (1990). *Georgia's alternatives to incarceration.* Unpublished manuscript, Center for Alternative Sentencing and Employment Services, New York.

Neises, E. (1993). *Report: The Center for Alternative Sentencing and Employment Services.* New York: Center for Alternative Sentencing and Employment Services.

Neville, L. (1989). *British Columbia electronic monitoring pilot project.* Ministry of Solicitor General, British Columbia.

New York Department of Correctional Services and New York Division of Parole. (1990). *The second annual report to the legislature: Shock incarceration in New York State.* Albany, NY: Division of Program Planning, Research, & Evaluation.

New York Department of Correctional Services and New York Division of Parole. (1991). *The third annual report to the legislature: Shock incarceration in New York State.* Albany, NY: Division of Program Planning, Research, & Evaluation.

New York Department of Correctional Services and New York Division of Parole. (1992). *The fourth annual report to the legislature: Shock incarceration in New York State.* Albany, NY: Division of Program Planning, Research, & Evaluation.

New York Department of Correctional Services and New York Division of Parole. (1993). *The fifth annual report to the legislature: Shock incarceration in New York State.* Albany, NY: Division of Program Planning, Research, & Evaluation.

Nuffield, J. (1982). *Parole decision-making in Canada.* Ottawa: Solicitor General of Canada.

Nuttall, C., with Barnard, E. E., Fowles, A. J., Frost, A., Hammond, W. H., Mayhew, P., Pease, K., Tarling, R., & Weatheritt, M. (1977). *Parole in England and Wales.* London: Her Majesty's Stationary Office.

Office of the Auditor General. (1993). *Performance audit of the use of electronic monitoring within the community control program* (Report No. 12011). Tallahassee: State of Florida.

Ohlin, L. (1951). *Selection for parole.* New York: Russell Sage.

Ohlin, L., & Duncan, O. (1949). The efficiency of prediction in criminology. *American Journal of Sociology, 54,* 441-451.

Oregon Department of Corrections. (n.d.). *Coos County DROP program: Report of the DROP committee.* Salem: Oregon Department of Corrections.

Oregon Department of Corrections. (1993). *DROP Statistics: Report of the DROP committee.* Salem: Oregon Department of Corrections.

Osler, M. (1991). Shock incarceration: Hard realities and real possibilities. *Federal Probation, 55*(1), 34-42.

Palmer, J., & Carlson, P. (1976). Problems with the use of regression analysis in prediction studies. *Journal of Research in Crime and Delinquency, 13,* 64-81.

Palmer, T. (1965). Types of treaters and types of juvenile offenders. *Youth Authority Quarterly, 18,* 14-23.

Palmer, T. (1967). *Personality characteristics and professional orientations of five groups of Community Treatment Project workers: A preliminary report on differences among treaters.* Sacramento: California Youth Authority.

Palmer, T. (1973). Matching worker and client in corrections. *Social Work, 18*(2), 95-103.

Palmer, T. (1974). The Youth Authority's Community Treatment Project. *Federal Probation, 38*(1), 3-14.

Palmer, T. (1975). Martinson revisited. *Journal of Research in Crime and Delinquency, 12,* 133-152.

Palmer, T. (1978). *Correctional intervention and research: Current issues and future prospects.* Lexington, MA: Lexington Books.

Palmer, T. (1983). The "effectiveness" issue today: An overview. *Federal Probation, 46,* 3-10.

Palmer, T. (1984). Treatment and the role of classification: A review of basics. *Crime & Delinquency, 30*(2), 245-267.

Palmer, T. (1991). The effectiveness of intervention: Recent trends and current issues. *Crime & Delinquency, 37*(3), 330-346.

Palmer, T. (1992). *The re-emergence of correctional intervention.* Newbury Park, CA: Sage.

Palmer, T. (1994). *A profile of correctional effectiveness and new directions for research.* Albany: State University of New York Press.

Palmer, T. (in press). *Individualized intervention with young multiple offenders.* Hamden, CT: Garland.

Palmer, T., & Grenny, G. (1971). *Stance and techniques of matched Nx, Na, Mp-Cfc, Cfm, and I₂ workers: A self-description of the treatment methods used as well as rejected by five groups of low caseload parole agents at California's Community Treatment Project.* Sacramento: California Youth Authority.

Palmer, T., Neto, V., Johns, D., Turner, J., & Pearson, J. (1968). *The Sacramento-Stockton and the San Francisco experiments* (Report No. 9, Part 1). Sacramento: California Youth Authority.

Palmer, T., & Wedge, R. (1989). California's juvenile probation camps: Findings and implications. *Crime & Delinquency, 35*(2), 234-253.

Palumbo, D. J., Clifford, M., & Synder-Joy, Z. N. (1990). From net-widening to intermediate sanctions: The transformation of alternatives to incarceration from benevolence to malevolence. In J. J. Byrne, A. J. Lurigio, & J. Petersilia (Eds.), *Smart sentencing: The emergence of intermediate sanctions* (pp. 229-244). Newbury Park, CA: Sage.

Palumbo, D., Musheno, M., & Maynard-Moody, S. (1984). *An evaluation of the implementation of community corrections in Oregon, Colorado and Connecticut.* Washington, DC: Department of Justice, National Institute of Justice

Panizzon, A., Olson-Raymer, G., & Guerra, N. (1991). *Delinquency prevention: What works/what doesn't.* Sacramento, CA: Office of Criminal Justice Planning.

Parent, D. (1989). *Shock incarceration: An overview of existing programs.* Washington, DC: National Institute of Justice.

Parisi, N. (1980). Combining incarceration and probation. *Federal Probation, 44,* 3-12.

Paternoster, R. (1987). The deterrent effect of perceived certainty and severity of punishment: A review of the evidence and issues. *Justice Quarterly, 4,* 173-217.

Payne, C., McCabe, S., & Walker, N. (1974). Predicting offender-patients' reconvictions. *British Journal of Psychiatry, 125,* 60-64.

Pearson, F. (1987a). Evaluation of New Jersey's intensive supervision program. *Crime & Delinquency, 34*(4), 437-448.

Pearson, F. (1987b). *Research on New Jersey's intensive supervision program: Final report.* Washington, DC: National Institute of Justice.

Petersilia, J. (1986). Exploring the option of house arrest. *Federal Probation, 50*(2), 50-55.

Petersilia, J. (1987). Georgia's intensive probation: Will the model work elsewhere? In B. McCarthy (Ed.), *Intermediate punishments: Intensive supervision, home confinement and electronic monitoring* (pp. 15-30). Monsey, NY: Criminal Justice Press.

Petersilia, J. (1988). House arrest. In *Crime file*. Washington, DC: National Institute of Justice.

Petersilia, J. (1990a). Conditions that permit intensive supervision programs to survive. *Crime & Delinquency, 36,* 126-145.

Petersilia, J. (1990b). When probation becomes more dreaded than prison. *Federal Probation, 54*(5), 23-27.

Petersilia, J. (1992). California's prison policy: Causes, costs, & consequences. *Prison Journal, 72,* 8-36.

Petersilia, J., & Deschenes, E. (1994). What punishes? Inmates rank the severity of prison vs. intermediate sanctions. *Federal Probation, 58*(1), 3-8.

Petersilia, J., & Greenwood, P. (1978). Mandatory prison sentences. *Journal of Criminal Law and Criminology, 69,* 604-615.

Petersilia, J., & Turner, S. (1987). Guidelines-based justice: Prediction and racial minorities. In D. Gottfredson & M. Tonry (Eds.), *Prediction and classification: Criminal justice decision making* (pp. 151-182). Chicago: University of Chicago Press.

Petersilia, J., & Turner, S. (1990). Comparing intensive and regular supervision for high-risk probationers: Early results from an experiment in California. *Crime & Delinquency, 36,* 87-111.

Petersilia, J., & Turner, S. (1993a). Evaluating intensive supervision probation and parole. *Overcrowded Times, 4,* 6-10, 16.

Petersilia, J., & Turner, S. (1993b). Evaluating intensive supervision probation/parole: Results of a nationwide experiment. In *Research in brief*. Washington, DC: National Institute of Justice.

Petersilia, J., & Turner, S. (1993c). Intensive probation and parole. In M. Tonry (Ed.), *Crime and justice: A review of research* (Vol. 17, pp. 281-335). Chicago: University of Chicago Press.

Pierce, N. (1991, January 14). Fiscal storms in the states. *Arizona Republic,* p. A-13.

Platt, J., Perry, G., & Metzger, D. (1980). The evaluation of a heroin addiction treatment program within a correctional environment. In R. Ross & P. Gendreau (Eds.), *Effective correctional treatment* (pp. 419-437). Toronto: Butterworths.

Pressman, J., & Wildavsky, A. (1973) *Implementation.* Berkeley: University of California Press.

Putnins, A. (1982). The Eysenck personality questionnaires and delinquency prediction. *Personality and Individual Differences, 3,* 339-340.

Quay, H. (1964). Personality dimensions in delinquent males as inferred from the factor analysis of behavior ratings. *Journal of Research in Crime and Delinquency, 1*(3), 3-37.

Quay, H. (1977). The three faces of evaluation: What can be expected to work? *Criminal Justice and Behavior, 4,* 341-354.

Quay, H. (1984). *Managing adult inmates: Classification for housing and program assignments.* Washington, DC: American Correctional Association.

Quinn, J., & Holman, J. (1991). The efficacy of electronically monitored home confinement as a case management device. *Journal of Contemporary Criminal Justice, 7,* 128-134.

Quinsey, V. (1981). The baserate problem and the prediction of dangerousness: A reappraisal. *Journal of Psychiatry and Law, 8,* 329-340.

Rand, A. (1987). Transitional life events and desistance from delinquency and crime. In M. Wolfgang, T. Thornberry, & R. Figlio (Eds.), *From boy to man, from delinquency to crime* (pp. 134-162). Chicago: University of Chicago Press.

Redlinger, L., & Shanahan, D. (1986). Planning forward and planning backward: Approaches to policy implementation. *Criminal Justice Policy Review, 1,* 76-90.

Reiss, A. (1951). Delinquency as a failure of personal and social controls. *American Sociological Review, 15,* 196-207.

Reiss, A. (1986). Co-offender influences on criminal careers. In A. Blumstein, J. Cohen., A. Roth, & C. Visher (Eds.), *Criminal careers and "career criminals"* (Vol. 2, pp. 121-160). Washington DC: National Academy Press.

Reiss, A., & Roth, J. (1994). *Understanding and preventing violence.* Washington, DC: National Academy Press.

Reitsma-Street, M. (1984). Differential treatment of young offenders: A review of the Conceptual Level Matching Model. *Canadian Journal of Criminology, 26*(2), 199-216.

Renzema, M. (1992a). Electronic monitoring primer: Version 0.90 [computer software]. Kutztown, PA: Tracking Systems Corporation.

Renzema, M. (1992b). Home confinement programs: Development, implementation, and impact. In J. Byrne, A. Lurigio, & J. Petersilia (Eds.), *Smart sentencing: The emergence of intermediate sanctions* (pp. 41-53). Newbury Park, CA: Sage.

Renzema, M., & Skelton, D. (1989). *The use of electronic monitoring by criminal justice agencies, 1989.* Kutztown, PA: Kutztown University Foundation.

Riley, D., & Shaw, M. (1985). *Parental supervision and juvenile delinquency* (Home Office Research Study No. 83). London: Her Majesty's Stationary Office.

Robinson, D., & Porporino, F. (1989). *Validation of an adult offender classification system for Newfoundland and Labrador* (Research Report No. R-04). Ottawa: Correctional Service Canada.

Rogers, R., & Jolin, A. (1991). Electronically monitored house arrest: Development and critique. *Indian Journal of Criminology, 19*, 2-8.

Romig, D. (1978). *Justice for our children.* Lexington, MA: Lexington Books.

Ross, H. (1992). *Confronting drunk driving: Social policy for saving lives.* New Haven, CT: Yale University Press.

Ross, J. (1980). Decision rules in program evaluation. *Evaluation Review, 4*, 59-74.

Ross, R., & Fabiano, E. (1985). *Time to think: A cognitive model of delinquency prevention and offender rehabilitation.* Johnson City, TN: Institute of Social Sciences and Arts.

Ross, R., Fabiano, E., & Ewles, C. (1988). Reasoning and rehabilitation. *International Journal of Offender Therapy and Comparative Criminology, 32*, 29-35.

Ross, R., & Gendreau, P. (Eds.). (1980). *Effective correctional treatment.* Toronto: Butterworths.

Ross, R., & McKay, H. (1976). A study of institutional treatment programs. *International Journal of Offender Therapy and Comparative Criminology, 20*, 165-173.

Ross, R., & McKay, H. B. (1978). Behavioral approaches to treatment in corrections: Requiem for a panacea. *Canadian Journal of Criminology, 20*, 279-295.

Rothman, D. (1980). *Conscience and convenience: The asylum and its alternatives in progressive America.* Boston: Little, Brown.

Rothman, J., Erlich, J., & Teresa, J. (1976). *Promoting innovation and change in organizations and communities: A planning manual.* New York: John Wiley.

Rush, G. (1988). Electronic surveillance: An alternative to incarceration: An overview of the San Diego County program. *American Journal of Criminal Justice, 12*, 219-241.

Rutter, M., & Giller, H. (1983). *Juvenile delinquency: Trends and perspectives.* Elmsford, NY: Pergamon.

Sampson, R., & Laub, J. (1993). *Crime in the making: Pathways and turning points through life.* Cambridge, MA: Harvard University Press.

Sandhu, H., Dodder, R., & Mathur, M. (1993). House arrest: Success and failure rates in residential and nonresidential community-based programs. *Journal of Offender Rehabilitation, 19*, 131-144.

Sanford, R. (1970). Whatever happened to action research? *Journal of Social Issues, 26*, 4-19.

Sawyer, J. (1966). Measurement and prediction, clinical and statistical. *Psychological Bulletin, 66,* 178-200.

Scheingold, S. (1984). *The politics of law and order: Street crime and public policy.* New York: Longman.

Schmidt, A. (1989a). Electronic monitoring. *Journal of Contemporary Criminal Justice, 5,* 133-140.

Schmidt, A. (1989b). Electronic monitoring of offenders increases. In *Research in action.* Washington, DC: National Institute of Justice.

Schmidt, P., & Witte, A. (1988). *Predicting recidivism using survival models.* New York: Springer-Verlag.

Schneider, A. (1986). Restitution and recidivism rates of juvenile offenders: Results from four experimental studies. *Criminology, 24*(3), 533-552.

Schneider, A., & Ervin, L. (1990). Specific deterrence, rational choice, & decision heuristics: Applications in juvenile justice. *Social Science Quarterly, 71*(3), 585-601.

Schneider, A., & Schneider, P. (1985). The impact of restitution on recidivism of juvenile offenders: An experiment in Clayton County, Georgia. *Criminal Justice Review, 10,* 1-10.

Schneider, A., & Warner, J. (1989). *National trends in juvenile restitution programming.* Washington, DC: U.S. Department of Justice, Office of Juvenile Justice and Delinquency Prevention, Restitution Education, Specialized Training and Technical Assistance Program.

Schrag, C. (1971). *Crime and justice: American style.* Washington, DC: National Institute of Mental Health.

Schrantz, D. (n.d.). *The five tenets of effective community corrections based on the Michigan experience.* Unpublished manuscript, State Office of Community Corrections, Lansing, MI.

Schumacher, M. (1973). Predicting subsequent conviction for individual male prison inmates. *New Zealand Statistician, 8,* 26-34.

Sealy, A., & Banks, C. (1971). Social maturity, training, experience and recidivism amongst British Borstal boys. *British Journal of Criminology, 11*(3), 245-264.

Sebba, L. (1978). Some explorations in the scaling of penalties. *Journal of Research in Crime and Delinquency, 15,* 247-263.

Sechrest, L., White, S., & Brown, E. (Eds.). (1979). *The rehabilitation of criminal offenders.* Washington, DC: National Academy Press.

Shaw, J., & MacKenzie, D. (1991). Shock incarceration and its impact on the lives of problem drinkers. *American Journal of Criminal Justice, 16,* 63-96.

Shaw, J., & MacKenzie, D. (1992). The one-year community supervision performance of drug offenders and Louisiana DOC-identified substance abusers graduating from shock incarceration. *Journal of Criminal Justice, 20,* 501-516.

Sherman, L., with Schmidt, J., & Rogan, D. (1992). *Policing domestic violence: Experiments and dilemmas.* New York: Free Press.

Sherman, M., & Hawkins, G. (1981). *Imprisonment in America: Choosing the future.* Chicago: University of Chicago Press.

Shore, M., & Massimo, J. (1979). Fifteen years after treatment: A follow-up study of comprehensive vocationally oriented psychotherapy. *American Journal of Orthopsychiatry, 49,* 240-245.

Short, J. (1991). Poverty, ethnicity, & crime: Change and continuity in U.S. cities. *Journal of Research in Crime and Delinquency, 28,* 501-518.

Simon, F. (1971). *Prediction methods in criminology.* London: Her Majesty's Stationary Office.

Smith, D., Wish, E., & Jarjoura, G. (1989). Drug use and pretrial misconduct in New York City. *Journal of Quantitative Criminology, 5,* 101-126.

Smith, L., & Akers, R. (1993). A comparison of recidivism of Florida's community control and prison: A five-year survival analysis. *Journal of Research in Crime and Delinquency, 30,* 267-292.

Smith, M. (1982). *Alternative forms of punishment and supervision for convicted offenders.* Conference paper, Conference on Public Danger, Dangerous Offenders and the Criminal Justice System, Harvard University, Cambridge, MA.

Smith, R. (1990). *A program assessment of Pride, Inc. house arrest program.* Unpublished master's thesis, West Virginia University, Morgantown.

Smykla, J., & Selke, W. (Eds.). (1995). *Intermediate sanctions: Sentencing in the 90s.* Cincinnati, OH: Anderson.

Solomon, H. (1976). Parole outcome: A multi-dimensional contingency table analysis. *Journal of Research in Crime and Delinquency, 13,* 107-126.

Sontheimer, H., & Goodstein, L. (1993). An evaluation of juvenile intensive aftercare probation: Aftercare versus system response effects. *Justice Quarterly, 10,* 197-227.

Souryal, C., & MacKenzie, D. (1995). Shock incarceration and recidivism: An examination of boot camp programs in four states. In J. Smykla & W. Selke (Eds.), *Intermediate sanctions: Sentencing in the 90s* (pp. 57-88). Cincinnati, OH: Anderson.

Spiegler, M., & Guevremont, D. (1993). *Contemporary behavior therapy* (2nd ed.). Pacific Grove, CA: Brooks/Cole.

Steffensmeier, D., & Harer, M. (1993). Bulging prisons, an aging U.S. population, & the nation's crime rate. *Federal Probation, 57*(2), 3-10.

Stojkovic, S. (1994). The President's Crime Commission recommendations for corrections: The twilight of idols. In J. Conley (Ed.), *The 1967 President's Crime Commission report: Its impact 25 years later* (pp. 37-55). Cincinnati, OH: Anderson.

Stott, D. (1960). A new delinquency prediction instrument using behavioral indications. *International Journal of Social Psychiatry, 10,* 27-29.

Sullivan, C., Grant, M., & Grant, D. (1957). The development of interpersonal maturity: An application to delinquency. *Psychiatry, 20,* 373-386.

Tarling, R. (1993). *Analysing offending: Data, models and interpretations.* London: Her Majesty's Stationary Office.

Tarling, R., & Perry, J. (1985). Statistical models in criminological prediction. In D. Farrington & R. Tarling (Eds.), *Prediction in criminology* (pp. 210-231). Albany: SUNY.

Taylor, R. (1993). *Research methods in criminal justice* New York: McGraw-Hill.

Texas Department of Criminal Justice. (1991). *Shock incarceration in Texas: Special Incarceration Program.* Austin: Texas Department of Criminal Justice.

Thomson, D., & Ragona, A. (1987). Popular moderation versus governmental authoritarianism: An interactionist view of public sentiments toward criminal sanctions. *Crime & Delinquency, 33,* 337-357.

Toborg, M., Bellassai, J., Yezer, A., & Trost, R. (1989). Assessment of pretrial urine testing in the District of Columbia. In *Issues and practices series.* Washington, DC: National Institute of Justice.

Toborg, M., Yezer, A., & Bellassai, J. (1987). *Analysis of drug use among arrestees* (Monograph No. 4). Washington, DC: Toborg Associates.

Toch, H., & Grant, J. (1991). *Police as problem solvers.* New York: Plenum.

Tonry, M. (1987). Prediction and classification: Legal and ethical issues. In D. Gottfredson & M. Tonry (Eds.), *Risk and classification* (pp. 367-413). Chicago: University of Chicago Press.

Tonry, M. (1990). Stated and latent features of ISP. *Crime & Delinquency, 36,* 174-191.

Tonry, M., & Will, R. (1988). *Intermediate sanctions: Preliminary report.* Washington, DC: National Institute of Justice.

Trevvett, N. (1965). Identifying delinquency-prone children. *Crime & Delinquency, 11,* 186-191.

Tuthill, J. (1986). *An evaluation of electronic home detention as a deterrent for offenders convicted of driving under the influence of intoxicants.* Oregon City: Oregon Corrections Division.

Tyre, M., & Orlikowski, W. (1993). Exploiting opportunities for technological improvements in organizations. *Sloan Management Review, 35*(1), 13-26.

Underwood, B. (1979). Law and the crystal ball: Predicting behavior with statistical inference and individualized judgment. *Yale Law Journal, 88,* 1408-1448.

U.S. General Accounting Office. (1990). *Intermediate sanctions: Their impact on prison crowding, costs, and recidivism are still unclear.* Washington, DC: Government Printing Office.

U.S. General Accounting Office. (1993). *Prison boot-camps: Short-term prison costs reduced, but long-term impact uncertain.* Washington, DC: Author.

Van Dine, S., Dinitz, S., & Conrad, J. (1977). The incapacitation of the dangerous offender. *Journal of Research in Crime and Delinquency, 14,* 22-34.

Van Ness, S. (1992). Intensive probation versus prison outcomes in Indiana: Who could benefit? *Journal of Contemporary Criminal Justice, 8,* 351-364.

Van Voorhis, P. (1987). Correctional effectiveness: The high cost of ignoring success. *Federal Probation, 51*(1), 56-62.

Van Voorhis, P. (1993). Psychological determinants of the prison experience. *Prison Journal, 73,* 72-102.

Van Voorhis, P. (1994). *Psychological classification of the adult prison inmate.* Albany: State University of New York Press.

Vaughn, J. (1992). *Evaluation of the electronically monitored home confinement program.* Warrensburg: Central Missouri State University.

Veverka, M. (1971). The Gluecks' social prediction table in Czechoslovak research. *British Journal of Criminology, 11,* 187-189.

Virginia Department of Corrections. (1992). *An evaluation of Southampton Intensive Treatment Center.* Richmond, VA: Virginia Department of Corrections, Research, Evaluation, and Certification Unit.

Visher, C. (1987). Incapacitation and crime control: Does a "lock 'em up" strategy reduce crime? *Justice Quarterly, 4,* 513-543.

Visher, C. (1990). Using drug testing to identify high-risk defendants on release: A study in the District of Columbia. *Journal of Criminal Justice, 18,* 321-332.

Visher, C. (1991). *A comparison of urinalysis technologies for drug testing in criminal justice: A research report.* Washington, DC: National Institute of Justice.

Visher, C. (1992). Pretrial drug testing. In *Research in brief.* Washington, DC: National Institute of Justice.

Vito, G. (1984). Developments in shock probation: A review of research findings and policy implications. *Federal Probation, 48,* 22-27.

Vito, G., Holmes, S., Keil, T., & Wilson, D. (1992). Drug testing in community corrections: A comparative program analysis. *Journal of Crime and Justice, 15,* 63-89.

Vito, G., Wilson, D., & Holmes, S. (1993). Drug testing in community corrections: Results from a four-year program. *Prison Journal, 73,* 343-354.

Vito, G., Wilson, D., & Keil, T. (1990). Drug testing, treatment, & revocation: A review of program findings. *Federal Probation, 54*(3), 37-43.

Von Hirsch, A. (1983). Commensurability and crime prevention: Evaluating formal sentencing structures and their rationale. *Journal of Criminal Law and Criminology, 74*(1), 209-248.

Von Hirsch, A. (1992). Scaling intermediate punishments: A comparison of two models. In J. Byrne, A. Lurigio, & J. Petersilia (Eds.), *Smart sentencing: The emergence of intermediate sanctions* (pp. 211-228). Newbury Park, CA: Sage.

Von Hirsch, A., Wasik, M., & Greene, J. (1989). Punishments in the community and the principles of desert. *Rutgers Law Journal, 20,* 595-618.

Wade, T., Morton, T., Lind, J., & Ferris, N. (1977). A family crisis intervention approach to diversion from the juvenile justice system. *Juvenile Justice Journal, 28,* 43-51.

Wadsworth, M. (1979). *Roots of delinquency.* London: Martin Robertson.

Wagner, D., & Baird, C. (1993). Evaluation of the Florida Community Control Program. In *Research in brief.* Washington, DC: National Institute of Justice.

Walker, S. (1989). *Sense and nonsense about crime: A policy guide* (2nd ed.). Pacific Grove, CA: Brooks/Cole.

Walter, T., & Mills, C. (1980). A behavioral-employment intervention program for reducing juvenile delinquency. In R. Ross & P. Gendreau (Eds.), *Effective correctional treatment* (pp. 187-206). Toronto: Butterworths.

Walters, G., & Grusec, J. (1977). *Punishment.* San Francisco: Freeman.

Wardlaw, G., & Millier, P. (1978). Psychologist's role on a New Zealand prison classification committee. *International Journal of Criminology and Penology, 6,* 185-190.

Warren, M. (1971). Classification of offenders as an aid to efficient management and effective treatment. *Journal of Criminal Law, Criminology, and Police Science, 62,* 239-258.

Warren, M. (1972, May). *Classification for treatment.* Paper presented at the National Institute of Law Enforcement and Criminal Justice Conference on the State of Research, Washington, DC.

Warren, M., Palmer, T., Turner, J., Dorsey, A., McHale, J., Howard, G., Riggs, J., & Underwood, W. (1966). *Interpersonal maturity level classification: Juvenile diagnosis and treatment of low, middle, and high maturity delinquents.* Sacramento: California Youth Authority.

Watts, R. K., & Glaser, D. (1992). Electronic monitoring of drug offenders in California. In J. M. Byrne, A. J. Lurigio, & J. Petersilia (Eds.), *Smart sentencing: The emergence of intermediate sanctions* (pp. 68-84). Newbury Park, CA: Sage.

Wax, M. (1977). *Effects of symbolic restitution and presence of victim on delinquent shoplifters.* Unpublished doctoral dissertation, Washington State University, Pullman.

Wedge, R., & Palmer, T. (1989). *California's juvenile probation camps: A technical analysis of outcomes for a 1982 release cohort. Camps, ranches, and schools study* (Report No. 4). Sacramento: California Youth Authority.

Weeks, H. (1958). *Youthful offenders at Highfields.* Ann Arbor: University of Michigan Press.

Weis, J. (1986). Issues in the measurement of criminal careers. In A. Blumstein, J. Cohen, J. Roth, & C. Visher (Eds.), Criminal careers and "career criminals" (Vol. 2, pp. 1-51). Washington, DC: National Academy Press.

Weisbord, M. (1992). *Discovering common ground.* San Francisco, CA: Barrett-Koehler.

West, D. (1981). *Delinquency: Its roots, careers and prospects.* London: Heinemann.

Wexler, H., Falkin, G., & Lipton, D. (1990). Outcome evaluation of a prison therapeutic community for substance abuse treatment. *Criminal Justice and Behavior, 17,* 71-92.

Whitehead, J., & Lab, S. (1989). A meta-analysis of juvenile correctional treatment. *Journal of Research in Crime and Delinquency, 26*(3), 276-295.

Wilkins, L. (1975). Perspectives on court decision-making. In D. Gottfredson (Ed.), *Decision-making in the criminal justice system: Reviews and essays.* Washington, DC: Government Printing Office.

Wilkins, L. (1985). The politics of prediction. In D. Farrington & R. Tarling (Eds.), *Prediction in criminology* (pp. 34-53). Albany: SUNY.

Wilkins, L., & MacNaughton-Smith, P. (1964). New prediction and classification methods in criminology. *Journal of Research in Crime and Delinquency, 1,* 19-32.

Williams, J., Johnson, D., & McGrath, J. (1991). Is the public committed to the imprisonment of convicted felons: Citizen preferences for reducing prison crowding. *Journal of Contemporary Criminal Justice, 7,* 86-94.

Williams, W. (1976). Implementation analysis and assessment. In W. Williams & R. Elmore (Eds.), *Social program evaluation* (pp. 267-292). New York: Academic Press.

Wilson, D. (1992). *A strategy of change: Concepts and controversies in the management of change.* London: Routledge & Kegan Paul.

Wish, E., & Gropper, B. (1990). Drug testing by the criminal justice system: Methods, research, & applications. In M. Tonry & J. Wilson (Eds.), *Drugs and crime: Crime and justice: A review of the research* (Vol. 13, pp. 321-391). Chicago: University of Chicago Press.

Wright, K., Clear, T., & Dickson, P. (1984). Universal applicability of probation risk-assessment instruments: A critique. *Criminology, 22,* 113-134.

Wright, R. (1994). *In defense of prisons.* Westport, CT: Greenwood.

Wright, W., & Dixon, M. (1977). Juvenile delinquency prevention: A review of evaluation studies. *Journal of Research in Crime and Delinquency, 14*(1), 35-67.

Yezer, A., Trost, R., & Toborg, M. (1987). *The efficiency of using urine-testing results in risk classification of arrestees* (Monograph No. 6). Washington, DC: Toborg Associates.

Yin, R. (1982). *Planning for implementation.* Draft mimeo, Case Study Institute, Washington, DC.

Zaleznik, A. (1992). Managers and leaders: Are they different? *Harvard Business Review, 70*(2), 126-135.

Zaltman, G., & Duncan, R. (1977). *Strategies for planned change.* New York: John Wiley.

Zimmerman, S., Van Alstyne, D., & Dunn, C. (1988). The national punishment survey and public policy consequences. *Journal of Research in Crime and Delinquency, 25,* 120-149.

Zimring, F., & Hawkins, G. (1991). *The scale of imprisonment.* Chicago: University of Chicago Press.

Index

About the Contributors

Brandon K. Applegate is a doctoral candidate in criminal justice at the University of Cincinnati. His published articles have focused on the determinants of public support for punishment. His current research interests are in the areas of effective correctional interventions, the social sources of criminal behavior, and citizens' assessments of criminal justice policies.

James Bonta received his Ph.D. in Clinical Psychology from the University of Ottawa. His clinical experience includes work with conduct-disordered children and their families, providing assessments of youths for juvenile courts, and as a psychologist at the Ottawa-Carleton Detention Centre, a maximum security remand facility for adults and young offenders. Since 1990, he has served as Chief of Corrections Research, Ministry Secretariat, Solicitor General of Canada, in Ottawa, Ontario. He is Adjunct Research Professor at Carleton University and on the Editorial Advisory Board for the journal *Criminal Justice and Behavior.* He has published in the areas of risk assessment, offender rehabilitation, and corrections. He recently coauthored (with Don Andrews) *The Psychology of Criminal Conduct.*

Francis T. Cullen is Distinguished Research Professor of Criminal Justice and Sociology at the University of Cincinnati. He is the author of *Rethinking Crime and Deviance Theory,* coeditor of *Contemporary Criminological Theory,* and coauthor of *Reaffirming Rehabilitation, Corporate Crime Under Attack, Criminological Theory,* and *Criminology.* He served as president of the Academy of Criminal Justice Sciences and as editor of *Justice Quarterly.*

His current research focuses on correctional policy, the prosecution of corporate crime, victimization on college campuses, and tests of criminological theory.

Paul Gendreau is Professor of Psychology and Director of the Graduate Program in the Department of Psychology at the University of New Brunswick in Canada. He received his Ph.D. in psychology from Queen's University, Kingston, Ontario. He has worked in criminal justice settings since 1961, primarily in prisons, as an administrator, clinician, and consultant. He has served as president of the Canadian Psychological Association and has worked on criminal justice projects in Australia, Jamaica, and New Zealand. He has published extensively, especially responding to the "nothing works" sentiment in criminal justice following Martinson. His research interests include the prediction of criminal behavior, the effects of prison life, and the evaluation of correctional programs. His Correctional Program Assessment Inventory (with Don Andrews) is becoming a widely used assessment protocol in corrections in Canada and in the United States.

Alan T. Harland is head of the Graduate Program and former Chair of the Department of Criminal Justice at Temple University in Philadelphia, where he teaches criminal law, legal philosophy, sentencing, and victimology. He received his Ph.D. from the School of Criminal Justice in the State University of New York at Albany, where he was Director of the Hindelang Criminal Justice Research Center. He also holds law degrees from the University of Pennsylvania and from Oxford University, England. His research on the topics of sentencing, victim compensation, and policy development and implementation have resulted in numerous publications in law reviews, social science and professional criminal justice journals, edited books, and government monographs. He is executive editor of *The Prison Journal.* He has served as a research and policy consultant to federal, state, and local agencies in the United States, Canada, and Europe.

Philip Harris is Chairman of the Department of Criminal Justice at Temple University in Philadelphia, where he teaches and conducts research on juvenile justice issues and organizational development. He received his Ph.D. from the School of Criminal Justice at the State University of New York in Albany. He spent 4 years as a juvenile corrections administrator in Canada, directing the assessment department, developing staff training, and designing the agency's management information system. He directs the Juvenile Corrections Leadership Forum for state-level juvenile corrections commissioners. His current research involves development of an evaluation information system for the Philadelphia Juvenile Justice System. His published works include articles, book chapters, and research reports on topics ranging from program implementation to the death penalty.

Francis X. Hartmann is Executive Director and Senior Research Fellow in the Program on Criminal Justice Policy and Management at the John F. Kennedy School of Government at Harvard University. His research interests include community responses to illicit drugs and the role of community policing in reducing violence. He is coauthor of *Lessons Learned: Case Studies of the Initiation and Maintenance of the Community Response to Drugs* and editor of *From Children to Citizens: The Role of the Juvenile Court.* He was formerly Director of the Hartford Institute of Criminal and Social Justice, Director of Research and Evaluation for New York City's Addiction Services Agency, and a Program Officer at the Ford Foundation.

Peter R. Jones is an Associate Professor in the Department of Criminal Justice at Temple University in Philadelphia. He received his Ph.D. in Social and Urban Geography from the University College of Wales at Aberystwyth. Prior to coming to the United States, he served as Senior Research Officer with the British Home Office Research and Planning Unit in London, where he conducted studies on pretrial decision making, sentencing patterns, prosecution policies, and public attitudes to the police. At Temple, his research and teaching interests include community corrections, risk prediction, and criminal justice decision making. His current research focuses on developing an information system in the Philadelphia Juvenile Justice System. He has served as research and technical assistance consultant for criminal justice agencies throughout the United States and has written extensively for both British and U.S. publications.

Ted Palmer recently retired as Senior Researcher in the California Youth Authority. He received his Ph.D. in Psychology from the University of Southern California. He was coprincipal investigator for the California Community Treatment Project and has conducted and directed research into group homes and juvenile probation camps, as well as statewide needs assessments of youth centers, shelters, and juvenile detention facilities. He has served as consulting editor to numerous correctional journals and has written numerous books and research monographs on juvenile and adult correctional research issues. His publications include *Correctional Intervention and Research, The Re-Emergence of Correctional Intervention,* and *A Profile of Correctional Effectiveness and New Directions for Research.*

Joan Petersilia is former Director of the RAND Corporation's Criminal Justice Program and currently a Professor in the Criminology, Law and Society program of the School of Social Ecology at the University of California at Irvine. She has directed several major research studies in policing, sentencing, and corrections. Resulting publications include *Intensive Supervision for High-Risk Probationers: Findings From Three California Experiments, Expanding Options for Criminal Sentencing, The Influence of Criminal Justice Research, Prison Versus Probation in California,* and *Granting Felons Probation.* She is a past president of the American Society of Criminology and has received awards for her work from the American Probation and Parole Association and the California Probation, Parole, and Corrections Association.

Stephen Smith is Student Coordinator at the Ambler Campus of Temple University's Department of Criminal Justice. Prior to his graduate work at Temple, he completed his master's level studies in criminology at Cambridge University in England. He is coauthor of articles and research reports on community service sentencing and correctional alternatives. His undergraduate teaching at Temple includes statistics and a wide variety of substantive criminal justice topics.

John Paul Wright is Assistant Professor of Criminal Justice at East Tennessee State University. He is completing his doctoral degree in criminal justice at the University of Cincinnati. He has published articles in the areas of white-collar crime, public opinion about the death penalty, and correctional policy. He is currently researching the impact of social support on delinquent involvement.